Diderot
and the Jews

Diderot
and the Jews

Leon Schwartz

Rutherford • Madison • Teaneck
Fairleigh Dickinson University Press
London and Toronto: Associated University Presses

© 1981 by Associated University Presses, Inc.

Associated University Presses, Inc.
4 Cornwall Drive
East Brunswick, New Jersesy 08816

909.04
D555xs

Associated University Presses
69 Fleet Street
London EC4Y 1EU, England

Associated University Presses
Toronto M5E 1A7, Canada

Library of Congress Cataloging in Publication Data

Schwartz, Leon, 1922-
  Diderot and the Jews.

  Bibliography: p.
    1. Diderot, Denis, 1713-1784—Views on Judaism.
2. Judaism. I. Title.
B2018.J83S38   909'.04924   78-73304
ISBN 0-8386-2377-8

82-4428

Printed in the United States of America

To my Polish-French-American-Jewish wife, Jeanne,
in memory of her family lost in the Holocaust . . .
and to Diderot's disciples
in the belief that mortals are all *different* and *equal*.

Contents

List of Illustrations   9
Acknowledgments   11
1. Introduction   15
2. Diderot and Judaism   26
    Diderot's Formation   26
    From Deism to Atheism (1745–1749)   28
    The *Encyclopédie* in the Making (1750–1757)   39
    The Years of Creative Maturity (1757–1773)   66
    Voyage to Holland and Russia and Last Writings
    on Judaism (1773–1778)   82
    The Private Correspondence   96
3. Diderot and Jewish Culture   100
4. Diderot and the Jewish Question   124
5. Human Diversity and National Character   141
6. Conclusion   158
    Notes   162
    Selected Bibliography   187
    Index   194

List of Illustrations

Diderot, painting by Michel Van Loo — 18

Diderot, painting by Fragonard — 18

Diderot, bust by Pigalle — 18

Diderot, bust by Houdon — 18

"Esther Being Presented to Ahasuerus," engraving by
Jacinto Gimignani after a painting by Poussin — 70

"The Dedication of the Synagogue of the Portuguese
Jews, in Amsterdam," engraving by Bernard Picart — 86

Moses, sculpture by Michelangelo — 120

Acknowledgments

In the various stages through which this book has passed between its original conception as a relatively brief "correction" of recently published notions on Diderot's attitude toward the Jews and its final metamorphosis into a full-length study of all the most significant aspects of Diderot's writings on this "exotic" people, many colleagues and friends have given me help and encouragement, and I am grateful to them. I am most indebted, however, to three people whom I have never met personally: Professor Paul H. Meyer, whose careful reading of the manuscript and whose numerous suggestions for improvement transmitted to me in writing reveal a generosity that is exceeded only by this same scholar's encouraging the publication of a work disagreeing in some respects with his own published views; Professor Otis Fellows, who also read the manuscript and graciously helped guide it toward publication even as he lay awaiting the surgeon's knife; and Professor Mara Vamos, who kindly brought the book to the attention of the editors. Grateful acknowledgment is also made to the late Professor Arthur Wilson for his advice on the acquisition of pictorial materials, and to Dean Gaby Stuart and the California State University, Los Angeles Foundation, for small but helpful grants received through their good offices. Finally, a list of acknowledgments would not be complete without including the members of my family who have helped in whatever way they have been able, Eric and Claire in Paris and Jeanne, directly in the line of fire at home.

Diderot
and the Jews

1

Introduction

What is the object of philosophy? It is to unite mankind
by a commerce of ideas, and by the exercise of a
mutual beneficence.
—Diderot[1]
The title "man" is recommendation enough.
—Diderot[2]

OF all the French writers of the eighteenth century, none better
than Diderot represents the humanist ideal, in direct line of descent
from Montaigne. "The goodness of the eighteenth century,"
writes Jean Thomas, "is basically Diderot's goodness. Do we say
that Voltaire was good, that Montesquieu was good? And Rousseau? It is Diderot who taught his century the spontaneous love of
humanity, the need to substitute for the abstract notion of generalized man, such as La Rochefoucauld or Racine depicted him, the
living reality of a flesh-and-blood being, touching in his weakness,
admirable in his universal curiosity."[3] "I love that philosophy
which exalts mankind," wrote Diderot to his soulmate Sophie
Volland in 1759.[4] Throughout his remarkable career as encyclopedist, man of letters, man of science, esthetician, and moralist,
the *philosophe par excellence*, as he was known to his contemporaries, pursued the phantom of this humanist philosophy. It is
hardly an exaggeration to characterize Diderot's pursuit of the
ideal of a moral society in an apparently godless universe as epic.
As relentlessly as Odysseus sailing from Mediterranean shore to
shore in search of Ithaca, did Diderot navigate on a sea of knowledge whose dimensions were constantly changing, whose shores
were constantly shifting, heroically tracking—with the aid of
every available instrument of learning, from geometry to philos-

15

ophy, from physics to the fine arts—the elusive haven of a godless "Heavenly City."

Diderot's personal quest uniquely characterizes the Age of Enlightenment, more so perhaps than that of any other philosophe. More dynamic and less tradition-bound than Montesquieu, more profound and less pessimistic than Voltaire, more eclectic and less dogmatic than Rousseau, he has been said to incarnate the eighteenth century itself: "in him all currents of that age, deep or shallow, crossed and went their separate ways."[5] Although Becker's aquatic metaphor transposes the current rider into the current carrier, it is consistent with the premises of quest and flux so fundamental to a study of Diderot. Diderot scholars familiar with these premises are aware that they are pursuing a moving object, that Diderot seen dallying on the island Calypso—or Tahiti, passing from myth to figurative reality—is merely a temporary image of Diderot rather than a definitive one, and that the latter—if it is possible to describe definitively—must be shown in motion in a time-space continuum. How typical of Diderot that, even in the realm of the visual representation of his physiognomy, he should invoke the principle of motion! "My children," wrote he to his as yet unborn grandchildren concerning Michel Van Loo's portrait of him, "I warn you that it is not I. I had in one day a hundred different appearances, as determined by whatever was affecting me. I was serene, sad, pensive, tender, violent, passionate, enraptured. But I was never such as you see me there . . . . I have a mask that deceives the artist, either because there are too many things blended together, or because, the impressions of my soul swiftly displacing one another and leaving their imprint each in turn on my face, the painter's eye no longer finding me the same from one instant to the next, his task becomes more difficult than imagined."[6] Even a portrait by Garand catching a fleeting Diderotian expression that the philosopher himself thought characteristic—*ecco il vero Polichinello*—is at best only an imperfect depiction. The ideal solution to the problem of capturing a visual record of Diderot's physiognomy, the cinematic medium, did not of course exist. But there is no doubt that a more reliable notion of Diderot's real appearance than is provided by the Garand pose alone can be had from the various Diderot faces as drawn, painted, or sculpted by Greuze, Carmontelle, Van Loo, Garand, Madame Therbouche, Fragonard, Levitski, Mademoiselle Collot, Pigalle, Houdon, and others, capturing as they do a variety of moods and moments of his existence.

The Diderot scholar is faced with a problem similar to the visual artist's. He can attempt, like Garand, to find *il vero Polichinello* in a single characteristic pose or expression, a much riskier expedient for him than for the artist, or he can apply the cinematic principle and portray his subject in motion, from the provincial Catholic port of embarkation of his childhood, through the deistic currents of his literary youth, threading his adult way on a sea of materialism between the Scylla of biological determinism and the Charybdis of environmentalism, ultimately to plant the flag of Senecan morality on a nameless strand of human existence that he believed as transitory as Nero's Rome.

Having observed with regret the distortion of the Diderotian message resulting from the stationary approach to Diderot's thought, one must strongly caution historians to avoid the temptation to draw definitive judgments from a single work or even several works dating back to a narrow segment of the time line of Diderot's literary career. Nowhere is this deficiency more apparent than in the now timely debate on the subject of eighteenth-century racism, and more specifically on the subject of Diderot's attitude toward the Jews.

Ever since the publication in 1884 of Theodore Reinach's article on "The Jews in Christian Opinion in the XVIIth and XVIIIth Centuries: Peuchet and Diderot,"[7] the false image of an anti-Semitic Diderot has been used to bolster the fashionable but dubious thesis that the French Enlightenment "set the stage for anti-Semitism in its modern form."[8] The Reinach article, a mere four pages of which dealt with Diderot, noted errors in Diderot's *Encyclopedia* article on Jewish philosophy[9] that "proved" to

Portrait of Diderot, by Michel Van Loo. Louvre. © *Arch. Phot. Paris/S.P.A.D.E.M.*

Portrait of Diderot, by Fragonard. ©*Arch. Phot. Paris/S.P.A.D.E.M.*

Bust of Diderot, by Pigalle. Louvre. © *Arch. Phot. Paris/ S.P.A.D.E.M.*

Bust of Diderot, by Houdon. Louvre. © *Arch. Phot. Paris/ S.P.A.D.E.M.*

Reinach Diderot's bad faith. Two stories about Jews woven into a later novel and Diderot's "superficial" observations on the Jewish community in Holland cast further doubt on his benevolence toward the Jews.[10] Probably inspired by Reinach, in 1932 Hermann Sänger wrote a German dissertation on *The Jews and the Old Testament in Diderot*[11] that studied in detail all the *Encyclopédie* articles on the Jews believed to be Diderot's. But the dissertation gave a cursory treatment to the rest of Diderot's vast body of writings, ignoring altogether such significant documents as the *Salons*, in which the genius of Hebrew poetry is the counterpoise of the genius of Greek philosophy in the Diderotian scale of human achievement, and the *Refutation of Helvétius' Work "On Man,"* in which Diderot clarifies his racial theories and theories on genius and morality. Sänger's conclusion, based on his limited and sometimes erroneous evidence (recent discoveries of the true authorship of some of the articles being unavailable to him) gathered preponderantly from Diderot's writings prior to 1759—his literary adolescence so to speak—was that Diderot's only interest in the Jews was to use them as a decoy in his fight with the Catholic church, and that, because of their "crudest concept of God," their "base morality," and their "ignorance in science and lack of skills," Diderot considered them a people "easy to despise." Beyond a philosophical interest in the Jews, Diderot "never had any real sympathy for the deprivation of their social rights in his time" (pp. 126–27). Sänger's thesis, not unimpressive as the academic exercise of a young scholar, is nevertheless a prime example of the nonevolutional approach to Diderot's thought. It was the principal source of the negative appreciation of Diderot's attitude toward the Jews in a long article by Paul H. Meyer and in Arthur Hertzberg's well-known study *The French Enlightenment and the Jews.*[12] Taking a more moderate position on Diderot, though still mostly negative, was C. C. Lehrmann in his book, *The Jewish Element in French Literature*. Also basing himself on the pre-1760 writings—except for the questionably attributed *The Moseiad* (see page 21)—Lehrmann concluded that Diderot was "completely indifferent to the fate of the Jews of his time."[13]

It is gratifying to note that not all scholars have accepted the dubious image of a Diderot unchangingly hostile or indifferent on the question of the Jews, but their pro-Diderotian judgments have tended to be either perfunctory or "ad hoc," that is, directed at refuting specific charges but offering no positive formulation of Diderot's position on the Jews. In the perfunctory category is Hannah Arendt, who based her surprising assertion that "Diderot [was] the only eighteenth-century philosopher who was not hostile to the Jews"[14] on an article written for the *Encyclopédie* not by Diderot but by his collaborator de Jaucourt.[15] In the "ad hoc" category this writer places Stephen J. Gendzier's intelligent article on "Diderot and the Jews," published in *Diderot Studies* XVI.[16] The Gendzier article summarizes the principal accusations against Diderot since Reinach, then limits itself to answering them. In this writer's view this is not enough, and it seems desirable that a positive evolutional formulation now be attempted on this subject both in its narrowest terms (Diderot and the Jews) and in its broadest terms (Diderot and the question of human diversity). It is the purpose of this monograph to propose such a formulation.

Pertinent Problems of the Diderot Canon and Relevant Texts

There are at least three supplementary problems, besides the overriding problem of evolution, inherent in a study of Diderot's beliefs. They are: (1) the problem of attribution or of what Diderot actually wrote; (2) the problem of used materials or the writings of others published under his name; and (3) the distinction to be drawn, if any, between what he published and what he withheld from publication.

The Problem of Attribution

This problem is particularly bedeviling in the study of Diderot's ideas in the *Encyclopédie*, for many of the articles are unsigned while others, clearly acknowledged by Diderot, were tampered with either by the editor LeBreton or by Diderot's less tolerant, anticlerical disciple Naigeon.[17] Several articles important to Sänger's thesis are now considered to be of doubtful attribution.[18] What degree of proof do such articles furnish toward the elucidation of Diderot's ideas? Should they be accepted as representative of his thought, ruled out entirely, or something in between? Jacques Proust, who inclines toward accepting Naigeon's attributions and "rectifications" (pp. 148–49), nevertheless warns that "for the historian of ideas who today wishes to form a valid appreciation of the breadth and quality of Diderot's personal contribution to the *Encyclopédie*, these practices [the disguising of authorship for protection from official persecution], however admirable they maybe from the moral standpoint, have had abhorrent consequences, and we shall see that more than one point of Diderot's thought has been totally deformed by commentators careless about verifying whether texts believed to have come from the Philosopher were really penned by him" (pp. 118–19).

Even more abhorrent than the introduction of evidence based on dubious *Encyclopédie* articles—for, when all is said and done, as chief editor of the project, Diderot selected the writers and approved their articles for publication, thus assuming a measure of identification with them—is the use of anonymous texts never acknowledged by Diderot or published in association with his name in his lifetime. Such an anonymous work was *La Moïsade* (*The Moseiad*), which, if really written by Diderot as Naigeon claimed, would lend some credibility to the Sänger-Hertzberg thesis. Fortunately, the evidence on this point is preponderantly negative, as will be demonstrated later.

A reasonable solution to the problem of attribution would therefore seem to take the following form. Dubious attributions of writings outside the *Encyclopédie* should be rejected, particularly if they appear inconsistent with ideas expressed in Diderot's acknowledged writings. This rule should be aplied even to works appearing in the Assézat-Tourneux edition of Diderot's complete works.[19] However, dubious attributions of articles written for the *Encyclopédie* may be admitted as evidence that they were at least acceptable for use by Diderot at the time, subject to the caution that Diderot, working under great pressure to meet deadlines, may at times have exercised minimal editorial restraints.[20] Again, the crucial criterion for the admission of such evidence would seem to be its consistency with verifiable original Diderot writings.

The Problem of Used Materials

The writings of others published under Diderot's name should be handled in the same manner as articles of dubious attribution. Let it be noted here that in the category of used materials are included not only articles penned by members of Diderot's team of collaborators (numbering about fifty) but also articles hastily "stitched together" by Diderot himself from other sources. To what degree can these articles, which a critic has said barely had time to register in Diderot's brain as he furiously copied Brucker, Basnage, Bayle, and Chambers,[21] be considered the product of his own mature thought or representative of his own unique view-point? Pierre Hermand considers them "the least significant" of Diderot's writings for a study of his beliefs.[22] Yet the cases built against Diderot by Reinach, Sänger, et al., rest very heavily on precisely this kind of evidence. *Caveat lector!* There is hardly a sentence in all of Diderot's articles on the Jews in the *Encyclopédie* that is not either taken textually from another source or added by Naigeon after Diderot's death! Good sense would therefore dictate that such materials be treated as used rather than original writings.

Published versus Unpublished Writings

Carl Becker (p. 57) notes the curious fact that "having published almost everything he wrote up to a certain date [1765], Diderot published, after that date, almost nothing, although he wrote more than ever before . . .'' Is it valid to maintain, as does Gendzier in his defense of Diderot, that texts unpublished by Diderot in his lifetime, should be regarded as less material to the issue of Diderot's liberalism that the published writings?[23] To elicit a negative response to this question one need merely ask which of Diderot's writings published prior to 1765 is more significant for an understanding of his position in French thought than the series of masterpieces flowing from his pen into his desk drawer between 1760 and 1775 and published only posthumously: *The Nun, Rameau's Nephew, D'Alembert's Dream, Jacques the Fatalist and His Master, Supplement to Bougainville's Voyage*, the *Salons, The Actor's Paradox, Refutation of Helvétius*, and the *Plan for a University*. One might with better logic argue that it is precisely in the works that Diderot consciously *reserved for posterity* that one may fully appreciate his liberalism and his humanism.[24] This is said in full cognizance of Becker's opinion that the unpublished writings were frequently paradoxes, reflecting the usually unresolved clash of "two Diderots," "the speculative philosopher . . . and . . . the emotional preacher of morality" (p. 64), and of Thomas's opinion that as paradoxes they sometimes appear to be mere intellectual games (pp. 40–41). It is this writer's contention that the dialectical obsession of the mature Diderot is *fundamental* to an understanding of the man and very relevant to any attempt to determine his position vis-à-vis the Jewish question.[25]

However, a special kind of problem is that of the pertinence of judgments expressed in Diderot's private correspondence. It is surely harder to demonstrate that such expressions were uniformly intended for public consumption. Yet, an author as sensitive as was Diderot to the opinion of posterity,[26] could not have been unmindful of it in his eloquent and moving letters to Sophie Volland, to the sculptor Falconet, and to others. A judicious use of Diderot's private correspondence would therefore appear justifiable.

Approaching the Question of Diderot and the Jews

The twentieth-century reader never ceases to wonder how
Voltaire could write in one place that all men, including the Jews,
are brothers,[27] and in other places heap so much abuse upon the
Jewish people.[28] Without excusing the excesses of Voltaire's language—which Diderot privately condemned (see chap. 2, n.
34)—and without attempting to justify the contradictions between
his universalism on the one hand and his apparent racism on the
other, it is necessary to draw some distinctions between the eigh-
teenth- and twentieth-century ideological climates and the status
of the Jews in European society.

Ever since the infamous Dreyfus Affair, anti-Semitism has
become an instrumentality of antiliberal political movements
reacting violently to real or illusory Jewish political and economic
power.[29] The attack on the Jews, especially since the Hitler period,
has automatically become associated with the general denial of
human rights. To the contemporary mentality it therefore comes as
a shock to read of the unsympathetic treatment of the Jews in the
writings of the leader of eighteenth-century French liberalism. The
position of the Jews in the eighteenth century was quite different.
Living in social and economic isolation, in communities dominated by a religious hierarchy and fossilized sumptuary laws, the
Jews appeared as the antithesis of a liberal social entity and of the
universalist philosophy. Thus it was not only not an anomaly for an
eighteenth-century French liberal to love all of humanity in the
abstract and to harbor a strong dislike for the Jews in the concrete
but rather a normal, though regrettable, state of affairs. Furthermore, the negative image of the Jews in eighteenth-century
French liberal eyes was intrinsically bound up with the liberals'
struggle against Christian dogma and with their concomitant desire
to undermine the authority of the Holy Scriptures, including of
course the Old Testament. The attack on the Old Testament involved three basic arguments: (1) its lack of credibility (contradictions, scientific and historical errors), (2) its immorality (stories of

perversion and cruelty), and (3) its lack of literary merit. In the course of the attack on Church dogma and the Old Testament, which had ironically been launched by the Jew Spinoza in the seventeenth century, it became a standard tactic to denigrate "Mosaism" and to characterize the people of the Old Testament as a morally and culturally base or inferior people, hardly a credible choice for the leading role in God's historical drama, as claimed by Christian theologians.[30] Unfortunately, the low state of Jewish culture in eighteenth-century Europe seemed to confirm this unflattering assessment of the Jews.[31] For a century addicted to dyadic oppositions, the Jewish tradition was the negative pole to the classical tradition's positive pole, and the opposition of Greek "truth and beauty" to Hebrew "myth and coarseness" became a commonplace.[32]

In light of the foregoing, it is essential, in order to formulate a comprehensive evaluation of a French philosophe's position on the Jews, to deal with a broad spectrum of considerations, including all of the following: (1) the Jews as a religious and historical phenomenon, (2) the Jewish cultural heritage, (3) the Jews as a contemporary social problem, and (4) the question of national character and human diversity. The study of the latter point will necessitate an examination of Diderot's theory of heredity. It is hoped that this study will accomplish for Diderot what near the end of his life he hoped to accomplish for the Roman philosopher Seneca[33] and will rectify the image of the "lover of humanity."[34] It is further hoped that, in the process, an additional significant facet of Diderot's fascinating writings will be illuminated.

Diderot and Judaism

Embrace the man of good will regardless of his beliefs.
—Diderot[1]

Diderot's Formation

DENIS Diderot was born in Langres, province of Champagne, in 1713, the eldest son of a well-to-do cutler, a devout Catholic who wanted his son to become a priest.[2] Young Denis studied in the local Jesuit school and was tonsured at age twelve. He was a precocious student and was rewarded for his success with an internship at the celebrated Parisian Collège d'Harcourt. He is believed to have attended classes in this Jansenist *collège* as well as in the leading Jesuit Collège Louis-le-Grand, and he received an excellent classical and biblical education. "I was suckled early on the milk of Homer, Virgil, Horace, Terence, Anacreon, Plato, Euripides, blended with that of Moses and the Prophets," recalls Diderot in old age.[3] He was undoubtedly also suckled on the sermons of Bossuet, like any typical French Catholic child, and exposed to what the poet Péguy has called "a virus that ceaselessly works in us," the virus of anti-Semitism.[4] It is unlikely that he saw a real, flesh-and-blood Jew in person before adulthood, for there were none in Langres and no more than several hundred living more or less clandestinely in Paris.[5]

Diderot's classical and biblical education laid the intellectual foundations for the future philosopher and encyclopedist: Pantophile, as Voltaire would call him. And so, to quote a Will Durant witticism, "The Jesuits lost a novice by sharpening a mind."[6] It did not take long for the sharp-minded provincial to perceive a fundamental antithesis between the two ancient cultures being taught him, between the rationalistic Greco-Roman and the irrational biblical,[7] and to develop a strong preference for the former. Furthermore, it wasn't long before the French ''virus'' would be crossbred with the Greco-Roman strain, as evidenced in the anti-Jewish writings of Plutarch, Pliny, Cicero, and Tacitus. Even the benevolent Horace, Diderot's lifelong passion, would indelibly associate in his mind Jewishness with simple-minded credulity in the Horatian formula ''*Credat Judaeus Appella*.''[8] Nor was it long before his aversion to Jewish credulity was equalled by his aversion to its Christian counterpart, and so Diderot soon rid himself of the last vestigial traces of a theological vocation.[9] Then he was pensioned out to a lawyer friend of his father's but spent his time studying Greek, Latin, Italian, English, and mathematics on his patron's time. One day, declaring his emancipation from his father's conventional expectations of him,[10] he gave up all thought of a normal professional career and avidly plunged into the cultural and intellectual stream of Paris, living a hand-to-mouth existence relieved by the generosity of friends or strangers and by the occasional sale of his services writing sermons for preachers or doctoral theses for theological students at the Sorbonne. It was then 1742.

For more than half a century, French religious thought had been infiltrated by subversive notions from abroad. Spinoza in Holland and Blount in England had begun what was to become an orchestrated attack on the divinity of the Bible. The Dutch Jew Spinoza had been followed at the end of the seventeenth century by the French Huguenot Bayle, exiled in Holland, while in England a new ''natural religion,'' based on the universalist and rationalistic doctrines of Lord Herbert of Cherbury, had won substantial support among English intellectuals. The English deists were Lockean, that is, they believed that man perceives God directly through his senses. They rejected the Judeo Christian doctrine of a single historical revelation. Their rejection of the divinity of the Mosaic Scriptures was later coupled with harsh judgments on the biblical Jews. The writings of the English deists were popular among the French freethinkers in exile. From England and Holland interest in the religious *nouveautés* spread out over the continent. Along with the interest in English deism was a revival of interest in Judaism.[11] The Englishman Bolingbroke, who met Voltaire in Paris in 1720 and inspired his attack on the Jews and the Bible in *Epistle to Urania* (1722),[12] exemplified the spirit of anti-Judaic deism. Matthew Tindal's *Christianity as Old as Creation* a decade later repeated the Bolingbrokian theme of ancient Jewish barbarity.[13]

By late 1742 Diderot's proficiency in English was such that he was able to translate Temple Stanyan's *History of Greece* for the publisher Briasson. He thereby learned at one stroke that he could, at one and the same time, satisfy his intellectual and economic needs.[14] After publishing a translation of *James Medical Dictionary* in collaboration with Eidous and the freethinking moralist Toussaint, he was drawn, possibly through the influence of the latter, to attempt a translation of a portion of Lord Shaftesbury's deistic *Characteristics*, the "Enquiry concerning Virtue or Merit," in which human virtue is treated as "natural" and independent of revealed religion.[15] The publication in 1745 of *The Principles of Moral Philosophy, or Essay on Merit and Virtue (Principes de la philosophie morale, ou Essai sur le mérite et la vertu)*, Diderot's free translation, or adaptation, of Shaftesbury, marks the beginning of his career as a philosopher, moralist, and religious critic.

From Deism to Atheism (1745–1749)

The two references to Jews in *L'Essai sur le mérite et la vertu* are in the form of Diderot's notes to the Shaftesbury text. Both concern the Jewish religion and are worthy of examination. Both purport to prove that Judaism illustrates the principle that religion not only doesn't guarantee virtuous behavior, it may actually impede it. In the first of these, which occurs near the beginning of the *Essai*, Diderot asserts that the Jewish practice of usury on non-Jews is allowed by Mosaic law. "Wouldn't you be better off dealing with 'a very bad Jew . . . who might even be suspected in the synagogue of being tainted with Christianism'?" he asks.[16] One cannot be sure whether Diderot was familiar with the history of usury in Christian Europe and the relative moderation of Jewish money-lenders compared with some of their Christian competitors.[17] But it was necessary for him to begin by at least pretending to exempt the Christian religion from attack on moral grounds, and the fact that Christians might actually be worse than Jews did not negate the thesis that formal religion had nothing to do with the practice of virtue, a thesis underpinning Diderot's constant devotion to religious tolerance. It is significant that this thesis would be reaffirmed in an unpublished Diderot text written twenty-eight years later, *with no exception made for Christianity*.[18]

The second reference to the Jewish religion (I, 56–57) is an expansion of Shaftesbury's contention that rewards and punishments do not guarantee virtue and that only a religion in which the reward promised is the chance to practise and exercise virtue in an afterlife is not incompatible with real virtue. Diderot contrasts the Jew, who has no other dream than temporal felicity; the Egyptian, who hopes to become a white elephant; the pagan, who counts on the delights of strolling in the Elysian Fields and partaking of its nectar and ambrosia; the Mohammedan, "deprived of wine by his law and voluptuous by temperament," who yearns to drink himself drunk eternally among his gray, red, green, and white houris; and the Christian, "who alone expects only a virtuous reunion with his God." In writing this passage, Diderot could only have had tongue firmly planted in cheek. It should be apparent to any student of the French philosophes that the Jewish expectation of felicity on earth coincided perfectly with their own materialistic aspirations and secular morality and would appear to them the least ridiculous of the four.

The "preference" shown by Diderot for Christian morality over Jewish in Book One of the *Essai* will be revealed in Book Two as a ruse, of the type perfected by Bayle in his bold examination of

Jewish and Christian Scriptures. It consisted of satisfying the
censor in the obvious places and suggesting elsewhere a more
subversive thesis. Thus, when Shaftesbury compares human and
animal morality and demonstrates that without religion and following only their natural instincts animals behave more "morally" than humans, that religious beliefs *sometimes* even encour-
age human cruelty, Diderot, in his notes, cites cases: Arab and
English religious wars, the cruel disposal of the ill in Asia, the
Mingrelian Christian practice of burying children alive, the Carib
and Peruvian practices of eating their young. He concludes by
saying that "The diverse customs, religions, and governments of
Europe would furnish us with a multitude of actions, less barbarous in appearance, but as fundamentally irrational and perhaps
more dangerous in their consequences."[19] It is clear that Diderot
did not consider Jewish practices, which are not mentioned here,
more irrational or dangerous than Christian.

In the following year Diderot published his first original work,
the *Pensées philosophiques* (*Philosophical Thoughts*), in effect an
expansion of his notes on Shaftesbury, bolstered by anti-Christian
themes expressed more directly in the clandestine manuscripts of
the period, such as Dumarsais's *Analyse de la religion chrétienne*
(1739) and La Mettrie's *Histoire naturelle de l'âme* (1745). Diderot also reached back to Spinoza and Bayle.[20] The principal
purposes of this anti-Pascalian work were to propose a deistic
alternative to Christianity, to advocate the uses of reason and the
experimental method in the search for truth, and to establish the
claims of esthetic sentiment and moral conscience. However,
Diderot takes a tentative step beyond deism and suggests an
atheist's argument, which he only temporarily rejects, for the
theory of a universe composed of eternal matter. This theory,
founded on ancient Greek atomism, had been revived in seven-
teenth- and eighteenth-century France especially by Gassendi and
the notorious *Testament* of the late curate Jean Meslier (1733).[21]

For the purposes of this study, what is most significant about the
differences between the *Essai* and the *Pensées* is the fact that until
the next-to-the-last *pensée*, the pretense of Christian superiority

obulus has developed a platonic theory of correspondences
lain the mysteries of life: "I realized that Cleobulus had
d a sort of local philosophy; that his entire landscape was
te and articulate for him; that each object furnished him with
its of a particular kind, and that the works of nature were, in
es, an allegorical book in which he read a thousand truths that
ed the perceptions of the rest of humanity" (p. 180). Aristes
irges Cleobulus to reveal systematically the philosophical
that he has discovered so that he may publish them and
ten mankind, "the most important service that one can
m in its behalf" (p. 181). After a brief debate on mankind's
ity for enlightenment, Cleobulus yields. The remainder of
ork is a triple allegory of the alleys of thorns, chestnuts, and
rs, symbolizing respectively Judeo-Christian asceticism and
cism, deistic moderation and tolerance in the Epicurean
ion, and atheistic hedonism and self-indulgence.
s in his allegory of the alley of thorns that Diderot writes of the
but, as might be guessed, they are not his principal target.
rincipal target is the Christian church, described as the army
e prince of the universe. Its uniform is an immaculate white
and a band covering the eyes (one recognizes here a reminis-
e of Voltaire's *Epistle to Urania*).[29] The guardians of the
er alley of thorns are the Doctors of the Church, "the nastiest
I know.[30] Proud, miserly, hypocritical, knavish, vindictive,
specially quarrelsome, they have inherited from Friar John of
unnels[31] the secret of smashing their enemies with their
ards; they would destroy each other for a word, if they were
rously allowed to do so" (p. 195).
r thirty-two numbered paragraphs Diderot, in a heavy-handed
orical satire, lampoons Church, pope, priests, monks, and
ogians, after which he is ready to take on the Bible itself.[32]
is code is composed of two volumes; the first was begun
nd the year 45,317 of the Chinese era, thanks to an old
herd who was expert in manipulating the quarter-staff, and a
magician to boot" (p. 200). The old shepherd is of course

over Judaism has been dropped, and it is the former that becomes
the primary target. This is not to suggest that there will be a
warming up to Judaism. To Diderot as to Montesquieu, the child is
the creature of the mother.

Yet, explicit references to Jews or Judaism are infrequent here.
There is an attack on the cruelty of the biblical God without
specific mention of either (VII, VIII, IX); there is an attack on
prophecy and revelation intended to debunk the contemporary
fantasies of the Convulsionaries (XLI); there are two attacks on the
divinity of the Bible, one based on its literary mediocrity (XLV),[22]
the other on its lack of textual integrity (LX). The few explicit
mentions of Jews are in *Pensée* XLII, where the deicide charge is
couched in hypothetical language—the intent is not to attack the
Jews but to deny the efficacy of miracles as an argument for
conversion; in *Pensée* XLIII, where Diderot quotes the appeal of
Julian the Apostate for mutual tolerance among the people of
Galilee—"It is by reason and not by violence that one should
influence men towards truth," says Julian after blaming the
"seditious priests" for fomenting trouble; and, finally, in *Pensées*
LXI and LXII, which purport to decide the question of which of the
major religions is the most acceptable. The fact that Christianity is
declared the winner in *Pensée* LXI will not fool any reader in the
know. In *Pensée* LXII, Diderot's true opinion is disguised in what
he cunningly calls the "singular" argument of the deists, to wit,
that deism, being the second choice of all the others, must therefore be preferred. There is no ranking of the others, but Judaism is
definitely not last, as Sänger would have us believe,[23] for in *Pensée*
LVI Diderot asks rhetorically, "What cult is more absurd than that
of the Egyptians?"[24] It will be noted that, in this entire work, the
only charge against the Jews that was not equally directed at the
Christians was raised against their seditious *priests*. But Diderot,
quoting Julian, was careful to make a distinction between the
priests and the people.[25] Diderot's hatred for fanatical, politically
meddling priests—"It is political religion that I abhor"[26]—would
be lifelong.

The *Pensées philosophiques*, published anonymously, were

condemned by the Paris *Parlement*. Diderot, whose authorship was known in the influential salons of Madame du Deffand, Voltaire's friend, and Madame Geoffrin, future patroness of the *Encyclopédie*, became overnight a leader of the rapidly coalescing movement of the philosophes, clearly identified with the school of Montesquieu and Voltaire. Like Diderot and Condillac, Montesquieu and Voltaire had their ideological roots firmly planted in the soil of John Locke and the English deists. Among other members of Diderot's circle at this time were Rousseau and d'Alembert. It was shortly after the success of the *Pensées philosophiques*, but probably more on the strength of his translation of *James Dictionary*, that Diderot and d'Alembert—the latter already recognized as a distinguished mathematician—were chosen to coedit the largest French literary enterprise of the eighteenth century, the *Encyclopédie*.

The essential spirit of the philosophic movement was humanistic. Its cardinal principle was that the primary concern of human life is the pursuit of terrestrial happiness; to approach this state, it is necessary to discover the true nature of man and to reorder his social and political environment in accordance with the natural law. This philosophic principle has two conditions. There must be absolute freedom of scientific inquiry. There must be absolute freedom to enlighten the public on its results, for it could only be through enlightenment that "the demons" of superstition and fanaticism barring the way to a better, more reasonable society might be dispelled. The Christian church, with its vested interest in preserving a God-centered, as opposed to a man-centered, world, with its fierce resistance to scientific and philosophic threats to its immutable doctrines, and with its unswerving support of despotic monarchies, had long been regarded as the major enemy of the enlighteners.[27] Diderot, like Spinoza, Bayle, and the English deists before him, felt that the time had come to strike a more direct blow at the Church. Such a blow had to meet head on the issue raised by Bossuet, the great seventeenth-century Catholic theologian, who in his *Histoire Universelle* had attempted to explain

the development of human society, from Charlemagne, as an epic drama with G protagonists and with the Jews used as t Providence. To Bossuet, who, as we hav the Jews, Judaism was the first divinel ancient Jewish civilization was absolutel cultures of classical antiquity. In order thesis, therefore, Diderot would be tempt of Bayle and the English deists. The *En* larger and more comprehensive Baylian scholarly articles of biblical criticism inclu of subjects. But, in the meanwhile, Didero satirical work in a pseudo-Voltairian man *sceptique* (*The Promenade of the Skeptic*) relation to the serious philosophical articles the same way that Montesquieu's satirical stand in relation to his more serious *Spirit* of its satirical intent, it contains Diderot's m Judaism and the ancient Jews.

Diderot imagines a dialogue between con with classical appellations, Aristes and Cle of such appellations was an established lite soon made clear that Cleobulus speaks Greco-Roman philosophy. His vestibule busts of Socrates, Plato, Atticus, and Cicero. is a tolerant man who welcomes free discus

> . . .he has never obliged anyone to accept his [parlor] that I have seen the Pyrrhonist the skeptic applaud a successful argumei atheist open his purse to the deist, the deis the Spinozist; in a word, all philosophical together and united by the bonds of friends! will find concord, love of truth, truth itsel and it is here that neither the hair-splitter, zealot, the doctor of theology, the priest, n set foot (A-T, I, 179).

Moses, and Diderot's point is clear. The reference to the antiquity of the Chinese is a blow at the Christian doctrine of the primordial antiquity of the Hebrews and their cultural supremacy in ancient history. The reference to Moses' reputation as a sleight-of-hand artist and magician is intended to underscore the credulity of the Jews and Egyptians. The exodus of the Jews from Egypt is described as the flight of a "seditious sect" who plundered the land as they withdrew.[33] In a similarly irreverent vein, Diderot mocks Moses' account of the history of the Jews and ticks off with relish four or five of the most absurd or scabrous stories in the Old Testament. "Such were the great things that the old shepherd handed down to posterity" (p. 202). This is a direct slap at Bossuet's exaltation of Moses the historian over Thucydides.[34]

After a short passage on the Mosaic code, in which Diderot proposes some dubious interpretations of the origins of customs like circumcision and the eating of unleavened bread, he concludes the story of Moses with the latter's final instructions to the Jews: give no quarter to your enemies and become great usurers, "two charges of which they have acquitted themselves splendidly" (p. 203). The rest of the allegory of the thorns is a satire on the New Testament, the divinity of Jesus, the doctrines of the Holy Trinity and transubstantiation, and Jesus' miracles. The Christian religion is depicted as even more absurd than the Hebrew, for only a small percentage of the Jews were credulous enough to follow Jesus (p. 207). And though Christ's moral teachings were admirable, there was really nothing new about them. "You spout them as though they were new," says Menippus to Mark, "and they are perhaps to a coarse and stupid people, but they are old to the rest of mankind" (p. 208). Finally on the question of the literary merit of the Bible, Diderot is derogatory. "I shall not follow [the shepherd's people] in their conquests, in their founding a new empire, or in their diverse revolutions You must look for these in the book itself, where you will see, *if you can*, historians, poets, musicians, story-tellers, and public criers announcing the coming of the son of our ruler . . ." (p. 203, emphasis added). But even if one were to

concede any poetic merit to it, Diderot much prefers fact and
science to myth and poetry: "The alley of chestnut trees provides a
tranquil abode, and resembles rather closely the ancient Academy . . . . The people who inhabit it are naturally grave and serious,
without being taciturn and severe. Fond of reasoning, they like to
converse and even to debate, but without that harshness and
obstinacy with which their neighbors [in the alley of thorns] yawp
their fantasies . . . . One sees amongst them, traced in the sand,
circles, triangles, and other mathematical figures. Here they create
systems, seldom verses" (p. 215). Thus does Diderot propose an
antithesis between cool right-thinking, the Apollonian character—to borrow a nineteenth-century designation—as exemplified
by the Hellenic tradition, and impassioned fantasy, the Dionysian
character, as exemplified by the Mosaic tradition. It is noteworthy
that this rejection of passion and poetry, representing a departure
from Diderot's stance in the beginning of the *Pensées
philosophiques*, is but a momentary pause at one extreme of the arc
of a pendulum swinging Diderot in his literary career between the
antipodes of poetry and science.

Were the *Promenade of the Skeptic* representative of the Diderot
who emerges in maturity, as is the case with Voltaire in his *Epistle
to Urania*, one could hardly quarrel with Sänger's characterization
of Diderot's scorn for Jews and Judaism. One finds here a totally
negative appreciation, couched in the clichés of Voltaire and the
English deists. The ancient Jews are depicted as arrogant, seditious, barbarous, superstitious, ignorant, and stupid. Their only
redeeming quality, and a dubious one at that, is their poetry. Their
major sin is the engendering of a preposterous and intolerant
religion, which in its turn engendered an even more preposterous
and intolerant one. One sees in the *Promenade* the endemic anti-
Semitism of eighteenth-century France, Christian or secular. To
the Christians, the Jews were damned for killing their God; to their
enemies, the Jews were damned for bringing him to life. But the
Promenade is as uncharacteristic of the real Diderot as Michel Van
Loo's portrait. Diderot himself must have realized it, for never

again, except in a private joke, would he borrow the gross manner of Voltairian burlesque in his writings on religion and the ancient Hebrews.[35]

The *Promenade* was not published in Diderot's lifetime. If it had been, he would probably have gone to prison for it or been exiled from Paris, as Voltaire had been for his *Philosophical Letters* in 1734 and as the younger Crébillon had more recently been for his erotic novel *The Sopha*.[36]

A short while after completing the *Promenade*, Diderot set down in twenty-seven new *pensées*, the articles of his faith in "natural religion." *De la suffisance de la religion naturelle (On the Sufficiency of Natural Religion)*, which was not published until 1770, provided a sharp contrast in tone to the *Promenade*. Its principal thesis was that revealed religions are based on man's word but that natural religion, the oldest of all, comes directly from God and that its only aims are the knowledge of "essential things" and the practice of "important duties," visible in nature (A-T, I, 261). Denying the Christian dogma of damnation of all pre-Christian peoples, Diderot wrote that the "natural religion was just as sufficient for the salvation of those who lived under its law, as the law of Moses for the Jews and Christian law for Christians" (pp. 262–63). "But if," continued Diderot, "natural law was improved by Mosaic law, and the latter by Christian law, why couldn't Christian law be [improved] by another that God hasn't yet chosen to reveal to mankind?" (p. 263). "Everything that has a beginning has an ending; and everything that has not had a beginning will have no ending. But Christianity had a beginning; but Judaism had a beginning; but there is not a single religion on earth whose date is unknown except natural religion. Therefore only it shall not end, and all the others shall pass on" (p. 268). In the twenty-second *pensée* Diderot asks whether Christianity explains more satisfactorily than natural religion the natures of God and man. "If the naturalist is asked: 'Why does one suffer in this world?' he replies, 'I haven't the vaguest idea.' If the Christian is asked the same question, he replies with an enigma or an absurd-

ity . . . . 'Don't you see' [say I to the Christian] 'that you are
explaining this phenomenon as the Chinese explained the suspension of the world in the heavens?' 'Men of China, what holds the
Earth up?' 'A great elephant.' 'And the elephant, who sustains
him?' 'A turtle.' 'And the turtle?' 'Who knows?' 'Well then! my
friend, leave the elephant and the turtle out of it, and begin by
confessing your ignorance' '' (p. 270).[37] ''Could one not say that all
the world's religions are but sects of the natural religion, and that
the Jews, the Christians, the Moslems, even the pagans are but
heretical and schismatic naturalists?'' (p. 271). ''The truth of
natural religion is to the truth of other religions as the witness I bear
unto myself is to the witness I receive from someone else, it is what
bridges the gap between civilized man and the barbarian, the
Christian, the infidel and pagan, the idolator of Jehovah, of Jupiter, and of God, the philosopher and the people, the learned and the
ignorant, the old man and the child, even the sage and the fool . . .
[while sectarian religion is] what separates father from son, arms
man against man, exposes the learned and the sage to the hate and
persecution of the ignorant and the fanatical, and periodically
inundates the earth with the blood of all of them'' (p. 272). ''O
mortals! How have you contrived to make yourselves as unhappy
as you are? How I pity you and how I love you!'' (p. 273). On this
note of elevation and sentiment, Diderot concludes his profession
of faith. The few mentions of Judaism contain nothing harsh,
nothing corrosive. The predominant theme of the work is the
universal brotherhood of man. The predominant note is a profound
wish for its realization.[38]

Diderot's faith in a benevolent nature did not long endure. The
existence of natural flaws argued powerfully within him against
the existence of a Divine Providence. One such flaw was the
human freak. Undeterred by the experiences of Voltaire, Crébillon, and others, and in the midst of his by now feverish editorial
efforts on the *Encyclopédie*, whose subscription campaign and
prospectus were of immediate concern to the publishers, he determined to write and to publish a boldly atheistic work, *Lettre sur les*

aveugles à l'usage de ceux qui voient (Letter on the Blind for the Use of Those Who See). From the time of his first association with Condillac, Diderot was fascinated by the potential consequences of sensationalist psychology in the field of ethics. The *Letter on the Blind* is a seriously provocative study of the correspondences between human moral perceptions and individual sensory acuity. Besides suggesting a relativist theory of human morality based on differing physiological characteristics—the influence of Maupertuis is noteworthy here—the *Letter* marked a clear break with deism and a step directly toward materialistic determinism. For this effort, which incidentally contains no references to particular religions, Diderot was arrested and imprisoned for three months in the tower of Vincennes and released only through the frantic efforts of his publishers, after being forced to beg for his freedom in humiliating letters of apology. Now, in the late fall of 1749, he was ready to complete the prospectus and assemble the materials for the first volumes of the *Encyclopédie*.

The *Encyclopédie* in the Making (1750–1757)[39]

The *Encyclopédie* of Diderot and d'Alembert was *not* a "war machine" of ideologues conceived for the purpose of destroying religion and the French monarchy, as has sometimes been alleged.[40] Rather, it was a positive reaction to the destructive practices of the Church aided and abetted by the *ancien régime*. This point is forcefully demonstrated by René Hubert, who describes how scientific, political, and economic progress was being impeded by French officials under the influence of the clergy and their allies.[41] An example of this interference with progress was the case of Buffon, some of whose writings in natural science were proscribed because he had failed to take cognizance of biblical "theories." "It is not the Encyclopedists who enthralled to polemics the sciences of human societies," writes Hubert. "They found them already in that state [of thralldom] . . . and one should thank them for having struggled to achieve the independence to which they owe their later progress'' (p. 3). The positive purposes of the *Encyclopédie* were set forth by d'Alembert and Diderot in the "Preliminary Discourse" and summarized in Diderot's article "Encyclopédie." They include the systematic collection and exposition of all available knowledge and its transmission to future generations, "in order that . . . our nephews, becoming more enlightened, may at the same time become more virtuous and happy, and that we should not die without having well served the human race" (A-T, XIV, 415). This humanistic statement of purpose clearly enunciates for the first time what became the underlying purpose of all Diderot's subsequent literary efforts and what identifies him as unquestionably the most ambitious moralist of the eighteenth century.

The team of writers assembled by Diderot for the *Encyclopédie* was far from homogeneous either in social or ideological status. There were churchmen and laymen, commoners and noblemen, monarchists and republicans, and Catholics, Protestants, deists, skeptics, and atheists. This is not to deny that the biases of almost all the collaborators were politically liberal and philosophically Lockean, nor that the prerogative of the editors to assign appropriate topics to particular specialists did not to a great extent predetermine the results. Yet this power to commission did not produce absolute ideological uniformity.[42] Thus Formey's article "God" could disagree with the conventional philosophic thesis that Chinese civilization predated the Hebrew. Rousseau's economic theories in "Économie politique" were opposed by Boulanger's "Œconomie politique." Boucher d'Argis's monarchical theory of early French society ("Noblesse") was answered by the article "Représentants," variously attributed to Diderot and to d'Holbach.[43] The articles dealing with religious topics alone were distributed among no less than a dozen different specialists. This, added to the diversity of Diderot's sources in the many articles "assembled" by him alone, accounts for the many differences in tone, style, emphasis, and viewpoint, and sometimes glaring contradictions. That the net result is hostile to revealed religion despite this diversity is less the result of a deliberate antireligious conspiracy by the Encyclopedists, than of the fact that the sum total of positive knowledge available to the best scholars of the day and ''enlightened reason'' did not support the orthodox position of the Church.[44]

The guiding spirit of the *Encyclopédie* was Diderot himself, and, thanks to him, it adhered faithfully to the spirit and methodology of his master, Pierre Bayle. This methodology, as Hubert has pointed out (p. 32), consisted of insincere defenses revealing the weaknesses and errors in Church doctrines[45] and direct attacks on Christian dogma or morality. The more direct attacks were usually concealed in articles purporting to deal with innocent matters (for example, ''Capuchon'' [''Cowl'']).

The central position of the Jews in the Christian theology and theory of history made them a prime target of most of the Encyclopedist writers on religious, philosophical, and historical subjects. The Mosaic doctrine of a ''chosen people'' was unacceptable to the philosophes, not only because it seemed to be contradicted by the known facts of history but more importantly because it offended their belief in the equality of all members of the human family before a hypothetically just God. It was precisely because they were not anti-Semites in the modern sense, that is, racists, that the philosophes refused to concede a special place in the Divine Plan or in nature and history to the Jews.[46] The denigration of the ancient Jews undoubtedly appears excessive to the enlightened twentieth-century reader. But the negative epithets used by eighteenth-century writers had been inherited from the classical tradition and had become a quasiliterary convention.[47] What is more significant in the standard philosophic position on the Jews, however, is that by debunking the historical role assigned to them by Christian theology, it freed them of the burden of theological guilt. To Bossuet and the Christian church, the Jews were *condemned* to wander the earth, forever ''carrying with them the mark of [God's] vengeance, a monstrous people.''[48] The philosophes rejected this baleful article of Christian faith.[49]

It shall not be necessary in this study to analyze each and every article referring to Jews in the *Encyclopédie*. The number is too great, and they are not all particularly significant. It should be sufficient in this chapter to consider only the most important which shed light on Diderot's attitude.

There are several articles intended to show resemblances between Jewish genesis legends and pagan mythologies. Sänger cites "Androgynes," "Antédiluvienne," "Chaos," "Mosaïque et Chrétienne," "Préadamite," and a section of the long article on Jewish philosophy ("Juifs, Philos. de"). Of the six, only "Androgynes," "Chaos," and "Juifs" were signed by Diderot; "Antédiluvienne" and "Mosaïque et Chrétienne" were attributed to him by Naigeon, and "Préadamite" is no longer accepted in the Diderot canon (Proust, pp. 531–38). Sänger objects to the "playful," sometimes mocking tone of the articles "Antédiluvienne" and "Mosaïque et Chrétienne," but admits that the same is found in Brucker, their source. One wonders by what logic Diderot's "playful" equating of Jewish and pagan legends could advance a thesis that the Hebrew religion was more absurd than any of the others in the ancient world. Can it be supposed that Diderot's opinion of Greek mythology is any more positive? "The mythology of the Greeks," he wrote, "was no more than a confused clutter of isolated superstitions; Orpheus formed a body of doctrine from it; he instituted divination and mysteries; he made secret ceremonies of them, a sure means of giving a solemn appearance to these puerilities" ("Greeks," A-T, XV, 50). And if Diderot narrates with a straight face some ludicrous Jewish stories for the purpose of discrediting them, what can one say of this narration of the Greek genesis story?

From the beginning, the children of the Earth and of the Sky fell out with the Sky, and remained hidden in the bowels of the Earth. Earth instigated her children against her husband, and Saturn cut off the Sky's testicles. The blood of the wound fell to Earth and produced the Giants, the Nymphs, and the Furies.

From the testicles thrown into the sea was born a goddess around whom the Cupids assembled: that was Venus . . . (p. 55).

In Diderot's article on the Greeks is a reference to the purity of the Hebrew tradition: "We know only the Hebrews amongst whom tradition has been kept pure and unaltered, and had they had only this privilege it would have sufficed to have them regarded as a very special race and truly cherished by God." It is not necessary to accept Diderot's sincerity in this passage—he obviously did not believe that the Jews were a race favored by God—to reject the offensive rewording of the passage by Naigeon after Diderot's death. This is how the passage appears in the Naigeon edition used by Assézat-Tourneux and subsequent unsuspecting readers: "The Christians claim that the Hebrews are the only people amongst whom tradition has been kept pure and unaltered; but this privilege, which is attributed exclusively to this ignorant and fierce nation, is not more proven than the inspiration of its prophets and the divinity of its religion" (A-T, XV, 50).[50] This is only one of a number of cases of Naigeon's envenoming of Diderot's references to the Jews.[51]

Akin to the Diderotian tactic of equating Jewish and pagan genesis stories for the purpose of debunking the supremacy of Jewish teachings amongst the ancient peoples, is the tactic of denying the originality of Jewish philosophy. The article "Egyptians" purports to show the Egyptians as Moses' teacher, rather than the reverse. Hubert points out that the philosophes could not free themselves entirely from biblical categories. Thus they accepted the notion of a single source of civilization but preferred to identify this source as Egypt, not Israel.[52] "The Egyptians assumed, in the Encyclopedist sociology, the place of the chosen people" (pp. 46–47).[53] On the other hand, the article "Asiatics"[54] falsely traces the Jewish cabala back to Buddha and calls the *Christians* "the most ignorant of all the peoples of Asia, and perhaps the most enthralled to superstition" (XIII, 374; emphasis added). In the article "Arabs,"[54] the Arabs' talent for philosophy is deprecated and the author denies that Moses, "this man learned in all the wisdom of the Egyptians" (p. 315), ever went to live among the Arabs to satisfy his avidity for philosophy. He then debunks the philosophical standing of Abraham (claimed as the father by Arab philosophy), calling his philosophy "pure Jewish imagination" (p. 317), but quotes Maimonides on the superiority of Jewish laws to those of their neighbors the Zabians.

> The famous Moses Maimonides has drawn from the *Arab* authors all that he says of this sect [the Zabians]; and it is by examining with a curious and attentive eye all the extravagant and superstitious ceremonies that he very ingeniously justifies most of the laws of Moses, which at first sight would offend our sensitivities, if the wisdom of these laws were not shown by their opposition to the laws of the Zabians, for whom God wished to inspire the Jews with a great aversion.

Diderot refers the reader to Spencer's thesis that Mosaic laws were divinely ordained to "furnish a perfect contrast with the superstitious ceremonies of the Zabians" (p. 320). Though Diderot casts doubt on this, he seems to confirm at least the *relative* superiority of Mosaic law in this instance: "One could not establish between Jews and Zabians a more powerful barrier" (p. 318). As for the holy books of the Zabians, they contained, according to Maimonides, "ridiculous stories" of Adam, Seth, Noah, and Abraham, "comparable to the fables of the Koran . . . . If you are curious to learn about these fine things, you may consult Maimonides. It would be an abuse of the reader's patience to present him here the fables with which those books are filled" (p. 321). Though there is little doubt that Maimonides himself is being belittled for wasting time on fairy tales,[55] the principal objects of the author's scorn in this passage are the holy books of the Arabs in general and the Zabians in particular. Thus it may be seen that the Jews were treated no more scornfully than other peoples whose religious beliefs and practices "shocked the sensibilities" of the philosophes.[56]

The fact that Christianity was regarded as but a "reformed Judaism" by the philosophes,[57] however, tempted them to seek to trace its most undesirable features in the parent religion. Thus, the author of the article "Resurrection"[58] notes that the dogma of the resurrection of the dead "is a belief common to Jews and Christians alike" (XVII, 22). In his article "Celibacy" Diderot traces this "socially pernicious practice" back to the biblical ideal of purity as exemplified by Adam and Eve before the Fall but acknowledges that the Jews, no less than the Greeks, regarded celibacy as a sin against nature (art. "Children"). And if Moses renounced the company of women after receiving God's laws, and if the Jewish Nazarenes and the purest of the Essenes followed this example, the practice was equally common among Egyptians, Gymnosophists, Brahmans, Athenian hierophants, Pythagoreans, and Cynics (XIV, 43, 47). The article "Divination" recites the history of this "system of absurdities" which "the light of reason couldn't prevent from spreading . . . among the Jews and the Christians" (XIV, 295) and traces it back to Egypt, where the Jews "became infected" with it, then the Greeks, and through them the Romans (p. 288). The article "Mosaïque et Chrétienne," previously referred to, ridicules Christian cosmogony based on Mosaic "physics." "The result is . . . that all these authors, more learned in religion than informed on the secrets of nature, have been of virtually no service to the progress of true philosophy . . . [and] it is not their fault that Moses has not been dishonored by their attributing all their fantasies to him" (XV, 131).

The article "Theocracy," which has now been identified as d'Holbach's (Lough, p. 121), traces the Christian practice of papal consecration of kings back to God's selection of Moses to lead his people out of bondage, a divine act institutionalized by the Hebrews until the time of Samuel, when "the Israelites, with an unprecedented display of ingratitude, tired of being governed by the orders of God himself . . . wished, like the idolatrous nations, to have a king . . ." (XVII, 238–39). The logic of the article is such that if one chooses to assume that d'Holbach is sincere in accusing the Jews of ingratitude, one must also assume that this atheist really believed that God had instructed Moses. D'Holbach is, of course, writing ironically, with an eye on the censor. And when he goes on to say that "the Jews are the only people who provide us the example of a true *theocracy*" (p. 240), it must be understood that he is not talking about a political system, but about the God-Moses relationship. When it comes to tracing the history of theocratic governments, which he calls "impostures," d'Holbach finds examples among the Arabs, the Japanese, the Gauls, the Ethiopians, and the Egyptians. It would be patently absurd to attribute all of these to Jewish influence![59]

The articles "Bible," "Canon," and "Chronologie sacrée" ("Sacred Chronology") all deal with the issue of the textual integrity of the Bible. In the first two, Diderot, copying Chambers, pretends to support the orthodox position of the Church, while noting problems such as the multiplicity of languages used and their relative age ("Bible"), and contradictions in biblical canon among Jews, Catholics, and Protestants ("Canon"). "Sacred Chronology" was written in the wake of and in response to the famous De Prades Affair. it is therefore necessary to digress momentarily from the *Encyclopédie* to consider that event.

In 1751, Abbé de Prades, a candidate for the degree of Doctor of Theology at the Sorbonne and collaborator on the *Encyclopédie*, presented a thesis containing ten propositions that were condemned by Church authorities and the Paris *Parlement* as pernicious, blasphemous, and destructive of Christian dogma. The thesis affirmed the Lockean principle that all human knowledge is acquired through the senses, proposed a rationalistic, utilitarian basis for law in society, established the superiority of theism over revealed religion, cast doubt on miracles and "witnessed" supernatural phenomena, raised the issue of inconsistencies in the cosmogony attributed to Moses, denied that the Mosaic system envisioned rewards and punishments in an afterlife, and challenged the infallibility of the Church. The enemies of the philosophes suspected Diderot of having ghost-written this thesis and urged the withdrawal of the royal privilege for the publication of the *Encyclopédie*. Diderot's response was twofold. First, he collaborated secretly on de Prades's apologia (*Apologie de l'abbé de Prades*), published in 1752. Then, he took pains in the third volume of the *Encyclopédie*, which appeared the following year, to reestablish his "orthodoxy." it is not within the scope of this monograph to treat in detail Diderot's defense of de Prades. There is only one significant reference to Judaism in the *Apologie*, an admission to rejecting the defective chronology of the Pentateuch (A-T, I, 481). A passage "defending" the Mosaic doctrine of the origins of society (p. 465) is intended only to confound the critics of the thesis and cannot be taken seriously. The third volume of the *Encyclopédie* contains two articles directly related to the De Prades Affair: "Chaos" and the aforementioned "Sacred Chronology." The former pretends to support the Mosaic story of creation. It is a masterful example of the Baylian technique of strangling an orthodox argument in a tangle of hypotheses. In this case Diderot plays the game semantically. Taking the Latin word *creavit* (he created), he concludes that depending on what the word means, "one may say of the *chaos* anything one wishes" (XIV, 93). In "Sacred Chronology" Diderot repeats (without defending it) the Pradean argument on conflicting chronologies attributed to Moses. Mention is made of the omission of Chinese chronology, which antedates the Deluge, and of the disparity in chronology between sacred and profane texts. Diderot pretends to reconcile these divergences. "The Christian does not imitate, in his respect for the books containing the foundations of faith, the faint-heartedness of the Jew or the scruples of the Moslem. He dares to apply the rules of criticism, subjecting their chronology to the discussions of reason, and seeking the truth in these occasions with all possible liberty, without fearing to be blamed for impiety" (XIV, 172). The "faint-hearted" epithet applied here to the Jews is a shield behind which Diderot hopes to fend off attacks on his own "impieties." It is an epithet he uses again elsewhere to describe *other people* who are disinclined to challenge religious authority.[60] The article also refers to the "prodigious antiquity of the Chaldeans, the Egyptians, and the Chinese" (p. 177), this after having apparently debunked the antiquity of the Chaldeans in a preceding article ("Chaldeans," p. 82). "The desire to be taken for the most ancient people in the world is a mania *that has commonly afflicted all nations*" [emphasis added].[61]

An objective reader of the *Encyclopédie* cannot fail to note, as is demonstrated above, that the bias of this work, as of its principal editor, is empirical and rationalistic, and consequently hostile to all religions rooted in revelation. The degree of attention paid to Moses and Judaism is proportionate to their importance in French religious and philosophical thought. In dealing with them, it was necessary to bow to the conventional ambivalence of the Christian church. It was both necessary and risky to praise and to blame. "If one dared to publish books openly favoring Judaism," wrote Rousseau in his *Émile*, "we would punish the author, the editor, the publisher."[62] On the other hand, publicly expressed skepticism of the common bases of Jewish and Christian orthodoxy could be equally dangerous. Rousseau's solution to the problem in *Émile* was to praise the Bible and Jesus and to denigrate the Jews.

> Is it possible that a book so sublime and at the same time so simple be the work of men? . . . Never could Jewish authors have found either its tone or its morality . . . . But where had Jesus gotten amongst his people his pure and exalted morality of which he alone has given the lessons and the example? From the depths of the most furious fanaticism, the highest wisdom made itself heard; and the simplicity of the highest virtues honored the basest of all peoples.[63]

To Diderot's credit, he never resorted to the argument that the Jews as a people were incapable of higher moral conceptions. His concern, quite to the contrary, was to demonstrate the universality of the moral impulse in mankind. As mentioned earlier, this theme was expressed in the treatise *On the Sufficiency of Natural Religion* in 1747. It is reiterated again and again in Diderot's works.

One of the chief bases of Diderot's antipathy for the Jewish religion was precisely the inadmissibility of its claim to exclusive moral superiority. In order to destroy this claim it was sometimes necessary to focus on the moral deficiencies of the Jews. This was done in an opportunistic manner in the course of articles dealing with other topics. An example is the story of Hypatia in the article on eclectic philosophy. The tragedy of this pagan woman philosopher is set against the conflicts between the Jews and Christians of Alexandria. In this account, the Jews are depicted as highly volatile, a quarrelsome people (XIV, 342, 343).[64] A more subtle criticism of Judaic ethics is contained in the article "Bois de vie" ("Wood of Life"). Here the description of the Jewish practice of allowing men to touch the Torah sticks as a healing device serves not only to expose Jewish superstition but at the same time to focus on a practice discriminatory of women. On the other hand, such negative characterizations are sometimes balanced by positive. For example, in his article "Enfants" ("Children") Diderot tells how Jewish girls could inherit from the father in the absence of a male heir and that, if a girl had to be sold to save an indigent family from starvation, the buyer "did not abase her in any lowly or demeaning service; she was by no means a slave. She lived in freedom and received appropriate compensations" (XIV, 504–505).

The only systematic treatment of the Jewish religion in the *Encyclopédie* appeared in the ninth volume, prepared in the early or mid-1750s but withheld from publication with volumes VIII–XVII after the publication privilege was withdrawn in 1758. This was in the articles "Judaism" and "Jews, Philos. of." However, before considering these articles, it is necessary to examine two other works of Diderot that were contemporaneous with the earlier volumes of the *Encyclopédie*.

In 1751, Diderot's interest in linguistic and esthetic conceptualization and the senses spurred him to write a sequel to the *Letter on the Blind.* His *Lettre sur les sourds et muets* (*Letter on the Deaf and Dumb*) less controversially theorized on the relation between the senses and esthetic concepts and conventions. Diderot's ideas on the relative esthetic merits of ancient and modern languages and literatures, pertinent to a study of his attitude toward Jewish culture, will be discussed in Chapter 3 of this work. What may be noted here is that the philosophe, always ready to entertain a seductive paradox, proposes to prove what most of his colleagues were denying and what he himself appears to doubt in the *Encyclopédie*, to wit, that the Hebrews are the oldest "race" on earth! He does this by linguistic analysis, and concludes: "If you examine Hebrew attentively you will necessarily come to the conclusion that it is the language of the first inhabitants of the Earth" (A-T, I, 381).[65] This is not the last time that Diderot breaks with a pet Philosophic position when what he regards as the best empirical evidence conflicts with it.

Another work, greatly significant to the understanding of Diderot's intellectual evolution, was published in 1753 (revised in 1754) under the title of *Pensées sur l'interprétation de la nature (Thoughts on the Interpretation of Nature).* Although primarily a declaration of faith in the experimental method, made under the influence of Diderot's latest philosophical beacons, Sir Francis Bacon and Count de Buffon, the *Pensées* contain a new theme that profoundly affected his philosophy. This is the theme of "inspirationism,"[66] or intuition. It is first expressed in *Pensée* XXX:

> The great habit of doing experiments gives the crudest technician a presentiment that has the character of inspiration. All that would be left for him to do would be to make Socrates' mistake, and call it a *personal demon.* Socrates had such a prodigious habit of considering men and weighing circumstances, that, on the most sensitive occasions, there quietly took place in him a prompt and correct calculation, followed by a prediction that scarcely ever went awry. He judged men as people of sensitive taste judge works of the mind, by feeling. It is the same, in experimental physics, with the instinct of our great technicians .... Thus, the most important service that

they have to render to those whom they initiate in experimental philosophy, is less to instruct them in the process and result, than to cause them to acquire that spirit of divination through which one *sniffs out*, so to speak, unknown processes, new experiments, undreamed of results (A-T, II, 24).

Jean Fabre has discovered here a Diderotian confrontation with cold rationalism and a bold step toward the recognition of inspired genius in whatever trappings: poetic, philosophic, or scientific. This new direction, which Jacques Chouillet sees as a marriage of science and the poetic imagination (pp. 366–67), and which may be considered as symptomatic of the preromantic genius principle of esthetics rampant in England and Germany in the 1750s, is later confirmed by the *Encyclopédie* article "Theosophists,"[67] wherein the intuitive genius of Socrates is compared to the other great intuitive geniuses of history: Pindar, Aeschylus, Moses, Christ, Mohammed, Shakespeare, Roger Bacon, and Paracelsus. "O men to whom nature has given this great and extraordinary imagination, who create, who overcome, whom we call fools or sages, who is there that can predict your future?" (XVII, 266). But it would be wrong to assume that Diderot has abandoned materialism for mysticism. To quote Fabre, Diderot is looking for a "psycho-physiological explanation of intuition, based on the memory of impressions and conforming to his sensationalism and material-ism" (p. 211).

There are no specific allusions to the Jewish religion in the *Thoughts on the Interpretation of Nature*. However, Diderot rejects the efforts of all theologies that seek to discover final causes in nature. "That is to substitute human conjecture for God's Creation," says Diderot in *Pensée* LVI. "Nowhere," comments Vernière, "has Diderot's Spinozism been clearer than in his attack on final causes."[68]

The year of the first printing of the *Pensées* was a fateful one for Diderot. For in that year a young German classical scholar and Francophile, Frederick Melchior (later Baron) Grimm, who had earlier met and befriended Diderot through Rousseau's good offices, began a secret literary correspondence with the crowned heads of several German states. Within a few years, this correspondence would be directed to some of the most powerful monarchs in Europe, including Frederick the Great, Catherine the Great, Emperor Joseph of Austria, the queen of Sweden, and the king of Poland. Grimm's *Correspondance littéraire*, mailed with immunity from censorship in the diplomatic pouches of various foreign governments, was able to disseminate abroad works written by Diderot that were deemed too dangerous for publication. Some of his greatest masterpieces, such works as *D'Alembert's Dream, Jacques the Fatalist*, and the *Salons*, would therefore be admired abroad before they were known in France.[69] Grimm also became a valuable agent for the *Encyclopédie*. His most important client would be Catherine the Great, who, in one of her first acts as empress, offered all necessary assistance to Diderot to complete publication of the vast work "in Riga or in some other city of the empire."[70] Although Diderot did not accept this offer, he would later welcome her substantial financial support and ultimately journey to Saint Petersburg to the feet of his benefactress, the empress with "the soul of Brutus and the charms of Cleopatra."[71] In several ways Grimm became indispensable to Diderot's operations and to his ability to weather the storms that began to break out, as the true nature of the *Encyclopédie* became apparent to the Church and its allies at the court of Louis XV.

Another important German expatriate ally of Diderot's and of the Encyclopedists was Baron d'Holbach, a wealthy atheist and aspiring philosophic author. Diderot first became an habitué of his salon, facetiously nicknamed "the Synagogue," in 1752. "The Synagogue" became the most important center of the Encyclopedist movement in Paris, and d'Holbach's estate of Grandval, in the countryside east of Paris, offered Diderot a quiet retreat for weeks at a time when the climate in the capital, political or otherwise, became oppressive.[72]

Both Grimm and d'Holbach manifested, on occasion, a profound dislike for Jews and Judaism, the former in his secret correspondence, the latter in his public writings. It was perhaps because of the secrecy of his letters that Grimm felt free to give unrestrained vent to his anti-Jewish sentiments. In one letter, for example, he attacked the Jews for their "dishonorable commercial instincts." [73] In another he referred to them as "the stupidest, most repugnant, and most abominable people on earth" (VI, 271). And in another he wrote of the vulgar insensitivity of the Jews of Berlin (VI, 421). [74] It is instructive, in order to achieve a better appreciation of Diderot's own writings on the Jews, to view them in comparison to the writings of his associates. [75]

Although they did not finally appear in print until the ban on the last ten volumes of the *Encyclopédie* was lifted in 1765, the articles "Judaism" and "Jews, Philos. of" were composed considerably earlier. [76] The first of these is a perfunctory article, almost entirely based on Chambers's text, so that the account of Judaism in Europe is disproportionate in the space allocated to the Jews in England. Because his major effort would be in the article on Jewish philosophy, Diderot did not bother to modify Chambers's article on Judaism, except to add what Sänger calls "a fanatical, orthodox-sounding argument for the confiscation of [Jewish] property" (p. 114). Sänger is offended by this and by Diderot's "unemotional" narration of the explusion of the Jews from France and England in the thirteenth and fourteenth centuries (p. 30). Unfortunately, Sänger has failed to recognize the irony of Diderot's "defense" of the Christian confiscatory policy directed against the Jews in this "orthodox-sounding" passage: " . . . as their wealth came mostly from usury, the purity of Christian morality seemed to require that they make general restitution of it" (XV, 317). [77] Also, Sänger does not seem to have recognized that the cross-reference to the article "Jews" is to de Jaucourt's article on the history of the Jews in Europe ("Juifs, Hist. de"), a very compassionate treatment of the subject, and not to the article on Jewish philosophy. If he had, he could not have taken seriously the dispassionate, "orthodox" account in "Judaism," which was obviously intended to satisfy the censor. [78]

The article on Jewish philosophy is one of the longest and most commented on in the *Encyclopédie*. It is the principal single piece of evidence used by Reinach, Sänger, and Hertzberg to support their charge that Diderot was fundamentally hostile to the Jews. Two important considerations should be noted in this regard from the outset: (1) the article deals with the Jews from antiquity to thirteenth-century Spain and has nothing to say about the Jews in modern Europe, who are the subject of the article by de Jaucourt; (2) the article is almost entirely a compilation from Brucker and Basnage and, as such, cannot be considered the product of Diderot's personal experience with primary sources. The composition of the article is unsmooth, as Diderot abruptly switches from a passage directly translated from Brucker's Latin to Basnage's French and back to Brucker. Taken as a whole, the article resembles nothing so much as the ugly hippogriff, the mythological monstrosity that Diderot symbolically used to describe literary deformity.[79]

The first thirty-eight pages of the article in the Assézat-Tourneux edition were taken almost verbatim from Brucker. The beginning is standard, with an acknowledgment of the Jews' reputation as the most ancient of peoples, a people that uniquely was never polytheistic, and to whose sages God spoke directly. Their first form of government was paternalistic and they were well versed in domestic and rustic economy. Their post-Patriarchal leaders were Moses, David, Solomon, and Daniel, "men of uncommon intelligence... [and] great legislators" (XV, 318). Without lending too much credence to the Jewish and pagan fantasies about Shem and Ham, one can put one's faith in historical accounts of the virtue, judgment, and innocence of Abraham, Isaac, and Jacob. Joseph was admired for his wisdom among the most advanced people on earth [the Egyptians] and governed them for forty years.

"But now we come to the time of Moses; what a historian! what a legislator! what a philosopher! what a poet! what a man!" (p. 318). If one knew only Diderot's *Promenade of the Skeptic* and

the spuriously attributed *Moseiad*, one would find it hard to disagree with Sänger's charge that Diderot's praise of Moses here is
deliberately, hypocritically exaggerated (p. 33). But let us look
elsewhere. Does not Diderot list Moses among the great geniuses
of history in his article "Theosophist"? And does he not exalt him
among the greatest of poets in his *Eulogy of Richardson* (following, p. 73) and in his *Salon of 1767* (following, p. 110)?[80]

The great figures of Hebrew antiquity prior to the Babylonian
captivity are known only through revelation and do not properly
belong to a history of philosophy.[81] The true history of Jewish
philosophy begins with the end of the Babylonian captivity, from
which time on the people are no longer called Israelites or Hebrews
but Jews.[82] The "true history" of Jewish philosophy follows. It is
divided into two major time segments. The first, taken almost
entirely from Brucker (II, 653–78), except for some of the material
on Jewish sects (from Josephus[83]), covers the period from the end
of the Babylonian captivity to the destruction of Jerusalem; the
second, taken almost entirely from Basnage (V, 1–180; XI, 346
ff.; V, 275–84; XIII, 254–80; VII, 6–12, 304–84, 117–302),
except for Naigeon's insertions and a subsection, the " 'Dogmas'
of the Peripatetics, Adopted by the Jews," from Brucker (II,
910-16), covers the period from the destruction of Jerusalem to the
end of the twelfth century.[84] The first part is subdivided in the
following manner: history and doctrine of the Samaritans, Jewish
colonies in Egypt, origin of Jewish sects, the Sadducees, the
Karaites, the Pharisees, the Essenes, and the Healers (Therapeuts).
The second part includes the period from the destruction of
Jerusalem to the publication of the Mishnah; the Talmud and
Gemara; great men among the Jews in the twelfth century; Jewish
ideas on the Divinity; Jewish ideas on Providence and free will;
and the dogmas of the Peripatetics and moral precepts of the Jews.

Taken as a whole, the article on Jewish philosophy is among the
fairest and most objective produced by a non-Jewish writer in the
eighteenth century. Sänger concedes that Diderot's sources were
the best available (p. 118) and that he wrote "only essentially what

his sources contained'' (p. 122). The editors of a recent comprehensive French edition of the *History of the Jews in France*
call the work by Basnage ''very remarkable for the period in its
effort towards objectivity and comprehension'' and Diderot's
contribution on the Jews in the *Encyclopédie* ''relatively moderate.''[85] Hertzberg, on the other hand, sees it as completely negative (p. 310).

It cannot be denied that the article on Jewish philosophy is
unfavorable in its broad lines. The treatment of the Samaritans
stresses their persecution by the Jews. In Egypt the Jews are
depicted as culturally inferior to the Egyptians and the recipients,
not the givers of the cabala and the allegorical method of teaching
religion. The Gemara of Babylon was full of nonsense and the
exoteric philosophy of the Jews is called a confused mixture of
principles that lead to fanaticism and a blind respect for the authority of ''the Doctors'' and for antiquity. Singled out for the harshest
attack is the Talmud and its place in Jewish philosophy is deprecated. Diderot deplores the ''blind obeisance'' paid to it by the
Jews and enumerates some of its absurdities and pernicious teachings. Hertzberg uses this attack on the Talmud to prove that
Diderot was echoing anti-Semitic writers who had preceded him.
But attacks on the Talmud have not been the province of anti-
Semites alone. By Hertzberg's own admission the ''pro-Jewish''
Mirabeau[86] would later warn of the ''dark phantoms of the Tal-
mudists'' (p. 294), and the Talmud has not been exempt from the
attacks of many Jews themselves: for example, Spinoza, Karaites,
Hasidim, and modern Jewish liberals.[87]

More significantly, though Diderot is obviously unfavorable to
orthodox Jewish religious thought, his treatment of the Jews as
people, with few exceptions, is balanced and often favorable.[88] He
reports that Prince Ptolemy Lagus appreciated the ''fidelity and
gallantry'' of the Jews, imported them into Egypt, and gave them
positions of authority (p. 329);[89] he reports that the Jews who
returned to Judea under Philadelphus's beneficent reign were motivated by love of their homeland;[90] he reports that the scorn of the

Egyptians for the Jews was part of their scorn for *all other na-tions*.[91] In his account of the origins of the Sadducean sect Diderot tells of the saintliness of Antigonus Sochaeus and of the Jews' tolerance toward this unorthodox sect until the time of John Hyr-canus (pp. 332–33). Diderot defends the Sadducees for their denial of the existence of spirits "because they had a clear and distinct idea only of sensory and material objects [and] placed God above their ability to comprehend" (p. 335). Furthermore, how could an eighteenth-century materialist disapprove of a sect that denied the immortality of the soul, the doctrine of rewards and punishments in the hereafter, and Divine Providence (p. 336)? Finally, to Diderot the Sadducees furnish the ultimate proof of the Baylian thesis that moral probity is separable from religion, a favorite philosophic tenet:

> A number of Christians have imagined that because the Sadducees denied the rewards and punishments of the afterlife and the immortality of the soul, their doctrine led them to a terrible licentiousness. But one must not draw these kinds of conclusions, for they are often false. There are two barriers to human corruption, the punishments of the present life and the torments of hell. The Sadducees had overturned the latter bar-rier, but they allowed the other to subsist . . . . The desire to be happy on Earth sufficed to hold them to their duty. There are plenty of people who would be little concerned about eternity, if they could be happy in this life (p. 337).

Diderot rejects Josephus's depiction of the Sadducees as fierce and barbarous. Josephus, after all, was a Pharisee!

The Karaites, though more mystical than the Sadducees, are also treated kindly. Diderot notes their "very simple and very pure notion of the Divine Being" (p. 340) and reports on their principal doctrines. His conclusion is benevolent: "Finally, their morality is very pure: they especially profess great temperance; they avoid eating too much or being too fussy over what they are served; they have an excessive respect for their masters; the doctors, for their part, are charitable and teach free of charge; they claim thereby to be distinguished from those who worship money, and exact large payments for their lessons'' (p. 341).

The treatment of the Essenes, which is based entirely on Josephus's *Jewish War*, is no less sympathetic, and the reader is made to appreciate their elevated moral precepts, their continence, their education of children toward virtue, their scorn for wealth, their ''admirable'' equalitarianism and sharing of worldly goods, their living in brotherhood (p. 347); their piety and industry (pp. 347–48); their quiet austerity, their charity, their cleanliness,[92] their peaceableness, and the sanctity of their given word (p. 338). The description of this last quality of theirs is reminiscent of the sympathetic portrait of the Quaker in Voltaire's *Philosophical Letters*: ''They even consider oaths as perjury, because they cannot believe that a man is not a liar when he finds it necessary to take God as his witness to be believed . . .'' (p. 348). Their manner of saying grace would touch the heart of the thickest-skinned philosophe: '' . . . but before sitting down to the table with the others, they solemnly swear to honor and serve God with all their hearts, to observe justice towards their fellow-man; never voluntarily to harm anyone; to help people of good will with all their might; to keep faith with everyone and especially their rulers'' (p. 348).[93] On their sense of honor and courage: ''They prefer death to life when honor is at stake. The war we [Josephus is being quoted] have had against the Romans has revealed in a thousand ways that their courage is invincible . . .'' (p. 349). Their belief in a place of reward for good souls and punishment for bad is similar to that of the Greeks, but they reject the notion of free will (pp. 349–50). Diderot finds it difficult to reconcile this with religion, ''for it is evident,'' he writes, ''that if man isn't free, religion perishes, actions cease to be good and bad, there is no longer punishment or reward; and one is right to claim that there is no more equity in God's judgment'' (p. 351). The passage on the Essenes concludes with the tongue-in-cheek assertion that their remoteness from the cities where Christ preached probably exempted them from his censure of their errors.[94]

According to Philo, there were two kinds of Essenes, one dedicated to good works and the other to contemplation. Of the latter type were the Healers or Therapeuts.

> Their principles were excellent; they left to their relatives all their worldly goods, for which they had a profound contempt, when they had enriched themselves with celestial philosophy . . . . This sect, which Philo has described in a treatise written solely for the purpose of honoring his religion against the Greeks who boasted of the morals and purity of their philosophers, has seemed so saintly, that the Christians envied the glory of their austerity. The more moderate of them, unable to deny absolutely to the synagogue the honor of having produced and nourished them in its breast, have held that at the least they had embraced Christianity from the time that Saint Mark preached in Egypt, and that, changing religion without changing their way of life, they became the fathers and first institutors of the monastic life (p. 352).

It is refreshing to note, in contrast to the contemporary deists' and atheists' usual denigration of the Jews as a means of subverting Christian doctrine, that in this passage Diderot does exactly the opposite. The fact that non-Christian Jews were capable of a moral purity generally thought to be impossible without the Christian Gospels, affords the philosophe the proof of the universal human capacity for moral purity and refutes a prime article of Christian faith. This is made clear when Diderot asks, "But doesn't one see similar examples of temperance and chastity among the pagans, and particularly in the Pythagorean sect, to which Josephus compared it in his day? . . . However, if one finds similar austere practices among the pagans, one should not be surprised to find them among the Jews, enlightened by the laws of Moses; and one should not steal this glory from them and give it to Christianity" (pp. 354–56).[95]

To the same degree that he is benevolent in his portrayal of these Jewish sects, Diderot is hostile in his portrayal of the Pharisaic, for it is in this sect that he sees the model of excessive religious fanaticism and superstition. The fact that this was the only Jewish sect condemned by Christ makes it convenient for Diderot, too, to condemn their excesses, which not surprisingly remind one of the excesses of medieval Christian fanatics, among which were the practice of self-mortification and the iron-handed regulation of all matters relating to religion.

There is no doubt that Diderot's version of the Jewish sects is inaccurate in some instances. The strongly negative picture of the Pharisees, for example, has been revised by contemporary scholars.[96] But is it fair to blame Diderot for what the historians of his time believed? And is the conformity of Diderot's portrayal of the Jewish sects with those of Voltaire and d'Holbach proof of a common malice, as Hertzberg implies (p. 311), or of a sharing of common sources of information? Had there been better sources available for Diderot to choose from, the first hypothesis might be convincing. But there were not. Even Sänger acknowledges the accuracy of most of what Diderot has written on the Jewish sects (p. 54). The "big distortions," he writes, come in the second part, in describing the Talmudic period. But anti-Semitism is not synonymous with hostility to the Talmudic tradition, as has already been noted.

This second part of the article, taken from the "objective, comprehensive" Basnage, begins with the following statement: "The ruin of Jerusalem caused among the Jews revolutions that were fatal to the sciences" (p. 356). The significance of such a statement is that whatever negative judgments on Jewish thought are made subsequently, a nonracial, causative basis has been established. This deterministic explanation of history is consistent with Diderot's later effort to deal with the Jewish question as a social and economic problem. The statement is significant in another respect. By thus dating the downfall of science among the Jews, Diderot-Basnage is contradicting Diderot-Brucker's assertion that the Jews "hadn't the slightest notion of exact sciences" from the time of the Babylonian captivity to the fall of Jerusalem (p. 319). One regrets finding Diderot thus precariously perched on the anomalous back of his hippogriff.[97]

The following passages contain a mixture of negative and positive observations. The "seditious spirit" of the Jewish refugees in Egypt caused a massacre (p. 356), and the Jews in Spain considered themselves superior (ibid.), but the Jews remaining in Jerusalem "could with better reason be proud of their origin" by the establishment of the academies (ibid.), and "The heads of the academies gave great luster to the Jewish nation" (p. 357). The most illustrious of these, "both in moral integrity and in the breadth of his knowledge," was Judah the Holy, who completed the Mishnah (pp. 357–58). But, says Diderot later on, Judah's holiness in reality appears banal, and the miracles attributed to him are not believable (p. 358). Furthermore, he became too proud and placed himself above the laws of his people (p. 359). The fabulous story of his funeral is told with ironic naiveté, but the editor Naigeon, worried lest Diderot be misunderstood, added the formula *"Credat Judaeus Appella, non ego"* (p. 360).[98]

The period of the Mishnah is followed by the period of the Talmud. The study of this period begins with the ironic statement that "Although the . . . Mishnah appeared to be a perfect work, [the Jews] didn't cease to see two great defects in it . . ." (p. 360). The Talmud was therefore conceived to perfect the Mishnah. After repeating Basnage's inaccurate history of its composition, Diderot gives a long section on judgments. It is here that the article on Jewish philosophy becomes most derogatory. But Diderot professes to maintain a "moderate" stance. The critics of the Talmud, he writes, fall into four categories: the Jews, who consider it equal to God's law; some Christians, who rate it too highly; those who would consign it to the flames; and the last, "who take a middle position" (p. 362). Diderot obviously associates himself with the latter. That Diderot has exaggerated his neutrality soon becomes apparent when he emphasizes the Jewish prescription that "those who sin against Moses may be absolved, but . . . those merit death who contradict the doctors" (p. 362). The resemblance between such a precept and the Christian Inquisition is too plain. The "perfection" by the Talmud of the "imperfect-perfect" Mishnah remains itself imperfect. As a result, writes Diderot, it is necessary to furnish commentaries on the Talmud (p. 364). The result of this process is a progressive degradation, and "one can find [in all this] an infinite number of things that could diminish the profound veneration in which this work has been held for so many centuries." In order to make his point, he enumerates some of the less edifying tales and precepts. The danger of the Talmud, in his mind, is that "one's taste is formed by this work, and one becomes accustomed to measuring beauty only by what conforms to the Talmud; but if you examined it as a compilation of different authors who could have been mistaken, who sometimes used very bad taste in the choice of matters they dealt with, and who could have been ignorant people, you would notice a hundred things that degrade religion, instead of showing its splendor."[99]

To the argument of Christian admirers of the Talmud who saw in it a sourcebook for the teachings of Christ, he responds sarcastically, "It seems that Christ and his apostles could be sensible only by copying the rabbis who came after them" (p. 366). Then he returns to a favorite universalist theme: "Christ followed his ideas and spread his thoughts, but one must admit that there are some that are common to all nations, and several men say the same things, without ever having known each other, or read each others' works.[100] All one may reasonably say in this matter is that the Talmudists made comparisons similar to Christ's, but that the application that the son of God made of them, and the lessons that he drew from them, are always beautiful and sanctifying, while the application of the others is almost always puerile and frivolous."[101]

The passages on the Talmud are followed by passages on cabalistic philosophy, "this so-called science" (p. 367). Diderot gives a brief and unsympathetic account of Rabbi Akiba and of his alliance with Bar-Kochba, "the false Messiah," but omits comment on Akiba's *Book of Creation*. As to the author of the second cabalistic text, Rabbi Simeon ben Johai, little is told of his life save the miraculous intervention of God through Elijah in the composition of the *Zohar*.[102] Regarding the latter, Diderot is predictably unappreciative. "If one should ask the meaning of all these mysteries, one must admit that it is very difficult to discover, because, since all allegorical expressions are susceptible to multiple interpretation and engender very different ideas, one can only situate oneself after much trouble and labor: and who cares to go to the trouble, if he has no hope of getting much use out of it?" (p. 370). Diderot notes, besides, that the *Zohar*'s manner of depicting the operations of the Divinity in human disguise "was much in use among the Egyptians" (pp. 370–71).

When he gets to the great Jewish sages of the twelfth century, Diderot is more appreciative, for among them at least one finds the reading worthwhile.[103] The first of these, Ibn Ezra, is called "the Sage, *par excellence*" (p. 372).

> He was one of the great men of his nation and of his century. As he was a good astronomer, he made such fortunate discoveries in that science that the cleverest mathematicians have had no scruples about adopting them. He excelled in medicine; but it was principally for his explications of Scriptures that he was recognized . . . . He showed the way to those critics who today maintain that the people of Israel did not cross the middle of the Red Sea, but that they took a circular route while the tide was low . . . . He didn't dare reject the Cabala outright . . . he simply declared that this method of interpreting Scriptures was uncertain and that if one respected the Cabala of the Ancients, one should not add new explanations . . . or leave Scriptures to the caprice of the human mind (p. 373).

On Moses Maimonides, Diderot quotes Scaliger's opinion that "he was the first of the Jewish doctors to stop dealing in trivialities, like Diodorus among the Greeks," and applauds his criticism of the Gemara (p. 373). The account of Maimonides' life is one of the longest in the *Encyclopédie*, which attests to Diderot's recognition of his importance. Sänger chides Diderot for using too much space on biographical and anecdotal material in proportion to that given the study of his works and thought (p. 73). The criticism is justified, with the qualification that Diderot is merely

following Basnage, here as elsewhere. The treatment of
Maimonides' works is indeed skimpy. His knowledge of medicine
and languages is reported perfunctorily, while most of the brief
sketch of his intellectual contributions deals with his metaphysics,
of which the philosophe is skeptical.[104] One regrets that Diderot
did not recognize in the sage, who had said, ''Teach thy tongue to
say 'I do not know' and thou shalt progress,'' a true precursor of
his beloved Montaigne.

The sections on the cabala (esoteric philosophy) and the Jewish
sages are followed by an exposition of Jewish exoteric philosophy.
This material is taken principally from Basnage. However a brief,
and very negative, introduction is based on Brucker.

> Before speaking of the principal dogmas of the exoteric
> philosophy, it will be worthwhile to warn the reader not to
> expect to find among the Jews soundness of ideas, correctness
> of reasoning, or precision of style; in a word, all that is neces-
> sary to characterize a sound philosophy. On the contrary, you
> will find nothing but a confused mixture of the principles of
> reason and revelation, a deliberate and often impenetrable
> obscurity, principles that lead to fanaticism, a blind respect for
> the authority of the doctors and for antiquity; in a word, all the
> faults that mark an ignorant and supersitious people (p. 378).

This passage effectively sums up the standard mid-eighteenth-
century philosophic attitude toward Jewish philosophic backwardness. There is no doubt that Diderot accepted this assessment as
readily as Voltaire, d'Holbach, and Grimm. The fact that exceptions to Jewish ignorance such as Ibn Ezra and Maimonides had
existed proved one thing, however, a very crucial thing that, as
will be seen in Chapters 4 and 5, distinguished Diderot from some
of his contemporaries: national ignorance is a geographical and
cultural, not a racial, matter.[105]

It would be tedious and not particularly fruitful to set forth in
detail here the subsequent long exposition of Jewish exoteric
doctrines of the Divinity, Providence, free will, grace, creation,
angels and demons, and the first human beings. Let it suffice to say

that the Jewish tendency to think in the allegorical or mythopoeic mode, to rely on visionary penetrations into mystic spheres of thought, contrasts sharply with the rationalistic, scientific mode of classical culture. Although Diderot was beginning in 1754 to show signs of sensitivity to the method of intuitive analogic thought, he was not prepared to accept the substance of Jewish visions.

The article on the Jews is concluded with a listing of fifteen so-called "Peripatetic Dogmas, Adopted by the Jews," and fourteen "Moral Principles of the Jews." The high moral tone and practical wisdom of the latter enable the article to conclude on an edifying note.

The composition of the article on Jewish philosophy coincided approximately with the publication of the *Thoughts on the Interpretation of Nature*. There is a double significance in this fact. Firstly, having written the *Pensées*, Diderot is no longer interested in pursuing the struggle against religion on the battlefield of religious polemics. "In the *Pensées*," writes Fabre (p. 292), "he does battle against all purely speculative forms of reasoning—of which his early materialism was itself the product—towards the goal of constituting a truly experimental science, and of philosophy based on that science." From this time on, therefore, there will be a greater tendency on Diderot's part to reserve judgment on matters for which he had no first-hand evidence. Such a matter was the nature of contemporary Judaism. There would therefore henceforth be very little written by Diderot on the Jewish religion per se until he had had a chance to observe Jewish religious practices at first hand. The opportunity would not present itself to him until his trip to Holland in 1773. The second significance of the *Pensées* resides in their establishment of a new and dominating principle of Diderot's empirical philosophy, the principle of *diversity*. This principle, expressed in *Pensée* LVII, maintains that there are no two individuals exactly alike in nature.

They say, *there is nothing new under the sun*; and it's true for those who go no further than the rough appearance of things.

But what is this maxim worth to a philosopher, whose daily business is to perceive the slightest differences in things? What should he think who says that there aren't two leaves of *exactly* the same shade of green on an entire tree? What would he think who, reflecting on the great number of causes, even known ones, that must coincide for the production of a single nuance of precisely such and such a color, would claim, without wishing to do violence to Leibnitz' opinion, that it is axiomatic that, with the difference in spatial loci in which bodies are placed, combined with the prodigious number of causes, there has probably never been, and there probably never will be in nature two blades of grass of *absolutely* the same shade of green? If things change successively, passing through the most imperceptible nuances, time, which never stops, must ultimately create the greatest difference between forms that have formerly existed, those that exist today, and those that will exist in the distant future (*Oeuvres philosophiques*, pp. 238–39).

Complexity of causative factors and temporal mutability (flux) combine inexorably to assure diversity.

Diderot's principle of diversity is antithetical to racial stereotyping. It is no more possible to find two Jews who are exactly alike than two leaves or two blades of grass. Had Theodore Reinach properly appreciated this Diderotian principle, he would not have mistaken the meaning of a Jewish episode in one of Diderot's novels.[106]

The Years of Creative Maturity (1757—1773)

Work on the *Encyclopédie* almost completely dominated Diderot's waking hours from the time of his release from the tower of Vincennes in 1749 to the publication of the seventh volume in 1757. Meanwhile the creative demons in him lay dormant like a butterfly in its chrysalis. The year 1757 saw the breaking out of a storm over the *Encyclopédie*. The year had begun badly for freedom of the press when Damiens, a religious fanatic, attacked and slightly wounded King Louis XV. A short time later an edict was decreed that authorized the death penalty for the printing of tendentious books or pamphlets. A fierce attack on the *Encyclopédie* was mounted by its clericalist enemies. The appearance in the seventh volume of d'Alembert's article "Geneva," with its praise of that city's government and its "Socinian" clergy, and the untimely publication the following summer of the "blasphemous" *De l'esprit (On the Mind)* by Helvétius, a suspected Encyclopedist, moved the authorities to take action. Helvétius's book was suppressed and its author forced to retract publicly. Shortly thereafter the book was consigned to the inquisitorial fire. In March 1759 the publication privilege of the *Encyclopédie* was revoked and in September the pope officially condemned the enterprise. Several of the Encyclopedists had by now been thoroughly intimidated. D'Alembert had already abandoned the "sinking ship" in 1757. Rousseau, Duclos, and Marmontel dropped out the following year. Diderot refused to quit or even to accede to the urgings of Voltaire and others to come abroad to finish the work in peace. The suspension of the privilege to publish lasted until 1760. The two or more years between the completion of the seventh volume and the resumption of strenuous work on the latter volumes allowed Diderot time to spring his creative demon from its cocoon.

In his "Introduction" to Diderot's *Entretiens sur le Fils naturel (Conversations on the Illegitimate Son)*, Paul Vernière speculates that Diderot began to feel the urge to write for the theater around 1755. "Is he tired of the masked games of the *Encyclopédie*, the dusty polygraphy, the far-out conjectures of the *Interpretation of Nature*? Does he wish to impress the French Academy with a purely literary achievement, as Fréron[107] will insinuate . . .? Does he believe, as is suggested by Felix Gaiffe[108] . . . that by reforming the theater and by creating bourgeois tragedy he will extend the Encyclopedist propaganda? All these reasons are excellent; but to these should be added the insinuative urgings of Grimm the impresario; in [the period] 1755–1757, before the great misfortunes, Diderot has assumed the posture of a factional leader susceptible to the heady wine of flattery. Never was he to believe more naively in his own genius."[109]

That there was genius, who would now doubt? But it did not run toward the theater. Diderot's two "bourgeois" or domestic dramas, *The Illegitimate Son* and *The Father of the Family*, composed in 1757 and 1758, were mediocre. More important than the plays themselves were the manifestoes that accompanied them, the *Conversations* referred to above and the *Discourse on Dramatic Poetry*. In the *Conversations*, says Vernière, "we ... feel the vibrations of a new sensibility" (p. 74). It is the sensibility of Romanticism in the making.[110] This new sensibility would profoundly affect Diderot's writings on the Jews.

Fortunately, the cajolings of friend Grimm were not limited to the theater. Having begun in 1757 to send reviews of the biennial art expositions at the Louvre (Salons) to his literary correspondents, Grimm was able to induce the harried philosophe, who had already written theoretical works on esthetics,[111] to take his place in 1759. Thus was born the twenty-two-year career of the foremost art critic of the eighteenth century. The *Salon of 1759* is but the first tentative flight of the infant critic but how different already are the tone and style of Diderot the esthetician, the enthusiast, the poet, from the plodding polygraph of the *Encyclopédie*! The caterpillar had indeed turned into a butterfly. As an esthetician Diderot began to look at religion and the Jews in a new light. He saw them as the generators of *passion* and *poetry* and as a rich source of inspiration for artistic creativity.

As early as his *Philosophical Thoughts* Diderot had written that there is no "sublime" in the arts without strong emotions (*passions*) (I, II). Though he greatly admired the purity and natural beauty of the Greek and Roman artistic heritage,[112] he was rarely moved by pagan mythology as a subject of visual art. Unlike Voltaire and other classical critics, he came to prefer the evocative power of "our own mythology." Thus, commenting in 1753 on a crucifixion scene in his "Observations on St. Roch Church," he wrote as follows of its poetic power: "A building such as I imagine it, with all the pathos that one could put into it, would convert more people than all the sermons of Lent" (A-T, XIII, 7). Not much later, reflecting Diderot's view, Grimm argued that the Christian religion, appealing strongly to human emotions, provides an effective vehicle for the expression of pathos in the arts, and he described for his readers six *tableaux pathétiques chrétiens* envisioned by Diderot (II, 486).

The *Salon of 1759* formally lifted the veil on Diderot's esthetic principle for religion. Recalling Rembrandt's "Resurrection of Christ," he was dissatisfied with the puny efforts of his eighteenth-century artistic compatriots. "Do you remember, my friend,[113] Rembrandt's 'Resurrection'; the disciples standing by; Christ in prayer, head all wrapped in a shroud, of which one sees only the top and two frightening arms protruding from the tomb? The people here think that all there is to do is to arrange figures. They don't know that the first step, the important step, is to have a great idea. . . ."[114] Two years later, in the *Salon of 1761*, he stands in rapture before Deshays's paintings of Saint Victor and Saint Andrew: "His picture holds you and touches you; it is great, *pathétique*, and violent" (p. 120). But it is in the *Salon of 1763* that Diderot finally enunciates the principle explicitly and broadens it to include a Jewish *pathétique*! In his review of Deshays's "Marriage of the Virgin," he writes:

> Let anyone tell me, after [seeing] that, that our mythology lends itself less to painting than the Ancients'.[115] Perhaps Fable offers more gentle and agreeable subjects, perhaps we have nothing to compare, in that genre, to the Judgment of Paris, but the blood that the abominable cross has caused to flow on all sides offers quite another resource to the tragic palette . . . . The crimes that Christ's folly has committed and makes people commit are just as great dramas and much more difficult [to depict] than the descent of Orpheus into Hades, the charms of Elysium, the torments of Taenarum, or the delights of Paphos . . . . Surely I prefer to look at the rump, the breasts, and the lovely arms of Venus than at the mysterious triangle; but where in all that is the tragic subject I seek? For the talent of a Racine, a Corneille, and a Voltaire one needs crimes. Never has any religion been as fertile in crimes as Christianity, from Abel's murder to Calas's execution,[116] not a single line of its history that has not been bloodied (*Salons*, I, 214).

"Esther Being Presented to Ahasuerus," engraving by Jacinto Gimignani after a painting by Poussin. *Courtesy of Phot. Bibl. nat. Paris.*

Diderot's new principle is that crime is a "beautiful subject" for art because of the powerful emotions elicited and the moral lessons to be derived therefrom.[117]

In contrast to the Christian religion whose crimes inspire a "delicious horror," Diderot finds a different sort of inspiration in Jewish themes: "In another genre, see how much Raphael and other great masters have done with Moses, the prophets, and the evangelists. Do you think that Adam, Eve, her family, Jacob's posterity, and all the details of patriarchal life are a sterile field for genius?" (I, 214).[118] And in Poussin's "Esther Fainting Before Ahasuerus," he experiences the delicious passion of sympathy: "It is surely one of the most beautiful things I know. How beautiful is Esther's grief!" (ibid.).[119] Revolted by Hallé's demeaning portrait of Abraham,[120] he chides the artist: "Your Abraham is a lewd old man, with a leering look, a hooked nose, and the sourly grimacing face of a faun . . . . Monsieur Hallé, you annoy me." Two years later, commenting on a Briard painting of the "good Samaritan," he writes: "Not a shadow of pathos . . . . Isn't this story a thousand times more interesting in my old Bible than on your canvas?" (II, 161). And in his *Salon of 1767*, his masterpiece, Diderot accuses Renou of creating a "caricature of Jews" in his painting of "Christ at the Age of Twelve Conversing with the Doctors of the Law" (III, 301). Instead, he wants to see idealized Jewish figures as in Poussin, Michelangelo, and Raphael, and defends these as conforming to the characters represented.[121]

> Our Abbé Galiani, to whom I enjoy listening as much when he defends a paradox as when he argues the truth . . . adds that Michelangelo had . . . rejected the flattened hair, the Jewish-style beards, the pale, thin, shabby, common, and traditional faces of the apostles, that he had substituted for them the Classical character, and that he had sent, to some monks who had asked for a statue of Christ, the Farnese Hercules with cross in hand; that in other pieces, our Savior is a fulminating Jupiter; Saint John is Ganymede; the apostles are Bacchus, Mars, Mercury, Apollo, etc.

I must first ask: is this actually true? Exactly which are these pieces? Where can one see them? Then I shall want to see whether Michelangelo could, with any judgment, make the figure of the man contrary to his manners, his history, his life . . . . But look at what Poussin did: he tried to ennoble the characters; he conformed to Classical proportions according to the standards of his day; he so artistically fused the Bible and Paganism, the gods of Classical fable with the characters of modern mythology, that only the eyes of scholars and experts can perceive it, and the others are satisfied. That is the wisest course. It is Raphael's; and I do not doubt that it is Michelangelo's (III, 315).

In idealizing Jewish characters the great painters treated Jewish heroes in a manner analogous to the treatment of the classical. This had offended Webb,[122] who had instigated Galiani's criticism. Webb, then, is the butt of Diderot's polemic. "That author didn't foresee that he would be asked why Hercules strangling the lion of Nemea should be beautiful in painting, and Samson doing the same thing should be displeasing" (III, 314). A bas-relief of "David's Triumph after the Defeat of Goliath the Philistine," by the art student Milot, is the subject of one of Diderot's most sensually idealized descriptions:

To the right there are three large Philistines, very contrite, very humiliated, one with arms tied behind him; a young Israelite is busy tying the arms of the other two. Then David is borne to his chariot by some women, one of whom, prostrating herself, embraces his legs, others raise him up, a third, in the rear, crowns him. His chariot is harnessed to two fiery steeds; at the head of these steeds a groom restrains them with the bridle and gets ready to hand the reins to the victor. In the foreground, a sturdy Israelite, completely nude, drives a pike into Goliath's head, which appears enormous, overturned, frightful, with hair spread on the ground. Farther to the left, there are women dancing, singing, tuning their instruments. Among the dancers, there is a sort of Bacchante striking a tambourine, moving with infinite nimbleness and grace, arms and legs raised high; her head is turned towards the spectator, who, incidentally sees her from behind. In front is another dancer holding her child by the hand; the child is also dancing, but her eyes are fixed on the horrible head, and her action is mixed with terror and joy. In the background, some men, some women, mouths wide open and arms raised in acclamation (p. 343).

How different are these noble Jewish characters from the vulgar caricatures of the *Promenade of the Skeptic*![123]

In 1760 Diderot the playwright and Diderot the art critic were joined by Diderot the novelist. The subject of the involuntary confinement of young women in convents prompted him to write *La Religieuse* (*The Nun*), a novel of philosophical and moral importance, philosophical in its theme of human *diversity* (all women are not temperamentally suited for the cloistered life); moral in its differentiation of religiosity and goodness. The model for this novel was the Richardsonian novel of pathetic realism. After Richardson's death in the following year, Diderot wrote a highly emotional eulogy, paying homage to the Englishman's lessons of virtue: "My fellow-men, come and learn from him to reconcile yourself to life's misfortunes; come, we shall weep together over the unhappy characters of his stories, and we shall say: 'If fate overwhelms us, at least good people will weep for us too.'"[124] Then, in a lyrical apostrophe, Diderot pledged to the departed moralist a permanent abode in his literary pantheon. The passage bears reproducing here for its testimony on Diderot's literary idols in late 1761: "O Richardson, Richardson, how priceless you are to me; you shall ever be my book! Forced by pressing need, if a friend falls into poverty, if the mediocrity of my fortune does not suffice to give my children's education the necessary attention, I will sell my books; but you shall remain in my possession, you shall remain on my shelf along with Moses, Homer, Euripides and Sophocles; and I will read you each in turn" (ibid.).

Diderot's exaltation of Moses with the poets of ancient Greece confirms the inclusion of the Hebrew patriarch's name among the great creative geniuses of history in the *Encyclopédie* article

"Theosophists." This article must have been written by Diderot around the beginning of 1760, as he was then working on the article "Saracens," in preparation for the hoped-for lifting of the ban.[125] The article "Saracens" itself is worthy of noting briefly. Besides containing a reference to the Jewish explanation of the diversity of individuals in the philosophical sense, as interpreted by Maimonides (XVII, 42), it contains two passages indicative of the sorry status of the Jews in widely separate parts of the Moorish empire: the first dealing with Averroës' destitution by Prince Al-Manzor, who "relegated him among the Jews" (p. 48), and the second relating the massacre of the Jews of Fez (p. 52). Describing Mohammed, Diderot calls him "a fanatical enemy of reason, who reconciled however he could his sublime fantasies with a few shreds torn from Jewish and Christian writings . . ." (ibid.).

Diderot worked for two more years writing and assembling the materials for the last volumes of the *Encyclopédie*. Finally, on September 12, 1761, he could announce with relief, "That wretched revision is finished. I've spent twenty-four days in a row on it, ten hours of work per day. My corsairs all have their manuscripts before them. It's an enormous mass that terrifies them" (ibid., pp. 209–10). The final completion of his polygraphic chore now freed Diderot once more to pursue his more creative literary interests. Stung by the increasingly virulent campaign of the clericalist enemies of the Encyclopedists and especially by Charles Palissot's satirical comedy *Les Philosophes* (1760) in which he personally was grossly caricatured, Diderot hardened his attitude toward the Church and its allies. The need to express himself in less evasive terms surely accounts to a considerable extent for his new practice of withholding his writings from publication. It also accounts for his desire to go back to an earlier work whose tone, too conciliatory toward religion, now no longer suited him. In November 1762, writing to Sophie Volland, Diderot announced that he was working on a supplement to the *Philosophical Thoughts* (II, 33).

Although it has been shown by Venturi that of the seventy-two new *Pensées* only fifteen are pure Diderot, most of the others having been suggested to him by the anonymous *Objections diverses contre les récits de différents théologiens* (*Various Objections to the Accounts of Different Theologians*), there is no doubt that the *Addition to the Philosophical Thoughts* is an authentic statement of Diderot's current views on religion. From the very beginning he enunciates the principle of reason over faith. A direct attack on Christianity begins in the fourteenth *pensée*. "A true religion," states he in *Pensée* XVIII, "being equally important to all men in all times and in all places, must have been eternal, universal, and evident; none has these three characteristics. All are therefore thrice proven false" (*Oeuvres philosophiques*, p. 60). Attacking the credibility of Christ's miracles, Diderot distinguishes the Jews for having refused to believe them: "One must admit that the Jews are a people like no other; everywhere we have seen people hoodwinked by a single false miracle; and Christ could not convince the Jews with a multitude of true miracles" (*Pensée* XXV).[126] In the thirtieth *pensée* Diderot uses the term *Égyptien imbécile* for people who blindly accept articles of Christian dogma. The contrast between the "stupid Egyptian" (negative) and the "skeptical Jew" (positive) reverses the standard philosophic stereotype, drawn from Shaftesbury, wherein the "stupid Jew" was the archetype of the credulous Christian, while the Egyptian was the true originator of civilization. The attack on the Bible begins with the thirty-fifth *pensée*. The image of a cruel and unjust God is the unfortunate heritage of the Old Testament. But the Christians have only made matters worse: "What horrid Christians have translated as *eternal* signifies in Hebrew only *long-lasting*. It is to the ignorance of Hebrew, and the fierce disposition of an interpreter, that the dogma of eternal punishment is due" (p. 68). In the sixty-ninth *pensée* Diderot unequivocally identifies his principal target as Christianity. Here he condemns not only Christian dogma but Christian morality. He thereby revokes any previous expressions on the superiority of the latter to the Jewish. In his concluding *pensée* Diderot notes in a Latin maxim that he is writing here not for the multitude but for an elite few capable of appreciating the truth.

Diderot's reaction to Palissot's satire had another, more important, consequence: the creation of a new fictional masterpiece, *Le Neveu de Rameau* (*Rameau's Nephew*). Though motivated by revenge and savagely satirical on the corruption of the antiphilosophic clique, this "novel" also plumbed the philosophical problem of the relative moral obligation of the individual to society and to himself. *Rameau's Nephew* has two Jewish episodes, both germane to the study of the Jew in European society. For this reason, an examination of the work is deferred to Chapter 4.

Rameau's Nephew, like most of what Diderot wrote at this time, was withheld from publication by its author. The fact is that, unlike Voltaire and d'Holbach, Diderot was no longer greatly interested in joining in the public assaults on the bastions of Christianity by the philosophic artillery.[127] His interests in the decade of the 1760s were almost totally dominated by two strangely opposite fields, art criticism and psychobiology. His *Salons* in the middle years of the decade had grown from the relatively brief reviews of 1759 and 1761 to the large tomes of 1765 and especially 1767, with additional *Essays on Painting* sandwiched in between. His interest in biology, and its importance to the solution of the mystery of human thought and personality, culminated in 1769 in the composition of his most avant-garde work, the brilliant *Rêve de d'Alembert* (*D'Alembert's Dream*). Nevertheless, for his own amusement, he would on at least one occasion return to the religious question.

In 1763 he was tempted into composing a short treatise in response to a theologian's "anti-Philosophic diatribe" (A-T, II, 73). The result, *Introduction aux Grands Principes* (*Introduction to the Great Principles*), reiterated the principle that no nation is favored by God's revelation.

Proselyte: But has God ever spoken otherwise [than through his works]?

Sage: Yes, he has spoken to his favorites.

Proselyte: To whom? Is it to Zoroaster? Is it to Noah? Is it to Moses? Is it to Mohammed? There's a crowd of people who boast that God has spoken to them. The sad part about it is that he has spoken to each in a different idiom. Which one can be believed? Imposters! why do you try to win me over? What have I to do with your supposed revelations? Isn't the voice of my conscience enough for me? That is a far more convincing way for him to speak to me than through your mouths; the way he speaks uniformly to all mankind, to the savage as well as to the philosopher, to the Lapp as well as to the Iroquois . . . (ibid., p. 82).

Diderot the humanist wanted "religion" that unites all mankind, based on man's inherent moral instincts: "Why not be content with those basic and evident notions that are found engraved in the hearts of all men? A religion founded on these simple notions would have no disbelievers; it would make but one single people of all mankind; it would not cover the earth with blood in times of ignorance, and it would not be a despised phantom in enlightened centuries."

The dialogue between the Proselyte and the Sage is followed by nineteen responses of a Christian to the objections raised to revealed religion. The tenth of these states Bossuet's argument that the survival of the Jews is a mystery explicable only by Christian theology: "Reason demonstrates that the Jewish people should naturally be extinct; yet the Jewish people subsists against all reason" (p. 92). The philosophe replies:

Reason demonstrates, to the contrary, that since the Jews marry and have children, the Jewish nation must needs subsist. But, you will say, how is it that there are no more Carthaginians or Macedonians to be seen. The reason for that is that they have been assimilated by other nations. But since the Jewish religion, and that of the people among whom they live, do not permit them to become incorporated together, they must needs constitute a separate nation.[128] Furthermore, the Jews are not the only people who subsist in this state of dispersion. For many, many years the Ghebers and the Banians have been in the same situation (p. 97).

In response to the Christian argument that the Jews had been given a mission to fulfill, Diderot asks, "And how have they proved it?

By miracles [you will say]. But how is it that the Jews, witnessing the spectacular miracles of Moses, did not acquiesce? How is it that they were in constant revolt against him? You will say that they were insensitive creatures. But I, who haven't seen Moses' miracles and who come five thousand years after him, am I guilty of being as insensitive as they?'' (ibid.). Interestingly, though Diderot cited Jewish incredulity as an argument against Christ's miracles in the *Addition to the Philosophic Thoughts*, this is the first time that he equates Jewish skepticism directly with his own! Furthermore, this is the first time that Diderot has provided a rationalistic exculpation of alleged Jewish rebelliousness. Then, in a plea for universal tolerance, he adds, ''Let there be a cult, that's fine; but let everyone have the right to the one belonging to his own country; and let those who pray to God in Latin refrain from damning those who pray in English or in Arabic'' (ibid.).

In 1766 Diderot's friend, the gifted sculptor Falconet, traveled to Saint Petersburg to execute a statue of Peter the Great for Catherine II, the new Empress of the Russias. On the way, he visited Berlin and reported his impressions to the philosophe. As Berlin had an important Jewish community, Diderot was curious about what Falconet would observe there. Remembering friend Grimm's malicious comment on the Berlin Jews (preceding, p. 53), one better appreciates Diderot's response to Falconet's obviously favorable report:[129] ''I have received your brief note from Berlin, dated September 28. I am very pleased and not very surprised that those Jews are not as disagreeable as they have been described to us'' (*Correspondance*, VI, 343). Diderot the empiricist would like to see for himself. But he would have to wait until 1773.

In the following spring there appeared a scurrilous anti-Semitic pamphlet, published in London under the initials M. F. *La Moïsade (The Moseiad)*, a mock epic of Moses, sneers at the patriarch of the Jews, exaggerates the barbarity of his people, and calls them ''vile and vulgar men, slaves worthy of the yoke you bear.'' Unfortunately, on the strength of its inclusion by Assézat and Tourneux in Diderot's *Oeuvres complètes* (IV, 118–27), critics like Sänger, Lehrmann, and Hertzberg have used it as their most damaging piece of evidence against Diderot. But is the *Moseiad* Diderot's? The case for it has not been made, and, as will be shown, there is much reason to doubt it. In the first place, this satire was a part of a longer *Letter from Thrasybulus to Leucippus*, generally attributed to Nicolas Fréret and included in the 1787 edition of Fréret's *Oeuvres philosophiques*. Secondly, Grimm reviewed the *Letter* on May 15, 1766, and unhesitatingly affirmed the Fréret attribution.[130] Subsequently, Barbier in his *Dictionnaire des ouvrages anonymes (Dictionary of Anonymous Works)* agreed with this attribution. Walckenaer, a nineteenth-century Fréret scholar and like Fréret a member of the Academy of Inscriptions and Fine Arts, rejected Fréret's authorship, "for the honor of the Academy,"[131] and named Diderot as the culprit on the basis of a perceived stylistic similarity. Assézat and Tourneux concede that they included the piece in Diderot's *Oeuvres complètes* "partly to invite the editors of the new edition . . . [of Barbier's *Dictionary*] to undertake a study [of this item], and partly out of condescension for M. Walckenaer's opinion" (p. 119).[132] While Fréret's responsibility for the pamphlet may be regarded as a separate matter from his authorship of the *Letter*, and while his authorship of the former may be dubious, the following facts argue strongly against the attribution to Diderot:

1. There is no trace of *La Moïsade* in Herbert Dieckmann's *Inventaire du fonds Vandeul et inédits de Diderot*,[133] which includes the lists of her father's writings drawn up by Madame de Vandeul.
2. Grimm, who had access to virtually all of Diderot's writings at this time, reported regularly to his freethinking correspondents on all antibiblical writings being published, and, since his correspondence was secret, freely identified or guessed at their authors with no danger to the latter. Not only did he not conceal Diderot's boldest writings from his correspondents, but he was even authorized by the philosophe to have them copied and sent

out with his letters. Grimm's attribution of this work to someone else is strong evidence that it was not Diderot's.

3. In his private correspondence, and particularly in his letters to
   Sophie Volland, Diderot usually reported on his current writings, sometimes sending her copies. There is no mention of this
   work in his correspondence.

4. Diderot refers to ''those rash artillerymen'' who risk ''ending
   up in a bad way'' in commenting to Sophie on the plethora of
   antireligious pamphleteers (see preceding, p. 76 n. 127).

5. Even Grimm complained of the glut of antireligious trash
   published abroad. In his letter of April 1, 1769, commenting on
   a tract entitled *The Three Imposters* (Moses, Christ, Mohammed), Grimm tells his readers that he does not read these
   ''drugs'' (VIII, 324).

6. Unlike Voltaire and d'Holbach, Diderot did not have an English connection for his writings. Instead, he circulated them
   among his friends or allowed them to be sent by Grimm to
   correspondents in Germany and Russia, where they were withheld from publication until after the philosophe's death.
   Around 1770, probably through Naigeon's influence, Diderot
   appears to have renewed his interest in publishing in Holland,
   which he had not done since the second edition of *Les Bijoux
   indiscrets* in 1756. He would also publish in 1773 a couple of
   his moral tales with Gessner's *Idylls* in Zurich.

7. The virulent scourging of Moses and the Jews in *The Moseiad* is
   not typical of Diderot's known writings of this period. One
   recalls his harsh criticism in 1769 of Voltaire's ''anti-Mosaic
   obscenities'' (preceding, n. 35). But Fréret is the acknowledged author of the nasty article ''Abraham'' used by Voltaire
   in his *Dictionnaire philosophique*!

It was not such ''drugs'' that would now tempt the philosophic
demon in Diderot. His mind and his pen were concerned with far
more serious matters. The work for Grimm on the *Salons* was
backbreaking. ''Sunday will make a week since I have left my

study: the work [*Salon of 1765*] is making progress,'' wrote he to Sophie in late October, 1765 (II, 79). On November 10 he announced its completion. ''It is certainly the best thing that I have done since I have begun writing'' (p. 81). But the *Salon of 1765* would be surpassed in volume, richness, and labor by the *Salon of 1767*.[134] The latter was not completed until well into the next year. And by then Diderot was to begin work on *D'Alembert's Dream* (to be studied in Chapter 5).

The years between 1767 and 1769 were marked by a major event of scientific, historical, and philosophical importance. These were the years of the circumnavigation of the globe by the French navigator Bougainville. A cultured man, both scientifically and philosophically inclined, Bougainville would publish in 1771 a long and detailed account of the voyage, describing the characteristics and mores of the natives encountered on the way.[135] He dwelt especially on the innocently idyllic lives of the natives of Tahiti. Bougainville's account, depicting as it did the natural goodness of the non-Christian Tahitians, prompted Diderot to write a *Supplement*, in the form of a series of dialogues, in which man in his pristine state, uncorrupted by the false and prudish morality of Christianity, is confronted by civilized Europeans. ''I find [your] singular precepts opposed to nature and contrary to reason; made to multiply crimes, and forever to anger the old workman [God],'' says the Tahitian Orou to the chaplain of the French ship.[136] ''The capital error of Christianity,'' comments Jean Thomas in regard to Diderot's *Supplement*, ''as in all metaphysical dogmatisms, is . . . to refuse to see man as he is, and to substitute for him some sort of unreal phantom, disembodied, lacking passions and instincts, 'an abstract man, moved by no motive, a man existing only in a dream, or in the mind of a polemist.' ''[137]

Diderot's *Supplement* was begun in 1771 and completed by the beginning of 1773, the year that he would add to *Rameau's Nephew* the episode of a Jew of Utrecht, the victim of his sexual passions (see Chapter 4). For Diderot, like Bougainville, was now engaged in his own voyage of discovery, and Holland's Jews,

Anabaptists, Lutherans, and other non-Catholics could be called his Tahitians.

Voyage to Holland and Russia and Last Writings on Judaism (1773—1778)

At the invitation of Catherine the Great, Diderot left Paris for Saint Petersburg in early July 1773. Within a few days he was in The Hague, Netherlands, for a one-month business stopover, then proceeded on to Saint Petersburg, where he arrived in early October. It was his hope, besides seeing the empress, to observe at first hand the life of the people of Russia, rich and poor, noble and common, Christians and Jews. In this hope he would be disappointed. "Perhaps you would rather I tell you about Russia; but I haven't seen it," wrote he to Madame Necker on his return to Holland. "I missed the chance to go to Moscow . . . . Petersburg is nothing but the Court: a confused clutter of palaces and thatch-roofed houses, great lords surrounded by peasants and purveyors" (*Correspondance*, XIV, 72). Of Jews he saw none. How could he? There were only "a handful" in all of Saint Petersburg.[138]

Most of his time in Saint Petersburg was spent either conversing with the empress or advising her in writing on politics, economics, and religion. Among these writings is an essay "On Tolerance," in which the philosophe warns Catherine of the evils of religious persecution: "It is important . . . to the protector of freedom of thought, or to the enemy of intolerance to hold theology in contempt and the priest in a state of mediocrity and ignorance." He goes on to tell of the evil consequences in France of the persecution of the Jansenists. He compares their wretched state in mid-eighteenth-century France to the wretched Jews and Galileans under Julian, the former weeping over the destruction of Jerusalem, the latter over the destruction of their "fanatical schools." Then "a stupid and stubborn prelate" [Christophe de Beaumont] sets out to harass the few remaining Jansenists, "and in no time at all the sect revives more numerous and violent than ever."[139] On God, he writes: "It is not God who has made man in his image, but men who every day make God in theirs. The Mohammedan God is not the Christian God. The Protestant God is not the Catholic God. The child's God is not the adult's, nor is the latter's the same as the old man's. There are as many ideas of the divinity as there are different temperaments . . . . Personally I don't believe in it, perhaps I shall when dying; 'tis a wrench of the neck that threatens the most firmly mounted head." To Diderot, a basic evil of religion is that it substitutes an arbitrary code for natural law.[140]

> Let's just examine what can result from this order of duties superior to natural human duties, to duties based on the essential relationships between one individual and another individual of the same kind. What becomes of natural law for the person who asks God's pardon for the evil he has done to his fellow-man, who thinks that his first obedience is to a Supreme Being, who places the maxims of the faith ahead of the counsels of conscience and the commands of the law, who imagines that the hope for future happiness requires the sacrifice of a present good?
> What becomes of natural law or the law of nations when I see the hatred of the Mohammedan for the Christian . . .? What becomes of the civil law . . .? What becomes of domestic laws, rights, or duties? No one knows better than I . . . .
> Christ has said: "I have come to bring the sword to Earth, I have come to separate the wife from the husband, the father from the child, the child from his brother." Did not Moses say the same? And what did he not do, in his own nation and in foreign nations, with this opinion? Armed with the sword, did not Mohammed devastate Asia? Just let the priests be turned loose on the philosophes from one parish to another in France, and you'll see what will be left of them in less than twenty-four hours . . . . Saint Louis, the good and just Saint Louis, said to Joinville: "The first time you hear someone speak ill of God (Saint Louis's and Joinville's God, that is), take your sword and cut his belly open for me" (pp. 304–306).

Diderot's admiration for "Moses as genius" is counterbalanced by his hostility to the Moses as bearer of God's terrible, swift sword. This ambivalence, typically Diderotian, can be compared to his ambivalence towards Rameau's fictional nephew; it is symptomatic of a curious dualism in Diderot: the esthetician versus the moralist, exclaiming on the artistic beauty of crime and shedding tears for the victims. Jean Thomas identifies a complementary dualism in Diderot between the artist and the scientist (p. 108). Paul Vernière describes the dualism of the Dionysian and the Apollonian.[141] Jacques Chouillet cites Diderot's antinomies, amongst which he identifies the antinomy of ethics and esthetics (p. 599). The explanation of such dualistic tendencies in Diderot is not intended to render suspect the sincerity of his conflicting expressions on Moses. There is no reason to doubt the sincerity of both in the eighteenth-century writer who perhaps more than any other was sensitive to the complexity of things.[142] But it is important to accept them in their alternate contexts. As an esthetician Diderot could well admire the greatest Hebrew poet. As a philosophe whose freedom and very life were threatened by an intolerant religion that found its precedents in the biblical injunction "they must be put to death,"[143] he could only abhor him. But Moses' greatness was now above Diderot's scorn, and the bantering deprecation of the *Promenade of the Skeptic* is no longer in evidence in Diderot's formal writings on this subject.

If Moses had become a villain-hero to Diderot, the Jews are now treated differently. Prior to his conversion to art, they were only a negative religious-historical entity to him, and could be written about in a coldly abstract manner.[144] Now he is anxious to study them *sur le vif*. Unable to do so in Russia, and refusing to visit Berlin because of his antipathy for the "king with the nasty soul,"[145] Diderot returned to Holland. He arrived in The Hague on April 5, 1774, for a six-month stay. Here, in spite of the pressures of his literary occupations and a heavy schedule of invitations from scholars and dignitaries,[146] he was able to satisfy his curiosity to observe a society different from his own. Diderot's *Voyage to Holland* is the fruit of his observations there. In it he comments on all aspects of Dutch life and on the various classes and religions. Though he is disappointed by the prevalence of superstition and the hostility to freethinkers, he is pleased that there is no real persecution. "Materialism is abhorred there, but it is left in peace" (A-T, XVII, 428). There is a diversity of religious communities, but no one is threatened. "Here a man may commit himself to the prejudices of his childhood and his education without any unpleasant consequence to his happiness and the happiness of others. He can be neither persecutor nor persecuted. The Jew, the Anabaptist, the Lutheran, the Calvinist, the Catholic serve each other and do business together without their religious differences affecting their sentiments of humanity" (p. 440).

In Holland Diderot did not fail to take advantage of the opportunity to visit the Jewish communities and to observe Jewish religious practices. He visited the synagogues of Amsterdam, Rotterdam, and The Hague and wrote approvingly of their beauty (p. 431). In Amsterdam he attended a Jewish service. His account of this visit is good-natured. "Please put on a hat," he is told. "I don't wear one," he replies. "You may enter" (p. 432). Diderot reports on the service in a lively narrative style. He is confounded by the "furious cacophony" of the various chanters, then, after the service, by the hubbub and worldly discussions: "It is enough to make you think you're in one of our churches." With this one sly phrase, Diderot levels the barrier between Jew and Christian and links them in a common bond of humanity.

> Back in The Hague, I asked a rabbi why such noise in the temple, enough to make God plug his ears. He told me that everyone chants his book and his verse, and that each book has its chant, which incidentally is very melodious and very sweet, as he proved to me on the spot.
> I asked him why this impropriety of actions and words after the prayer in the house of the Lord. "It's just that the Synagogue is then no more than a common room, where, like you, we drink, we eat, we chat, we sleep after the prayer. We recognize as a holy place only the temple of Jerusalem, which no longer exists, and we shall have no true synagogue until it is rebuilt, which will happen sooner or later. You may be sure that the Messiah will come if we just give him time" (pp. 432–33).

"**The Dedication of the Synagogue of the Portuguese Jews in Amsterdam,**" engraving by **Bernard Picart.** *Courtesy of Rare Book Division, The New York Public Library; Astor, Lenox and Tilden Foun-*

In light of Diderot's obvious disbelief in Messianism, Christian or Jewish, one might have expected a sly Diderotian quip at this point. But the account ends here with no further comment. Diderot's failure to comment negatively on Jewish religious practices in Holland represents a significant departure from his usual scornful treatment of religion. The complaisant attitude manifested in his dialogue with a real-life rabbi presents a sharp contrast to his conventional philosophic hostility toward the priesthood.

This does not mean that Diderot's recognition of the bond of humanity between the Jews of Holland and the Christians of France had softened him toward religion. His abstention from attacking Dutch Judaism must be interpreted as a growing sensitivity to the fact that a continuation of the earlier philosophic attack on the Jews as a means of undermining Christianity was no longer an appropriate tactic in the 1770s, when the question of civil rights for Jews in France, for the first time, was beginning to surface as a national issue.[147] In short, as Jews were perceived in more human terms by French liberals, it became less and less appealing to use them as a scapegoat in their war on religion.[148] In Diderot's case there was another factor. Since at this stage he rarely wrote for the French public of his own time, he could concentrate his fire more directly on the real enemy, political religion or the temporal power of the Church.

Besides studying Dutch life and institutions during his stay in Holland, Diderot used his time there to work on several literary projects for Catherine II. One of these was a series of commentaries on the empress's "Preliminary Investigation" (*Nakaz*) for the establishment of a new code of laws for the empire. In his *Observations sur le Nakaz*, he warns Catherine of the dangers of priestly power, referring her to Samuel's speech to the people in the Old Testament [149] The establishment of an official church and the use of religion to consecrate the power of the sovereign is a dangerous threat to that power.

> I do not like to give too much weight and importance to those who speak in the name of the Almighty. Religion is a buttress that always ends up overturning the house.

The distance between altar and throne can never be too great. . . . Priests are even more unreliable as preservers of the law than magistrates; *nowhere on earth* has it been possible to reduce them to the state of simple, ordinary citizens without resorting to force [emphasis added]. . . .

The priest is a sacred personage in the people's eyes; the self-interest and security of the monarch requires that he be deprived of this status. . . . The politics of Venice favors the corruption of the priests (pp. 346–47).

Nor does religion pose a threat only for monarchical government. "What man of any sense at all would not recognize immediately, looking at all the religions in the world, a web of extravagant falsehoods, a system of rank ordained as follows: God, the priesthood, royalty, the people? Can such an order be countenanced by a sovereign? Nor is religion any the less pernicious in its consequences for a democratic state. Diminish as much as you can a deceitful system that diminishes you. I say this to *all* sovereign powers" (p. 348).

This generalized attack on religion and the priesthood is echoed in two other documents intended for the empress's use. In his *Plan of a University for the Government of Russia*, Diderot warns again of the socially destructive role of the priestly class.

If it had been a pacifier of popular disorders, a conciliator of parents and children, of spouses and relatives with one another, the consoler of the afflicted, the defender of the oppressed, the advocate of the poor, however absurd the dogmas of such a useful class might have been, who amongst us would have dared to attack it? The priest is intolerant and cruel; the axe that butchered Agag has never fallen from his hands (A-T, III, 511).

The theme of religious intolerance is forcefully reiterated in Diderot's *Memoirs for Catherine II*. "Intolerance has been one of the great scourges of my country, not only because of the blood spilled, the vast multitude of outstanding men in all fields that it has chased out of the country and with whom it has enriched the

surrounding countries, but by the loss of excellent minds . . . .
What I have said about the loss of good minds in France is the very
story of their loss in Italy, in Germany, in Spain, in Portugal.''[150]
The last-named losses can only refer to the expulsion of the Jews.

But the most fundamental objection of Diderot to religion is its
diminishing of the human person.

> What is the nature of a holy book? It is to show man as a
> nonentity in the presence of God; as an atom beneath the hand
> that disposes of it however it wishes.
>
> What are the ethics of a holy book? There aren't any: there
> can't be any. It is necessary only to see therein the Supreme
> Being as master of the just and the unjust.
>
> What is the result? That such a book must be full of atrocious
> actions justified by God's command, of innocent actions
> punished, purely for having been done against His will . . . .
>
> It is a work of wisdom and of folly, of truth and of falsehood,
> of vice and of virtue, the instrument with which the good and
> bad king are killed without distinction, a nation spared or
> massacred (p. 112).

Thus, Diderot's objection to religion is essentially humanistic.
Religion reduces man to a mere object serving for the amusement
of a capricious God. Though Diderot does not mention the Bible
here, it is obvious that the Bible is the archetype of the holy book he
is describing.

But if religion diminishes man, what is one to say of the
deterministic materialism of most of the philosophes? Indeed, the
problem of man's moral autonomy may be considered the last and
most formidable barrier that the philosophy of the aging atheist
must overcome. The problem is enunciated in its most sentimental
form in an undated fragment of a letter believed to have been
addressed to his last mistress, Madame de Maux, in September
1769.

> Your question about the comet has given me a singular thought:
> it is that atheism is close to being a kind of superstition almost as

puerile as the other [religions]. Nothing is unimportant in an
order of things that a general law links and carries along. There
are neither large nor small events. The Constitution *Unigenitus*
is as necessary as the rising and setting of the sun.[151] It is hard to
abandon oneself blindly to the universal tide; it is impossible to
resist it . . . . If I think I love you freely, I am mistaken. It is not
so. Oh, what a fine system for ingrates! I'm furious at being
stuck in a damnable philosophy that my mind can't help believ-
ing, and my heart denying . . . . I could almost turn Christian in
order to assure myself of loving you in this world as long as I'm
here, and of rediscovering you in the next to love you again
(*Correspondance*, IX, 154).

The problem of free will versus determinism—the eighteenth
century called the latter *necessity* or *fatalism*—would prompt Diderot to write his longest and most ambiguous novel, *Jacques le
Fataliste et son maître* (*Jacques the Fatalist and His Master*),
whose title characters uphold philosophical positions curiously
contradicted by the examples of their lives. Thus the Master, the
spokesman of free will, is depicted as a puppetlike figure, manip-
ulated by his socially inferior companion and utterly dependent
on him and on objects like his tobacco pouch, gold watch, and
horse. Jacques, the spokesman for determinism, behaves strangely
like a person in control of his destiny. *Jacques le Fataliste*,
composed sporadically between 1769 and 1783, failed to resolve
the dilemma of a moral person in a deterministic universe. Yet, a
clear statement was necessary. It would come in response to
Helvétius's book *De l'homme (On Man)*, a starkly mechanistic
treatise denying to man any greater claim to moral freedom than
what resides in the plant or the animal.

Here again Diderot affirms from the start that religion is an
unacceptable solution to his philosophical problem. "I detest all
the anointed of the Lord under whatever title . . . . One needs
neither priests nor gods" (A-T, II, 289). But the mechanistic
atheist who reduces human motivation to mere sensation and
equates *feeling* and *judgment* is just as dangerous from the standpoint of the ethical philosopher.

Is it quite true that physical pain and pleasure, perhaps the only bases for the actions of animals, are also the only bases of human actions?

Doubtless we must be constructed as we are and have feeling in order to act, but it seems to me that those are the essential and primary conditions . . . . the immediate and proximate motives of our aversions and our desires are something else again . . . .

To take conditions for causes is to expose oneself to childish paralogisms and to meaningless consequences . . . .

Isn't the distinction between the physical and the moral as substantial as between the sentient animal and the reasoning man?

Aren't those qualities that are characteristic of a sentient being and of a thinking being by turns either the same or different in almost all actions affecting our life's happiness or unhappiness, happiness and unhappiness presupposing physical sensation as a condition, meaning that one can't be a vegetable?

To this degree was it imperative not to make *feeling* and *judging* two perfectly identical operations (pp. 302–303).

I am a man and I need causes in conformity with my humanity (p. 300).

The uniqueness of the human person is his ability to recognize and to react to the conditions of his life. One need merely change the word *conditions* to "situations," and one can perceive how close the latest Diderotian apothegm comes to the Sartrian formula for man as *"une liberté en situation."* Though the person can do little to change the genetic limitations imposed on him by nature and is thus "determined" in the physical sense, though he cannot escape the laws of chance that may cripple him in his mother's womb or thrust him into an unsought hero's role in battle, he may through his lucidity *collaborate* with fate and thus acquire a moral sensitivity. The moral sense in man is attributable to "identity of structure, the source of similar needs, of similar pain, of similar pleasures, of similar aversions, similar desires, similar passions" (p. 356).[152] "Nature, structure, purely physical causes prepare genius," writes Diderot in his *Refutation of Helvétius*, "but moral causes are what make it bloom'' (p. 369). And what of the genetically less endowed? What can the moral precepts of society do for him? "The moral [precept] cannot change the physical [condition], but it constrains it . . . . One can inspire daring in a faint-hearted child, moderation in a violent child, care in a flighty child; he can be taught these things as he can be taught to control his outbursts when suffering pain: he suffers, but he stops complaining'' (p. 379). Thus, without yielding to the temptation of religion, without succumbing to the nihilism of stark mechanism, Diderot salvages the ideal of man's moral perfectability. It is by no means a perfect solution. For how can one teach the "moral imbecile," if the capacity for morality is relative to the capacity to judge, if, as Rameau's nephew cries out, one is genetically bereft of the "moral chromosome" ("*la fibre*")? Not perfect, but, in Diderot's eyes, more just than the Christian solution, for the moral imbecile shall at least not burn eternally in hell. He shall merely be subject to the minimum degree of social constraint required to insure civility.

Diderot's faith in the universality of the moral impulse regardless of religion is diametrically opposed to the charge of unreconstructibility leveled against the Jews by anti-Semites.[153] Commenting on the effect a display of heroism such as one saw in the ancient Greek or Roman theater would have on an Asian unfamiliar with such theatrical spectacles and alien to their ethics, Diderot refuses to affirm, as might his friend Grimm, that they would not be moved (p. 391). The fundamental moral law is engraved in the hearts of all normal human beings, even in the savage (p. 396).

The theme of the universality of the moral impulse, a fundamental theme of the philosophes altogether contrary to racist dogma, is complemented by the theme of universal folly and superstition. There are no people so superior that they have not at one time or another in their history been the dupes of false gods. Though the Oriental people, with the exception of the Chinese, were frequently cited for their ignorance and susceptibility to superstition, this is never explained in racial terms.[154] Even the Greeks, Romans, and Chinese, conventionally praised by the philosophes among the ancient peoples, were no longer uncritically admired by Diderot. On the Chinese, as early as 1753 in his article "Chinese," while generally praising their philosophic spirit, Diderot ridiculed the Chinese myth of Fohi being sired by the rainbow and "tales of this ilk" (XIV, 124). This qualification suffices to demonstrate a characteristic hesitancy in Diderot to sacrifice objectivity for ideological orthodoxy. This tendency to refuse to hew uncritically to an ideological "line" grows stronger as Diderot grows older. Thus, even as he continues to write favorably of the Chinese—"the wisest of empires"—in his *Refutation of Helvétius* (p. 411), in the same work he minimizes their superiority: "The duration of the Chinese government is a consequence, not of its merit, but rather of excessive population . . ." (p. 328). On the religion of the ancient Greeks and Romans, Diderot challenges Helvétius's unqualified admiration. To the latter's statement that "The pagan religion has no dogmas," he responds: "Is it really true? Each of the gods had his story. What shall we call these stories? Anyone who cast doubt on Venus' flirtations or who made fun of Jupiter's love affairs was charged with impiety, persecuted, condemned to death. The Eumolpides were hardly less intolerant than a parish priest . . . . I hate all the anointed of the Lord under whatever name they go" (pp. 287, 289).

From the ethical standpoint, Diderot's objections to religion are based on its social deleteriousness, with its persecution of dissenters; political domination or trouble making by the priesthood; its chilling effect on freedom of speech, press, and scientific inquiry; its justification of cruelty as consistent with God's example; its institution of a moral code contrary to natural law; and its subordination of man to a capricious and chimerical divinity. The time-honored argument in support of religion as a necessary guarantor of civilized conduct, an argument defended by Montesquieu, Voltaire, and Rousseau, is demolished by Diderot in one lapidary phrase: "It is true, religion motivates the return of a piece of gold, but it slays Henry IV" (p. 425).

Diderot's last important work bearing on this study is his *Essai sur les règnes de Claude et de Néron* (*Essay on the Reigns of Claudius and of Nero*), written in defense of the Roman moralist and statesman Seneca. Published in 1778, it was a rare public statement by the aging philosophe. Almost from the very beginning, the issue of the social irrelevance of religious dogma is raised. "It is to the tribunal of Gallion, proconsul of Achaia, that Saint Paul . . . was dragged by some fanatical Jews. 'If this man,' he told them, 'was guilty of an injustice or of a crime, I would support the prosecution with all my power; but since all that's involved is the text of your [religious] law, a dispute over words, decide the matter yourselves: such matters are not in my competence, and I shall not take part'" (A-T, III, 18). Diderot praises Gallion's speech as a model for magistrates to follow, but when Gallion also refuses to protect the Jews from physical attack by the Greeks, Diderot deplores his inaction. "Until then Gallion spoke and acted as a man of wisdom; but when he sees the Greek Gentiles, who hated the Jews, hurl themselves upon Sosthenes, the high priest of the Synagogue, and mistreat him without regard for his authority, he forgets his duty. He should add, I would think: 'Argue all you want, but no violence; the first one who strikes a blow will be seized and locked up'" (p. 19).

Diderot's comments on ancient Roman society are predicated on the life of Seneca. One learns, for example, that at the time Seneca arrived in Rome under the Emperor Augustus, "Judaic and Egyptian rites were proscribed" (p. 23). In a footnote Tacitus is quoted on the deportation to Sardinia of four thousand freemen "infected with this superstition" and whose demise in the unhealthy climate of that island "was a negligible loss." Diderot fails to comment on Tacitus's insensitivity to the value of human life. But, though he spares Tacitus here, he later exclaims in the face of Roman cruelty: "What frightful customs the Romans had!" (p. 290).[155] And he blames even Seneca for his insensitivity toward the mistreatment of Rome's slaves: "As if the slave were not a man! As if it were permissible, to satisfy one's curiosity, to immolate one's fellow-man!" (p. 362).

The sort of ambivalence that has been demonstrated in Diderot toward Moses was partly rooted in his conflicting attitude toward individual genius on the one hand, and religious imposture on the other. As early as the *Thoughts on the Interpretation of Nature*, Diderot had linked creative genius to a singular turn of the mind: "extravagances" to be compared to the delirious dreams of illness (*Pensée* XXXI). Georges May, in his article "Diderot, artiste et philosophe du décousu," likens Diderot's concept of genius to mental derangement, "a superior form of thought."[156] Diderot's article "Theosophists" explicitly links men of great imagination, including Moses, Christ, and Mohammed, Aeschylus, Shakespeare, and Paracelsus, to a turn of mind verging on insanity—"Oh! How closely together come genius and madness!" (XVII, 266). The theme of genius as a form of *folie* is an important premise of the characterizations in *Rameau's Nephew* and *Jacques the Fatalist*, and it is not altogether absent from *The Nun* (Madame de Moni's saintliness is as abnormal as it is remarkable). The fantastic hypotheses of the dreaming protagonist of *D'Alembert's Dream* is a striking manifestation of the same. At this time, in the *Essay on Claudius and Nero*, Diderot reaffirms the principle but warns of its potential evils. "It has been said that there was no great genius without a nuance of insanity:[157] it seems to me at least as true of all great malefaction" (p. 102). Diderot is no longer thinking here of the power of religious leaders. The emphasis in the *Essay* is rather on the dangers of the abuse of political power by an arrogant monarchy, reflecting a shift in the philosophic perception of the source of France's late-eighteenth-century troubles and prefiguring the events of the last decade of the *ancien régime*. With the expulsion of the Jesuits in 1762, the clerical menace in France had abated. Already prior to his trip to Russia, Diderot had perceived the changing order of priority of the philosophic struggle in a letter to Princess Dashkoff: "Each century has its spirit that characterizes it; the spirit of ours seems to be liberty. The first attack against superstition has been violent, immoderate. Once men have dared . . . to lay siege to the barrier of religion, the most formidable barrier that exists as well as the most respected, it is impossible to stop. No sooner have they turned their threatening gaze on the majesty of Heaven, than they will certainly, in the next moment, direct it against the powers of the earth.''[158]

To Diderot, the struggle against religion was inextricably bound up with the struggle for human rights. It is not surprising, there-fore, that the *Essay* contains a eulogy of the new American Repub-lic. Diderot's characterization of the United States as a ''refuge for the children of men who groan or who will groan under the lash of civil or religious tyranny'' (p. 393), anticipates by a century the words of Emma Lazarus on the Statue of Liberty.

The Private Correspondence

Diderot's private correspondence is full of unfavorable allu-sions to Christianity. These occasionally attain a pitch of violence commensurate with his own persecution by the Church and its spokesmen. A single example will suffice to illustrate the inten-sity of his anti-Christian, and especially anti-Catholic, feelings:

> What shall I say, when I see a work of your making in favor of the Christian religion? I shall say that you have committed the greatest possible abuse of the mind; this religion being, to my way of thinking, the most absurd and the most atrocious in its dogmas, the most unintelligible, the most metaphysical, the most tortuous . . . the most threatening to public tranquillity, the most dangerous to the sovereign . . . the most insipid, the ug-liest, the most Gothic and the gloomiest in its ceremonies; the most puerile and anti-social in its ethics . . . the most intolerant of all. I shall say that you have forgotten that Lutheranism divested of a few absurdities is preferable to Catholicism, Prot-estantism to Lutheranism, Socinianism to Protestantism, deism . . . to Socinianism.[159]

Of Judaism he writes rarely in his private correspondence, although there are occasional allusions to the Old Testament. His letter to Grimm of June 5, 1759, informs him that his daughter Angélique will recite passages out of the Old Testament for him. She likes especially the account of crossing the Jordan and the story of Joseph, "which she calls its best tales. The word is hers, and her mother doesn't like it" (*Correspondance*, II, 154).[160] In a letter to Falconet written shortly after he had composed his *Salon of 1767* Diderot defends Rembrandt's biblical characters: "How the devil do you want a biblical subject to be rendered? A tattered wretch would be a fine subject for a boudoir or drawing-room! That kind of reasoning is the result of luxury and its petty taste. When I speak of luxury I mean the kind that hides poverty, and not the kind that comes from abundance" (ibid., VIII, 139). Such a statement confirms Diderot's theory of the Bible as a fertile terrain for the artist, not to be treated lightly. Sänger's thesis purports to prove the contrary. Quoting a letter to Sophie Volland of September 1767, Sänger gives this exchange:

"But the Bible is very good fiction."[161]
"In faith, you're right; I have never read it in that light; I'll begin tomorrow; perhaps it will make me laugh" (p. 19).

What Sänger fails to tell the reader is that Diderot is reporting a conversation with Madame d'Aine, the addle-headed mother of Madame d'Holbach and a frequent butt of his droll stories. The incident is intended to show her frivolous mentality. It would, of course, be foolish not to concede that Diderot enjoyed an occasional joke at the expense of sacred books. For example, there is good-natured levity when, reflecting on the treatment of the animals, he imagines the appearance of a scaly Moses among the carp to take personal credit for the bread thrown into the pond by people (*Lettres à S. V.*, I, 158). Similarly, in an irreverent letter to Abbé Le Monnier, he puns on the word "stick" and quips, "But, apropos of your stick, don't you think one would praise it just the same regardless of the forest in which it were cut. The bonze, the dervish, the iman, the disciple of Moses, of Fo, of Christ, and of any other stick merchant will adapt himself to your fable" (*Corre-*

spondance, VI, 205). Interestingly, however, such jokes were not always disparaging. Thus, in writing to Voltaire about the hope he had that his play *Le Père de famille* would show the public "the image of virtue and the sentiment of humanity," he added humorously, "Then Moses can at last lower his hands raised towards Heaven" (ibid., III, 292), the implication being that this Mosaic gesture is a plea for God-given morality, which he, Diderot, hopes to realize by secular means.

The most convincing testimony in the private correspondence to the sincerity of Diderot's belief in the value of the Bible as a source of artistic inspiration is to be found in a letter to his sister Denise, written in 1772, in which he answers her request for a play worthy of staging in a convent by proposing Racine's *Athalie*: "The subject is drawn from the Bible; the action, simple and interesting; the diction, noble and pure; the sentiments, religious and sublime . . . . It is the most beautiful drama that we have in our language" (ibid., XII, 22). As a second choice he suggests Racine's *Esther*. Proud of his knowledge of the Old Testament, Diderot could as easily spice his prose with a biblical allusion as with allusions from pagan mythology (see notably his letter to Falconet, *Correspondance*, VII, 87), and he twitted his brother, the Canon of Langres, on his inability to read the Bible in Hebrew or in Greek as Diderot the atheist could (ibid., XII, 170).[162]

In point of fact, there is nothing in the private correspondence to confute the conclusions of the preceding study of Diderot's "professional" writings. On the contrary, one is surprised to find, in view of the number of negative references to religion, so few in which the Jews specifically are mentioned. One rare reference occurs in a long letter to Sophie recounting the history and evils of priestly government. Forgetting here Samuel's speech to the people, Diderot traces theocracy back to the Egyptian priesthood, which by inventing hieroglyphics and arrogating all knowledge unto itself plunged the people into ignorance and superstition *(Letters à S.V.*, I, 139). This process was repeated among the ancient Persians and elsewhere in Asia. Diderot then tells of the claim of the priests "in several countries" of the right to the first night in the nuptial bed. "The Jews, who had long lived in a theocracy, were not exempt from this practice" (p. 142). As an example, a case is cited involving the prophet Hosea and a prostitute.

The reader of Diderot's private correspondence finds no propensity in the *philosophe par excellence* to single the Jews out for special unfavorable treatment. On the other hand, the themes of universality and tolerance are nowhere more eloquently voiced. Writing to his brother, then Abbé Diderot, in 1770, he stated his universalist creed in the following terms:

> I have written my archbishop several times. I have had the courage to tell him that, were he a mufti in Constantinople, he would be as beneficent and quite as respectable as a prelate in Paris, and he took no offense.
> Behavior, behavior, dear Abbé, that's the only thing on which it should be permitted to judge us in this world . . . .
> Embrace the man of good will, regardless of his beliefs. There are on Earth an infinite number of different cults; but . . . there is only one morality. The common welfare embraces all humanity and the greatest impiety is to destroy it (*Correspondance*, X, 63).

And in a letter to Catherine the Great, Diderot wrote: "It would be wise to order professors of theology to terminate the teaching of religion with a treatise on tolerance." [163]

Diderot's tolerance excluded no cult, no people.

3

Diderot and Jewish Culture

The style is too turgid, too unnatural, too imitative of
the Hebrew writers, so full of Asiatic bombast....
—Voltaire[1]

I have changed my mind since those days....
—Diderot[2]

FOR the philosophes, to speak of Jewish culture was to speak of
Jewish literature and to speak of Jewish literature was to speak of
the Old Testament. Postbiblical Jewish religious writings and the
writings of the learned Jews of twelfth-century Spain were rarely
evaluated as literature. There was no known Jewish painting,
sculpture, or science in the modern sense. There were no indigenous architectural masterpieces, almost no known Jewish inventions.[3] Little attention was paid to Jewish music. The one important Jewish historian was a Romanized Jew, and the one "true"
Jewish philosopher was an apostate.[4] Jewish ethics were biblical
and talmudic, and were generally viewed with disdain. Except for
the poetry of the Old Testament, therefore, Jewry as such was
regarded as having contributed virtually nothing positive to world
culture.

As has been shown in Chapter 2, the denigration of the Jews by
the philosophes was partly a disguised attack on Christianity,
partly an honest judgment based on the mean state to which Jewish
culture had fallen in eighteenth-century Europe. Of these motives
the first was surely the more vital, for, irrespective of what the
Jews had become in Christian Europe, the appreciation of earlier
Jewish literature was vitiated by partisan ideological considerations. Thus when Diderot denigrated the poetry of the ancient
Hebrews in his first original publication he was merely echoing
Shaftesbury and Voltaire.

100

How miserable is the Latin version [of the Bible]! Even the originals are no masterpieces of composition. The prophets, the apostles, and the evangelists wrote as they perceived things. If one were allowed to consider the history of the Hebrew people as a simple production of the human mind, Moses and his continuers would come out no better than Livy, Sallust, Caesar, and Josephus, none of whom surely are suspected of having written by inspiration. Isn't even the Jesuit Berruyer preferred to Moses?[5]

In order to combat Christian belief in the divine inspiration of the Old Testament, it was necessary to deny its literary merit, and Diderot, despite his having been "suckled on Moses," began his literary career by playing the game according to philosophic rules.

Then, in his *Promenade of the Skeptic*, Diderot echoed another philosophic theme by placing biblical "irrationality" in opposition to classical "rationality." Of the people of the Old Testament he wrote: "It is said . . . that they had fine dreams, saw stars in the middle of the night [?], were prone to finding spirits, and fought courageously against goblins. Such were the great things that the old shepherd [Moses] handed down to posterity" (A-T, I, 202). In contrast is the culture of the Old Academy [classical Athens] whose inhabitants "are naturally grave and serious without being somber and taciturn. Reasoning by profession, they love to converse and even to argue, but without the harshness and obstinacy with which their neighbors [the Jews and the Christians] yawp their fantasies. The diversity of opinions in no way affects the display of friendship or slows the exercise of virtue . . . Here you see traced in the sand circles, triangles, and other mathematical figures. Here they construct systems, but rarely verses" (p. 215).

Emerging from this antithesis of the oneiric Hebrew tradition and the intellectual classical is the concomitant antithesis of poetry and science. The preference of the young Diderot for the latter was clear and unambiguous. It was an attitude that would soon begin to undergo subtle modifications, as alongside the scientific conscience there began to stir a dynamic esthetic conscience.

It is not clear whether these two sides of the Diderotian personality had coexisted within him from the start or whether a bizarre mitosis was set in motion by some external event, as for example his reading of Shaftesbury. What is clear, is that Lockean sensationalism in combination with Shaftesbury's theory of passions had already sown the seeds of Diderot's first esthetic principle, as expressed at the beginning of his *Philosophical Thoughts*:[6] " . . . it is only the passions, and great passions, that can elevate the soul to great things. Without them, gone is the sublime either from manners or from works; the fine arts return to their infancy, and virtue becomes petty" (*Oeuvres philosophiques*, pp. 9–10). But another voice in Diderot, the dominant Apollonian voice of rational control, hastened to rein in the morally dangerous Dionysian principle: "It would therefore be an advantage, you will tell me, to have strong passions. Yes, of course, if they are in balance. Establish a perfect harmony amongst them and you shall not fear disorder. If hope is balanced by fear, sense of humor by love of life, the penchant for pleasure by attention to health, you will see neither libertines, nor hotheads, nor cowards" (p. 11). It is obvious that by balancing opposite emotional forces Diderot merely cancels them out of the creative equation, and what remains is a conventional principle of classical harmony.

The Diderot of 1746 was not yet ready to accept the moral and esthetic consequences of unbridled passion, the esthetics of *désordre*, nor was the still conventional Diderot of the *Promenade*. It was not until the beginning of the first decade of the *Encyclopédie* that the philosophe was forced to face up to the irreconcilability of the passional and the rational as creative principles. A profound Diderotian dilemma was in the making.

Diderot's article "Beau" ("Beauty"), written for the second volume of the *Encyclopédie* in 1751, was still faithful to the classical principle of harmony, and the critical method defined therein is more intellectual than sensational. Commenting on Hutcheson's theory of an "internal esthetic sense,"[7] Diderot wrote: "As soon as we are born, our *external senses* begin to operate and to transmit perceptions of sensory objects to us . . . But the objects of what I call the *internal senses*, or the *senses of beauty and goodness*, do not present themselves to our minds so soon. Time must pass before children reflect on proportions, resemblances and symmetry, on affections and characters . . ." (*Oeuvres esthétiques*, p. 398). Farther on he added:

> We are born with the faculties of feeling and thinking; the first step of the faculty of thinking is to examine one's perceptions, to link them, compare them, combine them, perceive relationships amongst them either of compatibility or incompatibility . . .
>
> When I say, *all that awakens in us the idea of relationships*, I don't mean that, to call a thing *beautiful*, it is necessary to recognize what kind of relationship prevails . . . It is enough that one feels that the parts of a piece of architecture, and that the sounds of a piece of music have certain relationships, either amongst themselves or with other objects. It is the indeterminacy of these relationships, the ease with which they are seized and the pleasure that accompanies their perception, that have led us to imagine that beauty was a matter of sentiment rather than of reason (pp. 415, 419).

But at the same time that the article "Beauty" was written, Diderot's interest in linguistic and cultural theories as promulgated by Van Helmont[8] and Boulanger provided a new standard for his esthetic criticism, the standard of *powerful emotion*.[9] Diderot made direct use of Van Helmont's principle of the relationship between the primitive simplicity of language and its ability to express powerful emotions in his *Letter on the Deaf and Dumb*. First noting the absence of present and imperfect tenses in Hebrew verbs and the double function of the aorist tense in ancient Greek (A-T, I, 362), he concluded that such "imperfections" in primitive languages made them less precise but also less wordy and consequently more capable of concentrated emotional power (pp. 363–69). "I would gladly add that the didactic and orderly movement that governs our language makes it more useful for science . . . that we can better than any other people give expression to the intellect, and that common sense would choose the French language; but the imagination and the passions give preference to the ancient languages and to those of our neighbors'' (p. 371).

Diderot also noted the primitive hieroglyphic function of sounds in the ancient languages in relation to poetic expression (pp. 375 ff.) and concluded that the language of poetry is an infinitely more demanding language than the language of science: ''Then the reading of the most intelligible poets also has its difficulties? Yes, of course; and I can positively state that there are a thousand times more people capable of understanding a geometrician than a poet, because there are a thousand people with common sense for every one with good taste, and a thousand people with good taste for one with the highest order of taste'' (p. 382).

The theories that the older the language the more effective it is as a poetic instrument, and that primitive poetic expression is an esthetically superior achievement represent a clear movement by Diderot away from a narrow classical esthetic standard.[10] These theories were bolstered anthropologically by his contact with Boulanger and his knowledge of the latter's ''blast theory'' of civilization. Boulanger, who specialized in Middle Eastern languages and civilizations, believed that human civilization had been set in motion by a single original physical calamity. This theory had two major implications for a study of comparative cultures: first, that there was a single original civilization, as proved by the ''fact'' that the superstitions of the Jews were universal in the ancient world; and second, that the closer a culture was to ''the original calamity,'' the greater was its creative potential. That Diderot was influenced by Boulanger is confirmed by his preliminary notice to d'Holbach's posthumous edition of Boulanger's *Antiquité dévoilée par ses usages* (*Antiquity Revealed by Its Customs*) (A-T, VI, 339-46).[11] Though the Boulanger theories were not published until the beginning of 1766, Diderot appears to have known them as early as 1751. Thus, as the Van Helmont-Boulanger-inspired principle of the superior power of primitive languages took possession of Diderot, as he concurrently developed a greater appreciation for the roles of imagination and poetry in human culture, the unambiguous preference of the *Promenade* for scientific cultures which "rarely make verses," diminished accordingly.

The Diderot of the earlier *Encyclopédie* articles and of the long article on Jewish philosophy was still essentially unappreciative of the oneiric, mythopoeic literatures usually identified with Oriental cultures. Either Diderot was not yet spiritually prepared to grapple with the disturbing consequences of his nascent cult of energy, or he deliberately ignored it in order to avoid muddying the waters in a work whose purpose was to advance the philosophic cause with its ideal of utilitarian science. It is surely no accident that, when he finally was ready to confront his dilemma, he renounced the broad national audience for a select few, for the one in a thousand endowed with the esthetic sensitivity needed to comprehend him. Thus, in spite of the purely formal homage to the poetic genius of Moses in the opening paragraphs of the article on Jewish philosophy, the accent throughout this as throughout all the articles on mythopoeic cultures, whether pre-Socratic Greek, Egyptian, Arab, Persian, or Jewish, was on their childish irrationality, and his favorite terms for their literary productions were "puerilities" and "insipid fantasies." A principal underlying theme of his articles on the Jews was their lack of a practical, utilitarian cultural bias.[12]

At the very end of his *Letter on the Deaf and Dumb*, Diderot had observed that in the hands of an ordinary man even the more emotionally expressive languages, such as Greek, Latin, English, and Italian, "produce but ordinary things," while less expressive languages, like French, "will produce miracles beneath the pen of a genius. In whatever language there may be, the work that genius sustains never falls" (I, 392). The concept of individual genius thus provided a new element in Diderot's esthetic system. Three years later, in his *Pensées sur l'interprétation de la nature* (*Thoughts on the Interpretation of Nature*), Diderot linked creative genius to intuition. Shortly thereafter, he composed the article "Éclectisme" for the *Encyclopédie*. In it one finds an interesting modification of the concept of relationships (*rapports*) that had been used earlier to support an essentially classical theory of esthetics in the article on "Beauty." Diderot now asserts that intuitive genius perceives among apparently dissimilar things relationships that no one else has perceived. Especially noteworthy is the following passage in which Diderot explains the remarkable similarity between the *yunges* of the ancient eclectics and the monads of Leibnitz:

> One may be all the less surprised at these resemblances, the better one knows the *disordered pace* [emphasis added] and the deviations of poetic genius, of enthusiasm, of metaphysics, and of the systematic mind. What is the talent of fiction in a poet but the art of finding imaginary causes for real and acknowledged effects, or imaginary effects for real and acknowledged causes? What is the effect of enthusiasm in the man who is *transported* [emphasis added] by it, if it is not to make him perceive among dissimilar entities relationships that no one has ever before seen or supposed in them? (A-T, XIV, 313).

It is not irrelevant to note in the tone, sense, and vocabulary of this passage a distinctly preromantic esthetic theory in the making. The orderly Apollonian processes of the creative mind explicitly indicated as a prerequisite to beauty in the earlier article have now fled the scene, and the field is left to the Dionysian enthusiast creating by *disordered* leaps of the mind in a state of transport—one could say delirium or oneirism—permitting the widest latitude to the imagination. How far Diderot has come from the cooly traced circles of the classical Academy described eight years earlier in the *Promenade*! Never mind that the article is a free translation of Brucker. The theory of imaginative genius promulgated here became a permanent part of Diderot's evolving esthetic system, and, as Vernière notes in his introduction to the *Encyclopédie* article on "Genius," would lead directly to Goethe (*Oeuvres esthétiques*, p. 8).

It is not certain whether the article "Genius," which appeared in the seventh volume of the *Encyclopédie* (1957), was written by

Diderot, as Naigeon believed, or by Saint-Lambert, as Grimm claimed. Recent scholarship tends to support Grimm. But there is no doubt that Diderot did at least collaborate on the article in his editorial capacity, and, what is more important, that the article faithfully expresses his views.[13] The description of the genius contained therein is absolutely Dionysian. He is described as a person of extraordinary sensitivity and a hyperactive sensual memory: " . . . in the silence and darkness of his room, he enjoys the lush, cheerful countryside; he is chilled by the whistling winds; he is burnt by the sun; he is frightened by storms . . . . His soul . . . is enthralled by all that can magnify it; using real colors and indelible features, it strives to give substance to the phantoms of its making, which transport or amuse it." The soul of the genius, unlike that of the emotionally controlled creative artist of the *Philosophical Thoughts*, is transported by great, overpowering emotions that uproot it from its psychic moorings:

> . . . now all things are stripped of their imperfections; only the sublime, the agreeable, are traced on the canvas; at such times *genius* makes everything beautiful. At other times [the soul] sees in the most tragic events only the most terrible circumstances, and in such moments *genius* daubs in the gloomiest colors, the powerful expressions of moaning and pain . . . in the heat of enthusiasm, it is cut off from the nature and sequence of its ideas; it is transported into the situation of the characters it sets in motion; it has assumed their characters. If it experiences heroic passions to the highest degree . . . it produces the sublime.

The genius need submit to no academic restrictions, for the rules of taste arc irrelevant to his case. He creates by inspiration, not by rule.

> Good taste is often distinct from *genius*. *Genius* is a pure gift of nature; what it produces is the work of a moment; taste is the work of study and time. It depends on the knowledge of a

multitude of rules, formalized or supposed; it produces conventional beauty only. In order that a thing be beautiful in accordance with the rules of taste, it must be elegant, finished, crafted without appearing to be. To be a thing of *genius*, it is sometimes necessary that it be rough-hewn; that it appear irregular, obtrusive, unrestrained. The sublime and the *genius* glow in Shakespeare like lightning in the long night, while Racine is always beautiful. Homer is all *genius*, and Virgil elegance.

The association of individual genius with primitive emotion, energy, and intuition curiously parallels the association of great poetry with primitive, vigorous, mythopoeic cultures. Prior to 1760 Diderot used Homer and the pre-Aristotelian Greek playwrights, never Moses and the Jews, as models of the poetic genius of the Ancients in his esthetic criticism. Even in the *Letter on the Deaf and Dumb*, while using both the Hebrew and Greek languages to illustrate the primitive poetic principle, he conspicuously omitted Hebrew in his concluding passages on the relative literary merits of the principal languages (A-T, I, 371, 391). The reason for this now appears obvious. The scientist, Appollonian, Voltairian philosophe in Diderot said yes to the Greeks and no to the Hebrews. But the growing ascendancy of the artistic personality in Diderot in the years between 1757 and 1760—with the commencement of his *Salons*, the discovery of his dramatic and novelistic muses, his creation of Dorval and his adulation of Richardson—brought a significant modification of his cultural ideology. Jean Thomas has linked this modification to the maturation of Diderot's humanism.[14] Not the least interesting aspect of this maturation was his changing attitude toward the Jews.

As has been stated in Chapter 2, work on the *Encyclopédie* suffered a hiatus of more than a year as a result of the suppression of its publication privilege in 1759. This interruption coincides almost exactly with the crucial period of Diderot's esthetic conversion. One of the first *Encyclopédie* articles written after the break was the article "Sarrasins" ("Saracens"). It is noteworthy that although he condemns Mohammed's fanaticism in this article, he now uses the term *sublime* to characterize his religious imagination (A-T, XVII, 52), in contrast to his earlier contemptuous treatment of the mythopoeic imagination.[15] The article ''Théosophes,'' written shortly thereafter, describes this kind of imagination in detail.

I conjecture that these men, of a somber and melancholy temperament, owed the extraordinary and almost divine penetration . . . that led them sometimes to wild, sometimes to sublime ideas, to nothing more than a periodic disruption of the machine. Then they thought themselves inspired and they were mad. Their attacks were preceded by a kind of stupor . . . . Drawn out of this lethargy by the sudden surge of humors in them, they imagined that it was a Divine Power descending, visiting them, stimulating them; that the divine breath that had originally been used to give them life was suddenly being revived and regaining a portion of its . . . original energy, and they handed down instructions for coming artificially to this state of . . . ecstasy in which they felt borne up above themselves, a state they longed for, like that felt by those who have tasted the delicious enchantment and delirium that . . . opium leaves on the imagination and on the senses . . . . Oh, how near together are genius and madness! Those whom the fates have marked for good and for evil are more or less susceptible to these symptoms. They have them more or less frequently, more or less violently. They are locked away in chains or have statues erected of them; they prophesy from thrones, stages, or pulpits . . . they are heeded, admired, and followed, or insulted, mocked, and pelted with stones. Their fate belongs not to them but to the circumstances in which they appear. It is in times of ignorance and great calamity that they are spawned, for at such times do men, thinking themselves threatened by a Divine Power, gather round these kinds of madmen who do with them as they wish. They command sacrifices and they are made; prayers, and there is prayer; fasts, and there is fasting; killing, and there is slaughter; songs of gladness and joy, and people don flower wreaths and dance and sing; temples, and they are built; the most impossible enterprises, and they succeed; they die, and they are idolized. In this category may be placed Pindar, Aeschylus, Moses, Christ, Mohammed, Shakespeare, Roger Bacon, and Paracelsus. Change the time and he who was a poet could have been a magician, a prophet, or a law-giver. O ye to whom nature has given that great and extraordinary imagination, who create, who hold sway, whom we call madmen or sages; who is there that can predict your destiny? You were born to march either to the applause of humanity or to ignominy, to lead people either to felicity or to misfortune, and to leave behind you the impassioned clamor of acclaim or condemnation (pp. 265–67).

Which of these fates did Diderot reserve for Moses? Condemnation in 1747, acclaim in 1761. In his *Eulogy of Richardson*, for the first time, Diderot explicitly ranked the books of Moses with those of Homer, Euripides, and Sophocles, and swore to cherish them alike *dans tous les temps* (see preceding, p. 73). Almost coincidentally, he was editing the articles for the last volume of the *Encyclopédie*. Among these was Faiguet's article on usury ("Usure"). Though it condemned the abuse of the practice by Jews and Italians in the European past, it defended usury as economically useful (XVII, 552a). But what is particularly surprising in the article is the idyllic picture it paints of ancient Hebrew society.

It is evident that these passages [from Exodus] present us with a series of precepts that were very good for maintaining the bonds of union and of beneficence that should prevail in a large family, such as the Hebrew people were. . . . [God] had just demonstrated his power by drawing Jacob's descendants out of the yoke of oppression. He destined a delightful country for them, and he desired that they live there as true brothers, sharing this fine patrimony with one another without being able to lose it; repaying their respective debts every seven years; lastly, helping each other to the degree that there should be no poverty amongst them . . . . Besides, it is necessary to observe here an essential difference between the [Ancient] Jews and us; this nation of farmers, [living] without ostentation and pampering, almost without trade and without litigation, were unlike us in [our] indispensable habit of borrowing. What would the Hebrews have done with such great sums? Acquire manor houses and fiefdoms? Such a thing was not possible. All their lands were exempt from vassalage, all, in a way unalienable, could be acquired only on condition that they be returned to their former owners in the year of rejoicing or jubilee which occurred every fifty years. They could buy neither offices nor positions, they hardly had any, and the few they had were not venal. Likewise, they did not know anything about finance or colonial upkeep, nor the numerous other enterprises that are common amongst us (pp. 542–43a).

The life of the Hebrews, as described by Faiguet, reminds one of Fénelon's utopian *Bétique*. The people lived a simple life, close to nature, "equally free of opulence and poverty," in an uncompetitive, equalitarian society, altogether different from the money-oriented society of eighteenth-century France, which Diderot satirized at about the time the Faiguet article was written in *Rameau's Nephew*.

It follows from these differences that the practice of the free loan was a stricter obligation for the Hebrews than for us, and one may add that in view of the influence of legislation on morals, that practice was perfectly natural and easy for them, all the more so because their government supported a certain spirit of union and fraternity amongst them that has never been seen amongst other peoples. . . . These dispositions, so full of humanity and so worthy of a theocratic government, were never customary among the Christians (p. 543b).[16]

Diderot would not be converted to theocracy by Faiguet's article, but it could not help but have an effect on his appreciation of Jewish culture. Gone now was the earlier stereotype of the arrogant, quarrelsome Jew. The *Salons* of the 1760s, with their disapproval of Jewish caricatures and their advocacy of noble Jewish figures in art styled after Michelangelo and Raphael appear to confirm this opinion (see preceding, p. 71).

The *Salons*, and particularly those of 1765 and 1767, are more than mere reviews of painting, engraving, and sculpture. They are esthetic and moral manifestos, and they demonstrate how far from

the calm, measured, Voltairian rationalism of his earlier period
Diderot had moved.[17] Relentlessly pursuing a new protoromantic
ideal, as earlier announced in his discourse *On Dramatic Poetry*—"Poetry needs something enormous, barbarous and un-
tamed" (*Oeuvres esthétiques*, p. 261)—a part of Diderot follows a
course that leads directly to Chateaubriand, Goethe, and Stendhal.
A part only, for Diderot is now more than ever at odds with
himself. The split personality that dazzles one with the brilliant and
moving dialectic of *Rameau's Nephew* argues ceaselessly with
itself in all Diderot's writings of the period of maturity. The basic
issues of the Diderotian dilemma, though its faces sometimes
change, may be summed up as *grandeur* (sometimes called genius
or poetry) versus *goodness* (sometimes called philosophy). This
dichotomy was clearly postulated in the discourse *On Dramatic
Poetry*:

> In general, the more civilized and polite a people is, the less
> poetic are its manners; everything loses strength as it is refined.
> When does nature supply artistic models? In times that . . .
> wild-headed widows tear the flesh of their faces because death
> has carried off a mate; that chieftains, in defeat, lay their
> humiliated brows in the dust . . . that pythonesses, frothing in
> the presence of a tormenting demon, are seated, wild-eyed on
> their tripods, making the dark recesses of caverns moan with
> their prophetic cries; that the gods, thirsting for human blood,
> are placated only by its letting; that bacchantes, armed with
> thyrsi, wander through the forests inspiring terror in mortals
> who cross their paths; that other women strip shamelessly, open
> their arms to the first comer, and sell their bodies, etc.
> I don't say that these manners are good, but they are poetic
> (pp. 260–61).

The same dichotomy finds expression near the beginning of the
Salon of 1767. Imagining a dialogue with Grimm on the subject of
the social and artistic consequences of affluence, Diderot wonders
what kind of country he would like to live in:

"Whenever you see a handful of dirt gathered up on the plain, carried in a wicker basket, to be spread over the bare tip of a rock, with a wattle fence keeping it there in the expectation of a stalk of grain, you may be sure that you will see few buildings, few statues, and that you will find few Orpheuses, that you will hear few divine poems."

"But what do I care about such sumptuous monuments? Is that where happiness lies? Virtue, wisdom, decency, the love of child for parent, the love of parent for child, the ruler's affection for his subjects, the subjects' affection for their ruler, good laws, good education, the general welfare; there now, that's what I long for."

"Show me the land where they enjoy all these advantages and I'll go there, were it China."

"But there . . ."

"I get you. Cunning, deviousness, no great virtue, no heroism, lots of petty vices, children with thrifty minds and contentious lives. There the government is ceaselessly busy staving off the treachery of the seasons . . . the individual filling his loft with grain. No semblance of honor, I must admit . . ."

"Where then should I go? Where can I find a state of permanent happiness? Here, opulence that hides misery, there opulence born in abundance that produces only a brief felicity. Where might I wish to be born or live? Where is the home that holds out to me or my descendants the promise of a durable happiness?"

"Go to where evils carried to the extreme will bring about a better order of things. Wait for things to be good and savor the moment."

"And my descendants?"

"You're a fool. You look too far ahead. What were you to your ancestors four centuries ago? Nothing. Look in the same way at the unborn of the future who are equally remote to you. Be happy. Your great-grandchildren will be what it pleases fate, which governs all" (*Salons*, III, 125–26).

Unable to decide between *grandeur* (art, honor, heroism) and goodness (peace, order, full grain lofts), Diderot concludes the dialogue with Grimm's egoistic injunction to be happy. But the *grandeur*-goodness dichotomy continues to torment him. And what, he wonders, is happiness anyway? What is goodness? What is man? The dialogue is resumed some twenty pages later:

> "What exact notion can we have of good and evil, beauty and ugliness, truth and falsehood, without a preliminary notion of man?"
> "But what if man cannot be defined?"
> "Then the jig is up for us . . . . How many philosophers, lacking these very simple observations, have attributed to man the moral standards of wolves as stupidly as if they had prescribed man's moral standards for wolves?"
> "All creatures desire happiness, and the happiness of one creature cannot be the happiness of another. The moral standard is therefore defined within the limits of a species."
> "What is a species?"
> "A multitude of individuals similarly constructed."
> "So construction is the basis of morality?"
> "I think so."

This train of thought leads Diderot in meditation to wonder whether the *exceptional individual* or group of similarly exceptional individuals even within a given species is not entitled to a different moral standard, for example, "a moral standard for the artist, or for art" altogether different from the usual. "The rule of the poet is to go to extremes, the rule of happiness is to maintain a perfect balance. [To be happy] one should not live poetically. Heroes, romantic lovers, great patriots, rock-ribbed magistrates, apostles of religion, advocates of extreme philosophies, all these rare and divine madmen live poetically, and are unhappy. It is they who in death make great artistic subjects . . ." (pp. 148–49).

One might suspect, on reading this passage that the artistic half of the Diderotian personality is prepared, like the decadents of the late nineteenth century, to make of art an autonomous morality and to deny the universal efficacy and need for social responsibility. Is not this hypothesis of a distinct morality for artists, "*le rebours de la morale usuelle*," a striking anticipation of Huysmans? Such an interpretation, while tempting, is indicative of the dangers of a superficial or incomplete reading of Diderot. Intensely conscious of the complexity and ambiguity of the human condition, Diderot could sometimes pursue a paradox to its ultimate and sometimes shocking conclusion. Far from proving the philosophe's penchant for playing dialectical games, such exercises are invitations to join his anguished quest for elusive truth. Diderot the artist is undoubtedly in conflict with Diderot the rational philosophe. But is he really in conflict with Diderot the moralist? The discussion of the relationship between art and morality should not lead one to conclude that for the "poet" or genius there should be no social restraints, but rather that genius is "high risk-high gain" commodity for society, and that, though society may be the less ruffled without it, it would be infinitely poorer. Such a conclusion seems warranted by the following passage in the *Salon of 1765*:

> Whose faults should one excuse if not great men's? I hate all the petty baseness that only reveals an abject soul, but I do not hate great crimes: in the first place, because beautiful painting and tragedies are made of them; and besides, it's a fact that great and sublime deeds and great crimes bear the same mark of energy. If a person were not capable of setting a city on fire, another would not be capable of diving into an abyss to save it. If the soul of Caesar had not been possible, Cato's would not either. Man is born a citizen either of Taenarum or of Olympus, he is Castor and Pollux, a hero or a scoundrel, Marcus Aurelius or Borgia ... (*Salons*, II, 144).

For Diderot there is no inconsistency in "excusing" the crimes of the great and yet punishing them. The problem may be a semantic one, and a key is furnished near the end of *D'Alembert's Dream*, which Diderot wrote at the end of the decade. Denying the doctrine of free will, the author, speaking through the character of Dr. Bordeu, asserts that one's behavior is the end product of an inexorable chain of causes and effects, and that the theological concepts of vice and virtue should be replaced by the more socially descriptive terms beneficence and maleficence.

> "Man is born to good or to evil, he is insensibly carried along by the tide of fate that leads one individual to glory, another to ignominy."
>
> "And what about self-esteem, shame, and remorse?"
>
> "Childish notions based on the ignorance and vanity of a creature who attributes to himself the merit or blame for a necessary eventuality."
>
> "And what about rewards and punishments?"
>
> "Means for correcting the modifiable creature that we call evil and for encouraging the one we call good" (*Oeuvres philosophiques*, pp. 364–65).

Society thus acts, as it must, to protect itself. It may morally "excuse," even admire the socially harmful genius, but it must also punish him. Thus it is that the genius, a social misfit, is born to unhappiness among his fellow men. "O poets, poets!" exclaims Diderot in his *Reflexions on the Ode* (1770), Plato knew what he was doing when he expelled them from his republic. They have no right ideas on anything. Alternately organs of falsehood and truth, their spell-binding jargon infects an entire people and twenty volumes of philosophy are less read and do less good than one of their songs does harm" (A-T, VI, 414). But Diderot is merely acknowledging here the Apollonian logic of Plato's act; for the passionate demon in him, the intensely sensitive spirit that could intellectually reject Christianity and yet be transported, moved to tears, by Catholic ceremonies,[18] could not, in the last analysis, drive the poets out of his own republic.[19] For Diderot, like Goethe after him, ultimately believed in the grand common denominator of a universal human culture. "The essence of humanist culture," writes Jean Thomas, "is to give to those who have received it a sense of continuity in space and time. Embracing in a single sweep of the eye the sequence of great works of the human spirit, from the Bible to Voltaire's tragedies, Diderot admired the persistence and the identity of the human passions" (p. 75). Thus, ultimately, human passions blur the boundary between *grandeur* and goodness. The long digression in the *Salon of 1767* finally makes this plain.

"Is the philosophic spirit favorable or unfavorable to poetry? A big question almost decided in these few words."

"How true. More verve among barbaric peoples than among civilized; more verve among the Hebrews than among the Greeks, more verve among the Greeks than among the Romans, more verve among the Romans than among the Italians and the French, more verve among the English than among the latter. Wherever verve declines, so does poetry; as the philosophic spirit progresses people stop cultivating what they disdain. Plato expels the poets from his city. The philosophic spirit requires tighter, stricter, more rigorous comparisons; its careful step is opposed to mobility and metaphor. The reign of imagery passes as that of objectivity spreads. Reason introduces exactitude, precision, method, a kind of pedantry—pardon me for saying so—that stifles everything. All civil and religious prejudices are dissipated, and it is incredible to what extent incredulity robs poetry of its resources. Manners are refined; barbarous, poetic, and picturesque customs cease; and it is incredible how much damage these good manners do to poetry. The philosophic spirit brings with it a dry and sententious style . . ." (*Salons*, III, 153).

What is especially noteworthy in the foregoing passage is that the second half of the *grandeur*-goodness antinomy has been stripped of its moral content. It is no longer *le bon* that competes with poetry, but method, precision, exactitude. It is wild and powerful Hebrew dreams lyrically sung versus the circles and triangles of objective philosophy. Which is better, more important to humanity? The imaginary dialogue continues:

"In your opinion, What kind of poetry demands the greatest verve?"
"The ode, without question. There haven't been odes composed for ages. The Hebrews composed some, and they are the most ardent; the Greeks composed some, but already with less passion than the Hebrews. The philosopher reasons, the enthusiast feels; the philosopher is rational, the enthusiast is rapt . . . . Go and stand under the trees of the Tuileries at five o'clock. You'll see there passionless debaters, lined up in parallel rows, measuring parallel alleys with even step, as

mechanical in their statements as in their pacing, strangers to the torment of the poet's soul that they will never experience; and you will hear them call the Pindaric dithyramb extravagant, and the eagle sleeping under Jupiter's scepter, swaying on its perch, with feathers stirring to the strains of harmony, relegated to the category of puerile imagery.[20] When do we see the rise of critics and grammarians? Right after the century of genius and of divine productions . . . . It is not that Nature, which produces oaks as great as those of yore, today no longer produces antique heads, but that these astonishing heads shrink beneath the pervasive force of the prevailing timid standards of taste. There is but one perfect moment, when there is enough verve and liberty for passion, enough judgment and taste for wisdom. Genius creates beauty, criticism sees its flaws. One needs the imagination, the other judgment'' (p. 154).

If there remains any doubt that among these astonishing ''antique heads'' of Diderot's is that of Moses, let one quickly turn the ardent pages of this *Salon* to a discussion of the great writers of antiquity:

It is a rather general observation that one rarely becomes a great writer, a great *littérateur*, a man of very good taste, without having a close acquaintanceship with the Ancients. There is in Homer and Moses a simplicity, of which one should probably say what Cicero said of Regulus' return to Carthage: *Laus temporum, non hominis;* it is more the effect of the times than of genius. People with such manners, such clothing, such ceremonies, such laws, such customs could scarcely have another character. But it is a character that one does not imagine [by oneself], and it is necessary to look for it there, in order to transplant it in our own times, which, though highly corrupted, or rather, highly affected, can still appreciate its simplicity. We must speak of modern things in the ancient manner (p. 238).

Moses' ''antique head'' is therefore inseparable from ancient Jewish culture. The simplicity of patriarchal Jewish life as described in Faiguet's article on usury, is now acclaimed as the matrix of Moses' poetic genius. Moses can no longer be regarded as merely an exceptional Jew. In hailing Moses, Diderot now exalts ancient Jewish culture. The significance of passages such as those quoted here, and particularly of the conclusion of the passage contrasting creative genius with criticism, for an understanding of Diderot's ultimate attitude toward Jewish culture, lies in their final reconciliation of what had usually been perceived as opposites. No longer was it simply a matter of Jews versus Greeks, poetry versus reason, *grandeur* versus goodness, but the "perfect moment" combining a measure of both. Diderot's long and anguished quest for a moral solution to the problem of art and culture brilliantly anticipated Hegelian dialectics. The thesis is the energy and passion of the Hebrews, the antithesis is classical philosophy, the synthesis is a blending of imagination and rationalism.[21] "I was suckled early on the milk of Homer, Virgil, Horace, Terence, Anacreon, Plato, Euripides, blended with that of Moses and the Prophets," Diderot would write in 1774 (see preceding, p. 26). It had taken him more than half a lifetime to overcome his philosophic colic, a feat that Voltaire would never accomplish.

The *Salon of 1767* is perhaps the most important single document for an appreciation of Diderot's esthetic humanism, and a passage such as the following, coming at the end of Diderot's long, ofttimes oneiric,[22] digression on poetry, should dispel any lingering doubts concerning his final position: "Poets, speak everlastingly of eternity, of infinity, of immensity, of time, of space, of the Divine, of tombs, of manes, of hells, of darkened skies, of deepest seas, of shadowy forests, of thunder, of lightning that shreds the heavens; be tenebrous..." (p. 166). For the first time Diderot equates the Jewish Mosaic with the Greek Homeric literary traditions and exalts them both as models of literary taste. For the first time he compares the Old Testament, even in its inferior Hellenized Latin version, to Virgil's *Aeneid*, and he prefers the former.[23] And he recommends it again as a source book for subjects of passion and drama in art.[24]

The preromantic opinions and tendencies expressed here are repeated and elaborated in the later writings.[25] In the *Salon of 1769*

Moses, sculpture by Michelangelo. Church of St. Peter in Vincoli, Rome. *Courtesy of The Bettmann Archive.*

he insists again on the primacy of feeling over reason and bemoans the inability of his compatriots to dream as artists must.

> They dissert, they examine, they rarely feel, they reason a great deal, they weigh everything on the scrupulous scale of logic, of method, and even of truth; and what will happen to the arts, which are all premised on exaggeration and fiction, among men who are constantly occupied with reality and opposed by condition to the phantoms of the imagination, which they blow away with their windy mouths. The science of economics is a fine thing, but it will make us less human. I can already see the next generations with price lists in their pockets and business-men's briefcases under their arms (A-T, XI, 451).

Seven years later, in his *Pensées détachées sur la peinture* (*Scattered Thoughts on Painting*), his last major contribution to French art criticism, he reconfirms his adherence to the "prophetic genius" principle in art, with its personal vision, enthusiasm, and freedom.[26]

> Illuminate your subjects by the light of your own sun (*Oeuvres esthétiques*, p. 771).

> In any genre it is better to be extravagant than cold (p. 826).

> The rules have made a routine of art . . . they have helped the untalented; they have hurt the genius (pp. 753–54).

> Who has seen Moses? Michelangelo (p. 821).

In Diderot's eyes Moses has become symbolic of an epic, poetic culture that, unlike the philosophes of the Voltairian mentality, he unabashedly admires.

It is not within the purview of this monograph to study the stylistic influences of the Bible on Diderot's prose. It would make an intriguing study. Since Diderot tells his readers that he was suckled on Moses and the prophets and recommends that would-be writers first study Homer and Moses, it does not seem far-fetched to suppose that positive stylistic influences can be identified. How much of the evolution of Diderot's prose, as of Rousseau's, away from classical terseness toward romantic exuberance, with long rhythmic periods; parallel structures; accumulations of nouns, verbs, and epithets; lyrical effusions; apostrophes; and other appurtenances of late eighteenth-century rhetoric, is attributable to reminiscences of biblical rhythms and literary devices? A goodly amount, no doubt.[27] Easier to document, perhaps, is the moderate use by Diderot of biblical allusions to enrich his prose, as, when he learns of Falconet's eight-year postponement of his return from Russia, he writes: "Must I say then, like a certain biblical personage, a poor king but a rather good father who had just lost his child: 'He can no longer come to me, I have no other choice but to go to him' ";[28] or, wishing to characterize the Encyclopedist Dr. Venel's abandonment of his scientific labors for a life of hedonistic indolence, he calls his *carpe diem* existence "profound in the moral code of Solomon."[29] These examples will suffice for the purpose of this work.

Of the greatest writers of eighteenth-century France, only Diderot not only praised the Old Testament but, in so doing, credited its composition to the Jews rather than to God. How ironic that the writer who had started his career by belittling the Old Testament as the work of mere human beings, should end his career by making a virtue of that fact! How unperceptive of Sänger (p. 113) to interpret the demythologizing of the prophets' inspiration only as proof of Diderot's hypocrisy in writing on the Jews! But, beyond the Bible, Diderot was as myopic on Jewish culture as his century. His knowledge of the great Jewish culture of pre-Inquisition Spain was sketchy at best. It is unlikely that he knew of this culture more than what Brucker and Basnage told him. Of firsthand knowledge he appears to have had none. The trip to Holland, his first opportunity to see a living, functioning Jewish community, might have stimulated a younger Diderot to further study of Jewish culture. His appreciation of the architecture of the synagogues and the beauty of Jewish liturgical music might have spurred his artistic curiosity to seek out their origins and filiations. But by this time his physical and mental energies, already waning, were committed almost entirely to projects commissioned by Catherine the Great and to a revision of his earlier writings for a posthumous publication of his complete works.

His last important work, the *Essay on the Reigns of Claudius and of Nero* (1778), is the work of a moralist rather than an esthetician. But the humanistic theme of the universality and continuity of human intellectual achievement and the indebtedness of the present to the past, the future to the present, is clearly sounded.

> What is the object of philosophy? It is to unite mankind through the exchange of ideas, and through the exercise of a mutual beneficence.
> . . . Is there a worthier hope than to leave to one's relatives, friends, descendants, strangers, to one's own, to the universe, a subject for admiration, for discussion, for fond remembrance? Who created this work, this poem, this painting, this statue, this colonnade?
> . . . A kind of delicate gratitude combines with praiseworthy curiosity to interest us in the private lives of those whose works we admire . . . . All that concerns them arrests the attention of posterity! (A-T, III, 210, 212–13).

As for the Jewish heritage, Diderot's feelings of gratitude were mixed. Though he rejected unequivocally its religious precepts, he came to appreciate the luster of its poetry and to accept, even to practice, the use of mythic metaphor. Thus would he complete Seneca's quotation that "In the breast of the virtuous man, there lives a God, I know not which," with its antithesis, "And in the breast of evil, though I know not which, there lives a demon" (p. 221). Diderot was willing to concede the moral utility of the poetic mind.[30]

4

Diderot and the Jewish Question

> In order to speak pertinently of the baker's trade, one
> should have had one's hands in dough.
>
> —Diderot[1]

It has been shown in the preceding chapters that Diderot's writings on the Jews through the 1750s tended to treat them as an ideological abstraction, the antithesis of the philosophic ideals of universalism and scientific rationalism. In his monumental study of Diderot, Arthur Wilson acknowledges the "unfair" treatment of the Jews by Diderot and the philosophes, blaming it on the "necessities of polemics" and "their inability to appreciate religious genius and religious insights in any group."[2] But the Wilson biography does not explore the matter further. Chapter 3 has shown that, through the influence of his evolving esthetic convictions, Diderot's attitude toward the Jewish cultural heritage underwent perceptible modifications in the 1760s, but it is certainly true that before the 1770s and the trip to Holland there were few references to Jews as a contemporary social phenomenon. Sänger and Hertzberg see in this omission evidence of Diderot's insensitivity to Jewish suffering and therefore of anti-Semitic tendencies. "The Jews were not so interesting, not so important to him; the struggle against *'la superstition,' 'les prêtres'* [the priests] stood in the foreground for him just as for Voltaire," writes Sänger petulantly (p. 13). Hertzberg accuses Diderot of attacking "the Inquisition and the Church all his life without mentioning the persecution of the Jews at its hands" (p. 281). However in his next sentence he concedes to Diderot "one such passage in defense of the Jews and not a very warm one" in his *Encyclopédie* article "Crusades." It is important to point out that, although Hertzberg's

124

strongest case for philosophic anti-Semitism is made against Voltaire, and although the case made against Diderot is based largely on Sänger's work, Hertzberg fails to discern a flaw in Sänger's comparison of Voltaire and Diderot that is conspicuous in the passage quoted here. For Voltaire, like any real anti-Semite, was *very interested* in the Jews, who were a constant target of his wit, and sometimes—alas—his venom. Diderot's "dispassionate" attitude, his "lack of interest," hardly argues convincingly for his credentials as a true anti-Semite, whose essential quality, as has been noted by Sartre, is unreasoning anti-Jewish *passion*.[3] This is not to deny that, like most of his French contemporaries, Diderot did early in life contract what Péguy has called "the virus that secretly works in us."[4] A fair depiction of Diderot's ideological progress should, however, take note of the fact that as he grew older, more experienced, and wiser, and as the Jewish question in France became a timely issue, Diderot's perception of the Jews changed and his interest in their role in society grew significantly. For it is a fact, as Hertzberg himself attests, that public consciousness of a Jewish social problem in France was not aroused until the 1770s and 1780s, especially after the pogroms in Alsace in 1778 (p. 121).[5] Even the philosophes of the Voltaire-Diderot generations who are cited by Hertzberg as having furnished pro-Jewish arguments to the philo-Semites of the French Revolution—writers such as Montesquieu—dealt with the Jewish question less as a social than a religious one, as part of their struggle against the intolerance of the Catholic church. One should bear in mind, in comparing Montesquieu's passionate defense of the Jewish victims of the Inquisition referred to by Hertzberg (*Spirit of the Laws*, Book 25, Chapter 13), with Diderot's "not very warm" defense of them in the Crusades, that the former appeared in an original literary work, the masterpiece of an author indigenous to the Bordeaux region—a former member of the Bordeaux *Parlement*—who must have had occasionally personal contact with Jews, while the latter was merely a condensation of materials found in Fleury's *Histoire ecclésiastique*[6] for inclusion in a dictio-

nary article by an Encyclopedist who, when the article was prepared in 1752 or 1753, had probably never personally known a
Jew. For a fairer comparison of *impassioned* expressions of horror
by Montesquieu and by Diderot, one might better compare the one
contained in the *Spirit of the Laws* to Diderot's story of the betrayal
to the Inquisition of a Jew of Avignon in *Rameau's Nephew*. For
the latter, like Montesquieu's *Spirit of the Laws*, comes during the
period of the writer's literary maturity.[7]

From our twentieth-century perspective, the philosophes appear
derelict in not themselves bringing the issues of Jewish social and
political emancipation before the French public at an earlier date.
But taking such a position is somewhat like criticizing Giotto for
not paying enough attention to perspective and Descartes for
neglecting experimental science. The dominant issue of discrimi-
nation in France since the Revocation of the Edit of Nantes in 1685
had been the persecution of the Protestants, not of the Jews, whose
position, quite to the contrary of the Protestants', began to improve
markedly from that time on, so that the attention of the enemies of
religious persecution would more naturally be focused on the
plight of the French Protestants than on the French Jews.[8] Other
important considerations in determining the focus of philosophic
writings on religious persecution were the relatively recent ostra-
cism of Acosta and Spinoza by the Jewish community of Amsterdam—may the philosophes not be pardoned for seeing in this
persecution of dissidents a parallel to their own persecution by the
Catholic church?—and the active participation of French Protestant writers in the philosophic movement.[9] It is no wonder then that
when Diderot attacked religious persecution, the issue of Jewish
suffering did not occupy the center of the stage.

The *Encyclopédie* article on the Crusades was but one of a series
of articles dealing with the theme of religious intolerance. The first
two, both in Volume III, were "Cotereaux," dealing with the
persecution of the Petrobrusian Christian sects in southwest France
by Pope Alexander III, and "Crusades," dealing with the atrocities committed against the Jews and other non-Christians. Both

articles were written objectively and dispassionately in encyclopedic style. It is only after 1754, when the *Encyclopédie* itself began to feel the heat of the contemporary inquisitors' fires, that Diderot abandoned for a while the "not very warm" style of the historian and "an avenging passion suddenly animates the Philosophe's pen." [10] The article "Eclecticism" (Vol. V) contains a strong denunciation of the killing of the eclectic woman philosopher Hypatia by "Christian fanatics," the article "Ionic" (Vol. IX) condemns the fury of the Greek priests who attempted to have the Ionic philosopher Anaximander put to death, and the article "Scholastics" (Vol. XIV) recounts how medieval witch hunters brought about Roger Bacon's unhappy downfall. Finally, the article "Intolerance," also by Diderot, is a moving plea for the toleration of all people of other beliefs, for if they err they are no less our brothers. [11] Is it mere coicidence that in defining intolerance—"The word *intolerance* is commonly understood to mean that fierce passion that leads to hating and persecuting those who are in error"—Diderot used almost the same language as Sartre does in defining modern anti-Semitism? [12]

Diderot's *Encyclopédie* may not have been the first eighteenth-century French publication to shift the debate on the Jews from one of an ideological abstraction to one of a continuing social injustice and economic misfortune, but it was certainly the most influential. While it is true, as Hertzberg notes, that economists from Colbert to Ange Goudar had been recognizing the economic utility of the Jews, none would *link the economic and moral issues* as tellingly as de Jaucourt's article on Jewish history, the companion piece to Diderot's article on Jewish philosophy in Volume IX of the *Encyclopédie*. Both were written in the 1750s but not published until 1765 after the ban on the *Encyclopédie* had been lifted. It was this article that caused Hannah Arendt to proclaim Diderot "the only one of the French Philosophes who was not hostile to the Jews and who recognized in them a useful link between Europeans of different nationalities" (p. 23). Hannah Arendt was not entirely wrong, inasmuch as Diderot was indeed the editor, if not the author, of the de Jaucourt article, and as such cannot be denied at least a share of the honor. The article, one of three singled out by the editors of the *Histoire des Juifs en France* (referred to in Chapter 2) as examples of a certain number of *Encyclopédie* articles bearing the stamp of true liberalism in their treatment of the Jews, begins with an evocation of the horrors to which the Jews had been subjected since the beginning of the Christian era, the carnage wrought on them "under several Roman emperors and in every Christian country," and marvels at the tenacity of faith of these "perpetual martyrs." allusion is made to Montesquieu's famous metaphor comparing Judaism to a mother whose two daughters, Christianity and Mohammedanism, have "heaped on her a thousand injuries." The article proceeds to describe the Jewish dispersion and its causes, to explain the separation and cohesiveness of the Jewish community as the guarantor of its survival, and to justify Jewish dominance in the commercial professions as a natural effect of historical determinism. The article then specifies the crimes and atrocities perpetrated on the Jews in Christian Europe, without failing to deplore the inhumanity of their treatment in France, where they were systematically robbed, accused of practising magic, of child ritual murder, of poisoning fountains, and from which they were expelled, then readmitted, under degrading conditions. The article concludes optimistically by applauding the recent disposition of princes who have

opened their eyes to their own interests and have treated the Jews with more moderation. In several regions of the north and of the south, they have recognized that they could not do without their help. But, without mentioning the Grand Duke of Tuscany, Holland and England, animated by nobler principles, have granted them every possible humane treatment, under the constant protection of the government. Thus, in our day spread out more securely than ever before in every European country in which commerce reigns, they have become the instruments by means of which the most far-off nations can converse and correspond with each other . . . . The Spanish have paid a heavy price for having expelled them, as has France for having persecuted subjects whose beliefs differed in a few details from those of the prince.[13] The love of the Christian religion consists in practising it: and from such practice there come only sweetness, humanity, charity.[14]

The de Jaucourt article, and the Faiguet article on "Usury," which both appeared in 1765 when the last ten volumes of text of the *Encyclopédie* were finally published, were not only representative of a new and more sympathetic kind of writing on the Jews coming from segments of the philosophic camp but also important as affirmations of principles of historical determinism that would underpin the arguments of all the pro-Jewish writers in the period from 1765 to the French Revolution. Why were the Jews separatist and close-knit? Because their religious laws, reinforced by persecution, had made them so. Why were so many of them usurers, peddlers, brokers? Because few Christians would practise these "degrading" professions and the Jews were allowed few others. Why did they not take up decent trades? Because the guilds would not permit it. Why did they not practise agriculture? Because they could own no land. Why were they so uncouth? For the same reason any outcast group is uncouth.

There are indications that Diderot's curiosity about the Jews as a flesh-and-blood phenomenon rather than an ideological-historical abstraction began to be aroused in the late 1750s and early 1760s, at precisely the same time that he began to feel the surge of literary creativity that would lead to the production of his greatest works. Having had virtually no personal experience with Jews until this time, he at first refrained from depicting them in his plays and novels, unlike Voltaire, who managed to find room for at least one unsavory Jew in three of his four major philosophical tales.[15] A true empiricist, Diderot adhered, in the characters he imagined for his creative works, to the principle of writing only about "real people," that is, people he knew: actors, urban bourgeois types, nuns and clerics, habitués of the Paris salons, and the like. For, as he would later write in his *Apologie de l'abbé Galiani*, "in order to speak pertinently of the baker's trade, one should have had one's hands in dough'' (n. 1). It was only after his trip to Holland, where he could observe a community of Jews at firsthand, that he would add two Jewish characters to a revised version of *Rameau's Nephew*.

As far as is known, there is only one Jew whom Diderot appears to have met personally before the trip out of France. Isaac de Pinto, a Dutch-born Sephardic Jewish financier, came to Paris after the death of Stathouder William IV of Holland, to whom he had served as counselor and financial supporter for several years. Diderot probably met him in or after 1761, when his literary endeavors in the French capital gained some recognition.[16] These were an *Essay on Luxury* (1762); a *Defense of the Jewish Nation or Critical Reflexions* (1762), which was a reply to Voltaire's anti-Jewish diatribes; and a *Treatise on Circulation and Credit*, circulated in manuscript form ten years before its publication in Amsterdam in 1771. Diderot's acquaintanceship with de Pinto in Paris must have been a fleeting one, as there is no documentation or testimony regarding it from among other members of the Diderot circle, and its only echo in Diderot's correspondence is a reference to de Pinto's "libertinism" in a letter to Madame d'Épinay.[17] In 1768 de Pinto published in London an open letter in French addressed to Diderot entitled *On Cardplaying*, in which the utilitarian aspects of cardplaying were related to the human passions. Diderot appears to have taken no notice of it. De Pinto's most serious works were published several years later: the aforementioned *Treatise on Circulation*, a *Summary of Arguments against the Materialists* (1774), and *Letters of Mr. de Pinto on the Occasion of the Troubles in the American Colonies* (1776). The thesis of the economic utility of circulation and credit proposed in the first of these is consistent with de Jaucourt's thesis of the economic importance of international trade, and de Pinto's conclusion hinting at the economic value of the Jews seems to parallel de Jaucourt's earlier conclusion. However, de Pinto's arguments against materialism in the *Summary of Arguments against the*

Materialists could not have served to raise his stock with the author of *D'Alembert's Dream* and collaborator on d'Holbach's *System of Nature*.[18] Nevertheless, he considered himself Diderot's friend, and he had "close" relations with other celebrities, such as Hume, Mirabeau, Péreire, and King Stanislas of Poland.[19] De Pinto would play a more important role in Diderot's life in 1773 and 1774 during the trips to Holland, and he will be dealt with again.

The 1760s were for Diderot years of frenetic literary activity. Two of his three major novels and the *Eulogy of Richardson*, his longest and most important *Salons* and an additional major work on painting, *D'Alembert's Dream* (regarded by some as his greatest masterpiece), and the publication of the last ten volumes of text of the *Encyclopédie*, not to mention an extensive correspondence, the work on eleven volumes of engraved illustrations needed to complete the twenty-eight-volume set of the *Encyclopédie*, and parental responsibilities, did not leave Diderot the time to travel to distant places where he could encounter Jewish community life in action. Although there were a few Jews living in Paris, their presence there, while tolerated, was not legally sanctioned, and they made themselves as inconspicuous as possible. They did not, therefore, constitute a typical Jewish community and Diderot makes no mention of them. His nascent interest in the current generation of "the descendents of Abraham" is reflected in his correspondence with the sculptor Falconet. As has been indicated in Chapter 2, Falconet was traveling to Russia by way of Berlin in 1766, and he made a point of describing the Jewish community there in a letter to Diderot. Diderot's reply expressing satisfaction with Falconet's favorable description of the Berlin Jews testifies both to his interest in the subject and to his willingness to revise the negative image of the Jews that had been fostered in him both by his education and by such prejudiced witnesses as Grimm and Voltaire.

The *Encyclopédie* was finally completed in early 1772, and Diderot's only daughter was married in September of the same year. Diderot could now no longer resist the siren call from Saint

Petersburg of his benefactress Catherine the Great. The reluctant departure from Paris of this notorious nontraveler,[20] came in June 1773, its ostensible purpose being to attend with Grimm the wedding of Grand Duke Paul, Catherine's son, to a daughter of the Landgravine of Hesse, a patroness of Grimm's. But Diderot and Grimm traveled separately using different itineraries. Diderot would go first to Holland to explore the possibility of having his works published there. Grimm was more interested in visiting the courts of his German patrons.

The philosophe arrived in The Hague on June 15 and was the guest of the Russian ambassador Prince Dmitri Galitzin, with whom he stayed for two months while awaiting the arrival of Prince Narishkin, his escort on the trip from Holland to Russia. During his first stay in Holland he had the opportunity to visit several cities and to visit their Jewish communities, recording his impressions in notes that he intended for publication.[21] These notes would be augmented during his second stay in Holland in 1774. (They will be dealt with here after the account of the trip to Russia.) But before leaving for Russia, the philosophe found his old acquaintance de Pinto. In a letter to Madame d'Épinay, partially quoted above (n. 16), Diderot relates the following piquant experience with him: "He has a love-nest where, if I had wanted to, I could have become acquainted with the Idumean of the female sex. But these courses in physics have never been to my liking, and I have by now outgrown them." Diderot, at sixty, was only four years de Pinto's senior, and the unseemly sexual adventures of the not-so-young economist would be referred to in two places in the manuscript of Diderot's *Voyage to Holland* (A-T, XVII, 405 and 416). According to Diderot, these adventures were serious enough to have caused de Pinto trouble with the law. If such were the case, one could accept Diderot's sly remark on the matter and the story in *Rameau's Nephew* of a lecherous Dutch Jew as a typical Diderotian reaction to a bizarre personality, of the kind with which his last two novels would be replete. The echo of the de Pinto incident in *Rameau's Nephew* is but one of two Jewish episodes added to the novel subsequent to the voyage to Holland, both of which were used by Reinach as proof of Diderot's anti-Jewish tendencies. The fact that Diderot continued to maintain good personal relations with de Pinto during both his first and second visits to Holland should by itself cast some doubt on Reinach's imputation to Diderot of anti-Semitic motives in the tale of the Jew of Utrecht.[22] A different perspective on this story will be provided in Chapter 5, in the course of the discussion of Diderot's racial views. The second tale is of the heartless betrayal to the Inquisition in Avignon of a generous Jew by a consummate blackguard, the Renegade of Avignon, who, having enjoyed his kindnesses, proceeds to get away with his fortune. It is told by Diderot as an example of the ultimate in villainy, an example of the perverse sort of genius to which Rameau's fictional nephew aspires, but of which, even he—as degraded as he is—is incapable. The destruction of the Jew—which may be seen as symbolic of the tragic fate of the Jews in Christian Europe—the perfidious triumph of the renegade, and the nephew's admiration of the renegade's exploit, cause the philosophe to cry out, "I don't know which of the two causes me the greatest horror, the villainy of your renegade, or the tone in which you speak of it (*Oeuvres romanesques*, p. 461). Reinach did not comment on the significant fact that a Jew has been pictured here as generous and hospitable, trustingly unsuspecting of duplicity. Rather, he belabored Diderot for not knowing that the Jews of Avignon were never threatened by the Inquisition (p. 142). Diderot is thus condemned for attacking injustice against the Jews where it doesn't exist—strange proof of anti-Semitism! Never mind that Diderot probably got the story from the Jews of Holland themselves, amongst whom it was current,[23] or that it may be read as a fable.

In August 1773, Diderot set out for Saint Petersburg with Prince Narishkin. After a strenuous seven-week-long voyage, he arrived in the Russian capital "more dead than alive" (*Correspondance*, XIII, 65),[24] just in time to see the festivities surrounding the wedding of the Crown Prince. The empress was much impressed by her Encyclopedist guests, and she soon made both Diderot and Grimm associate members of the Imperial Academy of Sciences. Other honors would follow, the most remarkable of which must be the frequent intimate tête-à-têtes that Catherine the Great accorded the inelegant but conversationally dazzling son of a provincial French cutler. One is surprised and amused to read of their encounters, with Catherine forced to place a small table between them to protect her thighs from the gesticulating hands of the irrepressible Frenchman.[25] This intimacy encouraged the philosophe to question the empress on all aspects of life in her empire. He would regularly draw up series of questions to be answered by her in their meetings. "Diderot's ambition," writes Wilson, "was to convert Catherine II to the philosophy of the Enlightenment, or at least to reinforce what there were of her liberal convictions. In order to accomplish this, he presented his views by tactful indirection or adroit analogy or skillful insinuation, rather than by open confrontation" (p. 634). Many of Diderot's questions and Catherine's answers have been preserved in Maurice Tourneux's *Diderot et Catherine II* and in Volume XIII of Diderot's *Correspondance*. Among these are four questions on the Jews: "Admission to Russia was prohibited to the Jews in 1764; then this prohibition was abrogated. Are there any Jews here? If there are, under what conditions? Are they treated like other foreigners? And approximately how many Jews are there?"[26] Catherine's answer was as follows:

The Jews were expelled from Russia by Empress Elizabeth at the beginning of her reign, around 1742. In 1762 the question of letting them return arose, but as the proposition was inopportune, things remained as they were. In 1764 the Jews were designated as merchants and inhabitants of New Russia beyond the Boristhena. White Russia is full of them. There are three or four in [Saint] Petersburg. For eight or nine years I had a confessor with whom they were lodged; they are tolerated in spite of the law; we pretend not to know what they are. Besides, their reintegration could do harm to our small merchants; for those people [the Jews] attract everything to themselves, and their return might bring more outcries than benefits (ibid.).

From Catherine's answer, it is possible to deduce her assessment of Diderot's motives in asking the questions. She is obviously at pains to demonstrate her enlightened spirit—"I have nothing against them personally, but I don't want to incite the merchant class"—and her justification for not provoking the merchant class responds to the Jaucourtian thesis, quite obviously Diderot's also (as will be demonstrated presently), that the Jews are an economically positive influence in modern society. Diderot cannot respond directly to Catherine on this issue, but there are several indirect responses. One of these is the philosophe's ingenious if somewhat tongue-in-cheek defense of Catherine's impotence to solve *all* Russia's social problems. "Why is Russia less well-governed than France?" he asks.

> It is that the freedom of the individual is reduced to nothing and the authority of the sovereign is still too great there, that natural liberty is still too limited there.
> The Empress to whom I made these observations said to me: "So it is your suggestion that I should have an English-style parliament?"
> I answered her: "If Your Imperial Majesty could have it by waving a wand, I believe that it would exist tomorrow" (ibid., p. 573).

Other indirect answers are his memoirs to Catherine on the economic utility of usury and the moral and political advantages of tolerance,[27] and on the relationship between laws and mores.

> Mores are everywhere the consequences of legislation and of government: they are neither African, nor Asian, nor European, they are good or bad . . . .
> It is necessary everywhere that a people should be educated, free, and virtuous. What Peter I brought to Russia, if good for Europe was good everywhere. Without denying the influence of climate on the mores of the present-day Greek and Italian states, the future state of Russia will show that good or bad mores have other causes.
> The object, the purpose of all government should be the happiness of its citizens, the strength, the splendor of the State,

and the glory of the sovereign (*Diderot et Catherine II*, pp. 568–72).[28]

By postulating a hypothesis of the general modifiability of national mores based on legislative reform, with no exceptions made on racial or religious grounds, Diderot appears more universalist in spirit than Montesquieu and clearly belongs in the company of the pro-Jewish writers who denied the Voltairian hypothesis of a peculiarly immutable Jewish national character.[29] If the writings for Catherine the Great are not specific enough to satisfy the doubters, the *Voyage to Holland*, on which Diderot would soon resume his work, would be clear and unambiguous.

Diderot left Russia as he had arrived, wretchedly ill, and he complained grumpily that he hadn't been able to see much. "I saw nothing but the Sovereign," wrote he with typical overstatement to Madame Geoffrin. This quotation, given in Ducros's long study entitled *Diderot, l'homme et l'écrivain (Diderot, the Man and the Writer)*,[30] is taken literally by Sänger, who then uses it to condemn Diderot for closing his eyes to injustice in Russia. "He was much more interested in the adventures of rich Jews and the consequences thereof or in tricks played on Jews" (p. 14).[31]

Diderot arrived in The Hague in April 1774, full of new projects to complete for Catherine the Great and dreaming of revising and augmenting the *Encyclopédie* under the sponsorship of the Russian empress. He was also planning to have his complete works published in Holland, and a part of his time was spent in haggling with publishers in The Hague. At the same time, he was much in demand by Dutch intellectuals, some of whom used de Pinto as a go-between. Diderot's *Correspondance* contains a letter from de Pinto to R. M. Van Goens, a professor of literature at the University of Utrecht, promising to read to Diderot "the article of your letter that concerns him" and apologizing for Diderot's not being able to see him. "He is very busy with Grimm's arrival."[32] Yet, in spite of these pressures, he took copious notes on Dutch life and institutions, notes which, in the Assézat-Tourneux edition of his *Oeuvres complètes*, run to over one hundred pages in octavo. It is

of especial interest for this study to note that the largest portion of
the section on the various religious communities in Holland is
devoted to the Jews, almost two-thirds of the section entitled "On
Religion" (XVII, 430–33).

This section on the Jewish community begins as follows:

The Jews are nowhere else so close to the condition of the
other citizens. They have their quarter; some are shaven, others
are bearded. They have thirteen synagogues in Amsterdam; it
[sic] is rather a school than a temple; after prayer one would
think them indecorous there; they talk of business and of
courtship. This apparent scorn for the benefits of their prayer
reminds them that the real temple is no more.

The synagogues are very beautiful in Amsterdam, in Rotterdam, and in The Hague. There is the German synagogue and the
Portuguese synagogue. The Germans claim to be the descendents of the tribe of Judah, and the Portuguese of the tribe of
Benjamin. They are engaged in all forms of commerce; they
practise medicine; but they have no trades. When a bill of
exchange contracted by a Christian falls due on Saturday, they
are authorized to be paid on Friday. On the Sabbath day their
shops are closed; but they can appear in court, as they can during
their Passover and principal holidays. They own real estate,
they inherit, they make wills, and enjoy every protection accorded to citizens; they do not become magistrates. The shaven
Jews are rich and are regarded as honorable people; one must be
careful with the bearded ones, who are not very scrupulous.
Some of them are very well-educated.

Several rich Jews were made barons under William III of
England, in recognition of the powerful financial support they
furnished him in 1682. Their number in Amsterdam, before the
disturbances in Poland and the famine in Bohemia, rose to more
than one hundred thousand; it has grown considerably there.

To bring stray consciences back into the fold, the government
allows no methods other than preaching. It is possible that
religion may do more good in other countries, but it is in this one
that it does the least harm (pp. 431–32).

The rest of this section deals with Diderot's visit to a synagogue,
which has already been described in Chapter 2.

There are three important themes that stand out in the passage quoted here, themes that sustain the pro-Jewish Jaucourtian thesis. First, Jews are capable of becoming like anyone else given the proper economic opportunities and legal protections; second, they can be a national asset as their assistance to William of Orange demonstrates; and third the nation is much the better off for its policy of religious tolerance. The second and third themes are repeated elsewhere in the notes for the *Voyage to Holland*. In the section on the Dutch admiralty (p. 397), Diderot writes that "It is the Jews seeking refuge in Holland who by their example have taught the Dutch to establish trading centers on the coasts of Barbary and in the Levant." And in the section on "Ecclesiastical Government" (p. 440), he writes, "Here a man can commit himself to the prejudices of his childhood and his education without any harmful consequences to his happiness or to the happiness of others; he can be neither persecutor nor persecuted. The Jew, the Anabaptist, the Lutheran, the Calvinist, the Catholic serve and do business with each other without their differing religious opinions influencing their feelings of humanity."

In spite of these clearly positive expressions by Diderot in the *Voyage to Holland*, critics have pounced on one or two seemingly negative aspects of the account. Hertzberg implicitly faults Diderot for preferring "enlightened" Jews and quotes the passage on the difference between the shaven and unshaven (p. 282). But he writes elsewhere (p. 312) that Diderot believed it virtually impossible for Jews to overcome their Oriental character and fanatical religion in order to be enlightened! And is Diderot not merely parroting de Pinto's prejudices against bearded Jews? Let us read what Hertzberg himself writes elsewhere on de Pinto:

> The point which Pinto was making in that passage was that today, in 1762, the Portuguese were to be distinguished from all other Jews: "They do not wear beards and are not different from other men in their clothing; the rich among them are devoted to learning, elegance, and manners...."
> Pinto admitted that other Jews, mostly German and Polish ones, were depressed in manners and culture, but there were

among them, especially in Amsterdam and London, where they had lived in some freedom, "men who are the most upright people in the world . . ." (pp. 181–82).[33]

From the foregoing it seems plausible that Diderot's distinction between the bearded and the shaven Jews of Holland came directly from his Jewish host de Pinto.

Sänger concedes that Diderot was pleased that the Dutch Jews were better off than the others but criticizes Diderot for not contrasting their condition with that of the French Jews (p. 12). One must respond that the *Voyage to Holland*, as it has come down to present-day readers, is not a finished work but rather a set of notes for a projected work, and that it is not possible to speculate on what its final form might have been. One must add that it was still a risky matter under the *ancien régime* to criticize French institutions directly. By praising English institutions, Montesquieu and Voltaire had effectively demonstrated the weaknesses of the French. By praising Dutch institutions, Diderot does likewise.

Paul Meyer ignored the *Voyage to Holland* but said that Diderot's use of the incident of the Jew of Utrecht in *Rameau's Nephew* was "the brainchild of a gratuitously uncharitable imagination" (p. 1178). But he also distinguished between a truly anti-Semitic Voltaire and Diderot, who "had no personal grudge against the Jews" (ibid.).

Diderot lived for ten years after his trip to Holland. Six major works—the revision of his earlier works for posthumous publication; collaboration with writers like Abbé Raynal, who wrote a moving plea for more humane treatment of the victims of colonial oppression,[34] with Meister, the inheritor of Grimm's *Correspondance littéraire*, and possibly with Madame d'Épinay on her *Pseudo-Mémoires* (intended as an answer to Rousseau's *Confessions*); and the composition of numerous smaller pieces—did not permit Diderot to complete his work on the *Voyage to Holland*. Since his notes resemble a finished text, it is conceivable that he decided to leave them as written. Diderot's primary concerns in the last years of his life were with esthetic, scientific, and especially moral problems. His greatest psychic need was to resolve the moral problem of *l'homme biologique* (biological man), and to that end he would write three important books: *Jacques the Fatalist*, the *Refutation of Helvétius' Work "On Man,"* and the *Essay on the Reigns of Claudius and of Nero*. Their significance for this study will be dealt with in Chapter 5.

5

Human Diversity and National Character

> Imagine the English with three Elizabeths in a row and
> the English would be the basest slaves in Europe.
> —Diderot[1]

EIGHTEENTH-CENTURY anti-Semitism was not racist in the modern sense of the term. It was not rooted in any genetic theory of racial differences but in what one scholar has called "very pervasive cultural attitudes that blur the identification of true racism in the contemporary sense."[2] These attitudes were perpetuated by religious prejudice and supported by the theological doctrines of damnation and redemption. Anti-Semitism was implanted in the psyche of European children by their Christian upbringing and became, in the paradoxical phraseology of one commentator, "an acquired instinct."[3] If Jews had come to be regarded by some European Christians as a different species,[4] their decline to "subhuman" status was generally regarded as reversible by the simple act of embracing Christ. The fact that so few Jews responded willingly to this generous Christian promise of regeneration merely reinforced the conviction of Christians that meanness, stubbornness, stupidity, and fanaticism were traits providentially laid on the Jews.

The philosophes, who rejected the Christian demonology, could not accept its theological explanation of Jewish differences. Their approach to analyzing cultures was scientific rather than religious. "For all their misjudgments and prejudices," writes Peter Gay (p. 38), "—and sometimes because of them—the Philosophes took first steps, no more, toward a scientific history of culture."

There is hardly a study on the philosophes and the Jews that fails to take note of Montesquieu's tolerant attitude toward cultural

141

diversity and his theory of the environmental influences on national mores.[5] The eighteenth-century scientific authority on
human differences would be the French naturalist Georges Louis
Leclerc (Count) de Buffon, whose *Histoire naturelle (Natural
History)* is regarded as laying the groundwork for the science of
"biological geography." Buffon attributed geographically determined characteristics to peoples inhabiting different climatic zones
but did not regard these differences as being permanently fixed in
any hereditary mechanism.[6] Most of the philosophes and Encyclopedists followed Montesquieu's historical anthropology and
Buffon's biological geography in varying degrees. Of the major
figures of the French Enlightenment, only Voltaire, in his introduction to the *Essai sur les moeurs (Essay on Mores)* directly
challenged Buffon's belief in the ability of so-called degenerate
forms of man to be regenerated through changes in climate and
nutrition, and postulated a distinctly pregenetic theory of races.[7]
Voltaire's handling of the Jewish issue in this regard is somewhat
ambiguous but tends toward racism. Although he always refers to
the Jews as a people or a nation, never as a race or species, he
writes in one place of their *"génie"* which dooms them to perpetual subjugation (*Oeuvres complètes*, XIX, 518). As Voltaire
uses the term, it means innate character or spirit and implies
unmodifiability. This does not mean that all Jews are necessarily
the same. Voltaire makes an exception for the Essenes, who
resemble the Quakers of his *Philosophical Letters*,[8] and for individuals like Spinoza,[9] but to him these are rarities.[10] At the other
end of the racial-nonracial spectrum was Helvétius, who denied
any hereditary mental or moral limitations. In Helvétius' view the
human mind is completely modifiable by education.[11]

   Diderot is harder to classify in terms of a racial spectrum, for,
from the time of his *Thoughts on the Interpretation of Nature*, his
system tends to be *individualistic*, so that he is more apt to stress the
differences between individuals within supposedly homogeneous
groups than their resemblances. "There is only one possible way
to be homogeneous. There are an infinite number of possible ways

to be heterogeneous," he writes in *Pensée* LVIII. In the preceding *pensée* he has written that "on an entire tree there are probably no two leaves *perceptibly* of the same shade of green," and added that

> without consciously flaunting Leibnitz's opinion . . . it is demonstrated, by the difference in the points in space in which bodies are placed, combined with the prodigious numbers of causes, that there never have been, and probably never will be in nature, two blades of grass of absolutely the same shade of green. . . . If things change successively, passing through the most imperceptible nuances, time, which never stops, must in the long run produce the greatest difference amongst forms that have existed very anciently, those that exist today, those that will exist in the most distant centuries.

Heterogeneity is thus related to change. No individual thing ever exactly resembles another, nor does its present form exactly resemble its past or its future. This principle of diversity and continuous flux and mutability is absolutely antithetical to the Voltairian concept of an immutable national *génie*.[12] It is a constant of Diderot's thought, which he will almost immediately apply to human cases.

In 1758 he published his *Discourse on Dramatic Poetry*. In it is found the following relevant passage:

> There are probably not, in the entire human species, two individuals who have any really close resemblance. The general organization, the senses, the outer features, the viscera, have their variables. Intelligence, imagination, memory, ideas, beliefs, prejudices, nutrition, exercises, knowledge, states, education, tastes, luck, talents, have their variables. Objects, climates, mores, laws, customs, habits, governments, religions, have their variables. How then would it be possible for two human beings to have exactly the same tastes, the same notions of the true, the good, and the beautiful? The differences in the lives and varieties of occurrences would by themselves be enough to produce some [differences] in judgments.
>   Nor is that all. In the same person all is in a state of perpetual

vicissitude, whether he is considered in his physical or in his moral being (*Oeuvres esthétiques*, p. 283).

Diderot's insistence on the principle of individuality, which is essentially opposed to any form of stereotyping, is evident in his three major novels written after 1758. In *The Nun*, a Christian girl, the fruit of her mother's illicit love affair, is confined to a convent against her will and her nature. When she petitions the Mother Superior for her freedom, she is told that her request is contrary to what society and decency require of her.

> "Could it be that the temptations that surround us constantly, and that try to corrupt us, have benefited from the excessive freedom you have been given lately, to inspire in you some sinister impulse?"
> "No, madam, you know that I do not take my oaths lightly. I take God as my witness that my heart is innocent, and that there has never been a shameful sentiment in it."
> "I can't believe it."
> "But, madame, nothing is easier to believe. Everyone has his own character, and I have my own . . . . I am and always shall be a bad nun" (*Oeuvres romanesques*, p. 286).

Although Diderot does not in this novel offer a scientific explanation of the unwilling nun's unique character, it is made clear in the novel that Suzanne Simonin cannot overcome her nature regardless of her religious convictions, her education, and the pressures of society. Diderot has already conceded that these factors are not negligible in the formation of character, as is evident in the passage quoted from the *Discourse on Dramatic Poetry*, but, as will be demonstrated in *Rameau's Nephew*, the biological factor is the *primordial* one determining character.

Diderot began writing *Rameau's Nephew* in the year after he had written his novel of the nun, and the problem of the individual in conflict with a system of values imposed by society is once again the central issue. However, the character of Rameau's nephew, almost the complete opposite of Suzanne's, complicates the moral problem of the author. For Suzanne, though a "bad nun," was fundamentally a good person. She was kind, sensitive, forgiving, charitable, and endowed with great courage and rectitude. In her war with the conventual system she represented innocent nature which was being defiled by unnatural religious and moral customs and precepts. Her individuality and revolt were socially positive phenomena, for, as is made clear by the author, the system she opposed was a pernicious one in its effects both on the individual and on society itself. *Rameau's Nephew* confronts us with an individual whose natural propensities are at odds with the welfare of society, and the moral and philosophical problems posed in the claims between the rights of the immoral individual and of society are more difficult to resolve. In "justifying" his position, the nephew resorts to two principal arguments: he is innocent first because he was born without the moral "fiber" necessary for him to experience compassion, and second because society is so ordered that to succeed in it one must be dishonest, one can achieve success only at the expense of others, and only the foolish and the lazy refrain from the universal knavishness.[13] Both of these arguments are pertinent to this study, since the first is significant for an understanding of Diderot's theory of human diversity as it relates to morality, and both hold the key to his purpose in using the two Jewish episodes in the novel.

Rameau's nephew tells his philosophic interlocutor the story of the betrayal of the good Jew of Avignon by the renegade, and he tells it with great relish, for he adulates the perverse artistry employed by the renegade in his pursuit of the Jew's wealth. The philosopher expresses his horror both at the story and at the nephew's enjoyment of it. But the nephew blithely urges the philosopher to join him in a song in honor of the great rogue Mascarille.[14]

> And thereupon he began to do a most unusual song in fugue . . . .
> I did not know whether I should stay or run, laugh or be angry. I stayed, with the intention of turning the conversation

towards a subject that would drive from my soul the horror that
filled it. I began to find it very hard to stand the presence of a
man who discussed a horrible act, an execrable crime, as a
connoisseur of painting or poetry analyzes the beauties of a
work of art, or as a moralist or historian picks out and shows in
all their luster the circumstances of a heroic act. I became
somber in spite of myself; he noticed it and said: "What's
wrong with you? Are you ill?" "A little, but it will pass" (ibid.,
p. 462).

The nephew proceeds to give a lecture on the art of song, in the
course of which he sings arias from several operas and is completely transported by the melodic beauties of the voices and
accompanying instruments whose sounds he skillfully imitates.
The philosopher, struck by the incongruity of the character before
him, asks

"How is it that with such a fine tact, such a great sensitivity to
the beauties of musical artistry, you are so blind to beauty in the
moral realm, so insensitive to the charms of virtue?"
"It is apparently due to the fact that for those things there is a
sense that I don't have, a fiber that was not given to me, a slack
fiber you can pluck all you want and that doesn't vibrate; or
maybe it's because I've always lived with good musicians and
bad people, so that my ear has become very keen and my heart
has become very dull. And then, it could have something to do
with family.[15] My father's blood is the same as my uncle's[16]
blood. My blood is the same as my father's. The paternal
molecule was hard and blunt, and that damned first molecule
took over all the rest" (p. 473).

The theory enunciated here that some men are born without the
necessary biological sensitivity to the moral good would be sys-
tematized in *D'Alembert's Dream*, which Diderot wrote four years
after he completed a first draft of *Rameau's Nephew*. Having
painstakingly demonstrated the dependence of personality on biological characteristics, he pronounced these portentous sentences:
"We must substitute [for the idea of virtue] that of beneficence,

and for its opposite that of maleficence. We are born either for good things or for bad; we are inexorably swept up by the flow of events that carries one man to glory, the other to infamy.''[17] How then can one explain Diderot's passionate declaration in a letter to Sophie Volland that ''nature hasn't made us evil; what has is bad education, bad example, bad legislation . . .''?[18] One can explain it as a sentimental outburst, the product of a fervent philosophic wish that his moralistic heart desired to believe in spite of what his mind derived from science.[19] This humanistic wish would not be completely extinguished in the decade of *Rameau's Nephew* and *D'Alembert's Dream*, but would lie dormant in the Diderotian psyche to become in his later years a counter theme to his stark hereditarian hypothesis.

This hereditarian hypothesis is nowhere postulated as descriptive of entire ethnic groups. Indeed Diderot expresses in various places in his writings his disapproval of stereotyping on the basis of ethnicity. In his *Conversations on the Illegitimate Son* he has André, Lysimond's servant, proclaim, ''Sir, there are honorable people everywhere'' (A-T, VII, 111). And twenty years later, in his *Refutation of Helvétius*, he asks, ''Is it just to reproach a whole nation for the vice of a particular class? . . . It would be a very serious misjudgment of the general spirit of a people to draw conclusions about its strength or its weakness, the purity or corruption of its morals, or its poverty, from the actions of a few individuals, and to say 'Apicius let himself die of hunger because it wasn't possible for him to live with eight or nine hundred thousand pounds that he had left; therefore a Roman, in those days, was impoverished with that amount of capital' '' (ibid., II, 425–26).[20] Conversely, even where the corruption of morals is rampant in a degenerate society, there are always examples of virtue: ''In spite of tyranny, corruption, baseness, and the uselessness of virtue, there are virtuous men born everywhere, who live and die according to their principles'' (p. 391).

We can therefore approach the two Jewish episodes in *Rameau's Nephew* with the following assurance: it was not Diderot's intent in either of them to stereotype Jews either as necessarily generous, hospitable, trusting like the Jew of Avignon, nor prodigal, sensual, and dishonest like the Jew of Utrecht. What then was his purpose in telling these stories? Let us recall the nephew's second argument in justification of his egoistic conduct: Success in society depends on participating in the universal knavishness. The stories of the renegade of Avignon and of the Jew of Utrecht are two illustrations of the nephew's cynical view of humanity. That the first succeeds and the second fails is a typical Diderotian illustration of the principle that human calculation, no matter how cunning or ingenious, is sometimes confounded by the unpredictability of the intended victim's response.[21] The clever scheme of the Jew of Utrecht to escape payment to a Dutchman for the sexual use of his wife is confounded by his inability to predict that the Dutchman would be willing to expose his own and his wife's dishonor to force payment.

At a first reading the story of the Jew of Utrecht appears to perpetuate a stereotype of the lustful Jew as earlier portrayed by Hogarth, Cibber, Fielding, Voltaire, and others. Reinach, Meyer, and Hertzberg think it significant that the story as told in the *Voyage to Holland* had no Jewish character in it and conclude that Diderot gratuitously made the old lecher Jewish, in the image of de Pinto, when he wrote in into *Rameau's Nephew*. But, besides the fact that the Dutchman trading in his wife's charms and honor appears more ignoble than the Jew in the story,[22] Diderot had a valid philosophical motive as the basis for his revision of the incident. Recall now the nephew's first argument in justification for his immorality, his biological inheritance. Then, read the description of the Jew of Utrecht: " . . . he was a wealthy, prodigal Jew who loved music and my wild antics. I fiddled to the best of my ability; I played the fool; I lacked nothing. My Jew was a man who knew his law and observed it as rigidly as a bar, sometimes with his friends, always with strangers. He got himself into an ugly situation, that I must tell you about, for it is amusing. There was in Utrecht a charming courtesan. He was tempted . . ." (p. 482).

Diderot, like his precursor Pierre Bayle, did not believe that one's religious convictions significantly influence one's behavior. In his *Pensées diverses sur la comète* (*Divers Reflexions on the Comet*) (Chapter CXLVII), Bayle had written that "men can be at one and the same time very disorderly in their morals, and very convinced of the truth of a religion," and that "spiritual knowledge is not the cause of our actions." Far more important than one's religion as a cause of behavior are one's biologically determined characteristics. Just as the nephew is morally insensitive, the rich Jew, like de Pinto, is a born voluptuary.[23] Thus, *in spite of his law*, the Jew of Utrecht illustrates both the Baylian principle of the moral inefficaciousness of religion and the Diderotian principle of biological, ergo moral, diversity. It is pertinent, in order to judge this Jewish episode more properly in the context of the novel as a whole, to note that the Jew's lust is not a "Jewish" characteristic, for a dominant motif of the novel is *human* sexuality, as demonstrated repeatedly by the sexual antics of Rameau's Parisian circle and the philosophe's admission of his own sexual susceptibility (*Oeuvres romanesques*, p. 431). It is also pertinent to compare the fictionalized de Pinto to the description of another Dutch Jew in Diderot's *Encyclopédie*. The article on Spinoza is worded as follows:

> Benedict Spinoza, born a Jew, then a deserter of Judaism, and finally an atheist,[24] was from Amsterdam. . . . Everyone agrees that he was moral, sober, moderate, peaceful, unselfish, even generous; his heart was stained by none of the vices that dishonor. This is strange; but, after all, one should be no more surprised about it than about seeing people who behave very badly though they are firm believers in the Gospels. What the attraction of pleasure did not accomplish in Spinoza, *natural goodness and equity* did (*Encyclopédie*, XV, 463; emphasis added).[25]

Spinoza, the "virtuous Jew" by nature, and the fictional (?) de Pinto, the "unvirtuous Jew" by nature, illustrate that there is no *Jewish nature*: there are austere Jews and licentious Jews. Diderot's principle of diversity is thus confirmed.[26]

His last novel, *Jacques the Fatalist*, rounded out the trilogy of novels on human diversity. That there are no Jewish characters in this, the most populated of all his novels, is not irrelevant to a study on Diderot and the Jews. For the rogues' gallery of usurers, brokers, and shady dealers in second-hand goods depicted in the Saint-Ouin episode afforded the author an admirable opportunity for the inclusion of Jewish stereotypes, one that Voltaire, Balzac, and Dickens would not have failed to avail themselves of. But not Diderot, all of whose swindlers and thieves have good French Christian names like Le Brun and Mathieu de Fourgeot, and whose prime lecher is Father Hudson, a Premonstratensian monk!

Although Diderot treats individual character as being determined principally by heredity, and makes no attempt to characterize ethnic or national groups in racial terms, this does not prevent him from generalizing about the character of nations. But such generalizations are based on external factors, such as geographical and sociological. Thus, when he characterized the Egyptians as superstitious, he cited the influence of climate (A-T, XIV, 388). When he deplored the ferocity of the Parsees of Surate, he blamed their religion: "Superstition produces the same effects everywhere. Men must necessarily be miserable whenever they obstinately persist in unintelligible notions [religion, mythology], to which they attach more importance than to their own lives." [27] When he described the English as a melancholy people, he suggested that the national character was influenced by the foggy climate, heavy food, and strong drink, or the coal smoke that always enshrouded the country.[28] The Chinese are called a cunning, practical, and unheroic people, the result of the particular conditions of their agricultural life (preceding, p. 113). At times, particularly when he writes for monarchs, Diderot lays greater stress on political factors in the molding of national character. "Manners are everywhere the consequences of legislation and government," he writes to Catherine the Great in 1774, but he insists on the *universality* of moral standards:

. . . they are neither African, nor Asian, nor European; they are good and bad. A slave is a slave at the pole, where it is very cold. He is a slave in Constantinople, where it is very hot; it is necessary everywhere that a people be educated, free and virtuous. What Peter I brought to Russia, if good in Europe was good everywhere.

Without denying the influence of climate on mores, the present state of Greece and Italy, the future state of Russia, will show that good or bad mores have other causes.[29]

In 1772 Helvétius's book *On Man* was published posthumously. Its thesis was that at birth all human beings are intellectual equals and that education and sociological conditions alone account for all intellectual and moral differences in individuals and in nations. Diderot could not accept this extreme equalitarian hypothesis, and in the next two years he wrote his famous *Refutation*, which was a book-length response. What is significant in this response is that it tends to lay the emphasis on differences between individuals, rather than between nations. Thus Diderot concedes Helvétius's claim that nations differ very little from one another ("Who denies it?"), and that the French, if educated like Romans, would have their share of Caesars, Scipios, Pompeys, and Ciceros (A-T, II, 279). Also, he reiterates what he has written to Catherine the Great, that political conditions do strongly influence the national character, so that the freedom-loving English, under three consecutive despots like Elizabeth, would lose the spirit of liberty (preceding, n. 1).[30] But he refuses to concede the principle of equality at birth. "Ah! my philosopher friend, among the Greeks, among those Romans over whom you make such a to-do, you can count the geniuses on your fingers, and the imbeciles and fools were as numerous as amongst us. For it is eternally ordained that the freak called a genius shall always be infinitely rare, and that men of sense and intelligence never be common" (p. 290).

In general terms, one may say that Diderot believed that the incidence of genius in nations was primarily a matter of the accident of birth, and that genius and heroism were universal human qualities. Thus, he would write that "There is no nation at the pole or at the equator that is not capable of producing Homers, Virgils, Demosthenes, Ciceros, great legislators, great captains, great magistrates, great artists, but such men will everywhere be rare, whatever government there may be" (p. 326), so that even "under the Caliphs there were a Saadi and great physicians" (p. 357), and "there are heroes everywhere: . . . in the depths of the forests of Canada . . . in the shanties of slaves" (p. 409). And he repeats the universalist principle of morality: "The nation in which vice was honored and virtue scorned has never been and never will be" (p. 397). But, despite these more persistently voiced universalist expressions, and the deemphasizing of his earlier strongly geographical explanations of national character, he does not completely reject Montesquieu and Buffon. Replying to Helvétius's statement that geographical factors do not influence the mind, he writes:

> I don't believe this at all, if only because of the fact that every cause has its effect, and that every constant cause, however small, produces a great effect over a period of time. If it manages to determine the national spirit or character, it is important, especially in relation to the development of the fine arts, in which the difference between good and excellent is not merely the breadth of a hair.
>
> These general assertions about the air, the climate, the seasons, the diet are too vague to be decisive in such a tenuous matter.
>
> Is it thought that it is of no consequence to the inhabitants of a region, to their way of eating, of dressing, of doing things, of thinking, of feeling, whether it is humid or dry, forested or bare, arid and mountainous, flat or marshy, plunged into darkness eighteen hours a day, and buried under snows for eight months at a time? . . .
>
> There is hardly a man, in whatever clime, whose disposition doesn't show to some extent the clear or cloudy state of the weather . . . .
>
> Let us not overemphasize these factors, but let us not deny their effect altogether (pp. 320–21).

Several pages farther on he writes: "Just considering the diversity of climates, I could easily surmise that it is the same for minds as for certain fruits, good everywhere, but excellent in a particular country" (p. 326). And he proposes the following compromise between extreme physical determinism on the one hand and extreme environmentalism on the other:

> Say that laws, manners, government are the *principal causes* of the diversity of nations, and that if a given public institution is not enough to equal one individual [of genius], it does allow one large group of people to reach the level of another large group; and we shall bow our heads down before the experience of the centuries that teaches us that a Demosthenes, whom Greece will not produce again, may appear some day in the frosts of the glacial zone, or beneath the brazen sky of the torrid zone (p. 316).

One may say, in looking at the *Refutation* in its totality, that Diderot is strongly elitist as regards individual and relatively equalitarian as regards national differences. This paradoxical position is nowhere more strikingly expressed than in the following dialogue near the end of the examination of Helvétius's Tome I:

> "There were just as many knaves and fools, and just as foolish and knavish in Athens or in Rome as in Paris."
> "And great men?"
> "I think that they were less rare, and that is what, in my view, all the excellence in legislation boils down to.[31] As for people, I mean the masses, they remain alike everywhere . . . .
> An entire nation from which we are separated by a great lapse of time becomes nothing more, in our minds, than a small number of famous names that have come down to us in history" (p. 393).

The apparent contradiction between expressions such as "Imagine the English with three Elizabeths in a row and the English would be the basest slaves in Europe," and "the masses . . . remain alike everywhere," which appear within eleven pages of each other in the *Refutation*, may be explained by Diderot's belief that the masses follow their geniuses and heroes, to liberty or slavery. These great men are born in *relatively* equal numbers amongst all peoples, from the poles to the equator, but the blossoming of their genius and the direction it takes are determined by the external factors of geography, culture, and institutions. Thus, to recall the article "Theosophists" (preceding, pp. 51, 109), a Moses, a Pindar, a Christ, a Shakespeare may, in different times and places, be a poet, a magician, a prophet, or a legislator, and may lead his people to glory or to misfortune.

Diderot's theory of national character is evolutional. The Greeks were once great; they no longer are. The English are the freest men on earth, but they could easily become slaves. The Russians are ignorant, but Peters and Catherines may lead them out of the darkness. The Jews are not specifically dealt with in the *Refutation*, among examples of diverse national characters. The younger Diderot would not have missed the opportunity of reminding the reader of their ignorance and their superstition. But times have changed, and, with the exception of Voltaire's case, the Jewish *bête noire* of the earlier philosophic writings has virtually disappeared from the philosophic rhetoric of the 1770s.[32] When Diderot needs an example of stupidity, he now refers the reader to the inhabitants of Kamchatka (p. 395), for has he not already seen the enlightened Jews of Amsterdam? Has he not admired the beauty of their synagogues? Has he not found their liturgical music to be sweet? Has he not seen their contribution to Dutch commerce? And what if de Pinto is a womanizer? Was not Helvétius one too? And so, when Helvétius makes the startling assertion that a descendant of Abraham has as much right by venerable ancestry alone to a title of nobility, Diderot does not make sport of the idea, as we may imagine Voltaire would, but writes an objective etymological note on the word nobility, and circumscribes its use to feudal and postfeudal times (p. 444).

To a reader with an oversimplified or oversystematized notion of eighteenth-century French philosophic thought, who regarded

Diderot, for example, as unalterably hostile to the Judeo-Christian tradition compared to the classical pagan, and excessively smitten with the virtues of the Greeks, the Romans, the Chinese, and the English, it should be enlightening to read the *Refutation* in its entirety, thence to consult Diderot's last important work, *The Essay on the Reigns of Claudius and of Nero*. He will find in these works such heretical observations as the following:

A priest of Eumolpus was hardly less intolerant than a parish vicar (*Refutation*, II, 287).

The populace of Athens was baser than ours (*Essay*, III, 330).

Ancient Rome seems to me like a great slaughterhouse where the lesson to be learned was inhumanity (*Essay*, III, 326).

The duration of the Chinese government is a necessary consequence not of its goodness, but rather of the excessive population of the country (*Refutation*, II, 328).[33]

The English, enemies of tyranny at home, are the most ferocious despots abroad (*Refutation*, II, 422).[34]

Diderot was just as willing to revise his earlier judgments concerning the moral superiority of the traditional philosophic models of goodness as he was of the Jews. ''I seek what is truth, honesty, decency, and I give myself wholly to this search,'' wrote he in the *Essay on Claudius and Nero* (III, 196). One is not inclined to doubt his sincerity.

In the Europe of the late 1770s, the sight of the enlightened Jews of Amsterdam could only suggest to Diderot the probability of the future regeneration of European Jewry under more liberal governments. That he still regarded the Jews in the main as culturally depressed and addicted to centuries-old commercial habits that were unworthy of honorable men is evident in one or two of his private letters wherein he jestingly used earthily derogatory ethnic epithets.[35] But such expressions are extremely rare in the private correspondence and are carefully avoided in works intended for eventual publication. If one surveys the entire range of Diderot's formal writings from 1760 until his death twenty-four years later, one finds among his characters a single dishonorable Jew, in contrast to the abundance of "Christian" rogues that people his fictional writings. All other Jews, and there are a number of them if one includes the *Salons*, are portrayed with dignity or sympathy.[36]

Diderot did not survive to see the flowering of modern Jewish thought that was prefigured by his admirer Gotthold Lessing's friend Moses Mendelssohn. One should not be too hard on him for failing to recognize in Mendelssohn's *Phädon*, of which a French translation was published in 1772, the beginning of a Jewish enlightenment. To a French rationalist, Mendelssohn's Socrates appeared more like a disciple of Leibnitz and Wolff than the teacher of Criton and the Athenian philosophers.[37] Far more congenial to his philosophic spirit were the half-Jew Montaigne, father of modern skepticism, and the Dutch Jew Spinoza, whose "God as Nature" was Diderot's sole divinity.[38] Did Diderot need any additional proof that Jewish backwardness was anything but racial? But, though Diderot did not survive to see the new age of the Jews in Europe, he did live to see and to hail the birth of a new land across the sea.

> What simpler and more natural occasion . . . to record one's reflections, than to pause for a moment over one of the most extraordinary phenomena that the history of the world has afforded us, a people enslaved to a people, a nation that suddenly shakes off the yoke of servitude, that liberates itself from despots with the help of despots, and that, pondering over the means of forever ensuring its happiness together with its liberty, prepares a refuge for all the children of men who cry out or who will cry out beneath the lash of civil or religious tyranny (*Essay on Claudius and Nero*, III, 393).

That Diderot's dream for the future involved not only universal political and religious tolerance, but universal political and religious *equality*, is certain. In his last letter destined for publication, his passionate defense of Abbé Raynal's democratic *History of the Two Indies*, he described a deputy of the people in the following terms: "He is the organ of virtue, of reason, of equity, of humanity, of justice, of clemency, of law, or of any other of those sublime Quakeresses before whom mortals are all equal" (*Oeuvres philosophiques*, 641). Thus did Diderot, in 1781, ten years before the emancipation of France's Jewish population, proclaim the equality of all mankind.

6

Conclusion

Is he good? Is he bad?

—Diderot

THREE years before his death, in the year in which he wrote his defense of Abbé Raynal's condemnation of colonial oppression, Diderot made the final revision of the best of his three plays, entitled *Est-il bon? est-il méchant?* (*Is he good? Is he bad?*). In it he created Monsieur Hardouin, a character who in order to do good appears to others to be doing the opposite. Diderot consciously intended Monsieur Hardouin to reflect an image of himself.[1] It is a fascinating bit of historical irony that the fate of Diderot's reputation on the question of eighteenth-century anti-Semitism should exactly parallel Monsieur Hardouin's reputation for good or for evil. Diderot's reputation is based largely on two early works whose motivation was fundamentally humanitarian. The *Promenade of the Skeptic*, while unappreciative of the Mosaic tradition, and while given to the use of some offensive caricature of both Jews and Christians, was not motivated out of a desire to do injury to the Jewish people, but rather to weaken through ridicule the power of the oppressive institution of the established Church and its doctrines, which appeared to mock both science and humanism. Clearly the most offensive of the latter to the philosophes was the doctrine of a chosen people. The intent of the long article on Jewish philosophy, compiled by Diderot from what were then regarded as the fairest of the available sources, was, again, to attack the foundations of Christian belief by destroying the credibility of its Jewish sources and the plausibility of the theological explanation of the Jewish role in history. That Diderot's interpretation of certain events in Jewish history now appears gratuitously negative

158

may be ascribed both to the limitations of the available historical materials and to the desire of the philosophes to stress the pernicious effects of religious fanaticism. This was the overriding concern of eighteenth-century French liberalism. In this regard, one may paraphrase Diderot's defense of Seneca in his last major work: "Judge not Seneca according to the lights of your own time but according to the lights of his."[2] Diderot's negative assessment of the evolution of Jewish philosophy in Volume IX of the *Encyclopédie* was directly preceded by de Jaucourt's sympathetic article on secular Jewish history. It is clear from Diderot's pairing of these articles and from their complementary subject matter that, although the philosophes could not approve of aspects of the Jewish religious heritage that appeared to them to have served as the model for Christian superstition and priestly power, their intent was to improve the situation of European Jewry through liberalization of political, social, and economic policies governing their treatment. But, in recent writings on Diderot and the Jews, only the article on Jewish philosophy is remembered, and is made to appear as Diderot's most authentic personal statement on the Jews, which it was not. While it is evident that Diderot's universalist ideology made it hard for him to acquire a genuine feeling of warmth and amity for the Jews, a people that in his day still seemed wedded to the notion of their divine election, Diderot succeeded, especially after 1760, in eschewing in his writings the anti-Jewish biases of philosophic associates like Voltaire, d'Holbach, and Grimm, and in dealing objectively, even sympathetically, with Jewish subjects, to earn a place among the more sensitive, perceptive, and humane writers on the Jewish question in its diverse ramifications. Unfortunately for Diderot's reputation in this regard, he left no single, comprehensive statement of his position on the Jews, so that it has had to be synthesized from among his diverse writings, most of which remained unpublished until after the French Revolution and remain unfamiliar to the general public. Also, since he is given no credit for the publication of the de Jaucourt article,[3] which as early as 1765 contained the basic arguments to be used by all

Jewish and pro-Jewish writers from Valabrègue, Turgot, and Mirabeau to Abbé Gregoire, Diderot's role in preparing the ideological climate for Jewish emancipation in France is unappreciated.

The nineteenth century was slow in recognizing Diderot's merits, and when it did it tended to seize upon his supposed confirmations of its own ideological proclivities. Thus a presumed "Germanism" in Diderot made him the hero of late French Romanticists like Sainte-Beuve and the Jewish drama critic Jules Janin, while Marxists regarded Diderot and d'Alembert's *Encyclopédie* as the forerunner of nineteenth-century philosophical materialism.[4] Although nineteenth-century Marxists did not speak with one voice on the Jewish question, certain Marxist ideologues associated Jewishness with the negation of universality[5] and with the system of banking and finance.[6] In the first of these charges against the Jews, Karl Marx, who claimed to be an avid reader of Diderot,[7] could find some justification in the *Encyclopédie* article on Jewish philosophy, but it is doubtful that he could have shared the Diderot-Jaucourt approval of the Jewish role in European commerce or Diderot's enthusiasm for Jewish themes in religious art and ancient Hebrew poetry, attitudes that found expression elsewhere in Diderot's writings.

One regrets that the subtlety of Diderot's thought has often eluded partisan and dogmatic drinkers at the Diderotian stream. For it is obvious to the serious and conscientious student of this most advanced and complex of eighteenth-century French thinkers that coexisting with his hatred of religion and authoritarian social patterns was an immense capacity to appreciate creative genius in its most diverse productions and a profound sense of the inherent worth of all mankind.

Where then would Diderot have stood were he to have lived in the nineteenth century to see the French socialists, his admirers and professed spiritual descendants, bitterly divided on the question of the Jews? Would he have stood with xenophobic dogmatists like Pierre Joseph Proudhon, or would he have joined Zola and Jaurès in their philanthropic denunciations of anti-Semitic political demagoguery?[8] One suspects that it would have been the latter, but only after he had written essays on Bizet's music, Pissarro's painting, Bergson's philosophy, Bernhardt's acting, and corresponded with Freud on the physiology of dreams!

Notes

Chapter 1

1. *Essai sur les règnes de Claude et de Néron (Essay on the Reigns of Claudius and of Nero)*, in *Oeuvres complètes (Complete Works)*, ed. J. Assézat and M. Tourneux (Paris, 1875–1877), III, p. 210.

2. Ibid., p. 290.

3. *L'Humanisme de Diderot* (Paris, 1938), p. 71.

4. *Lettres à Sophie Volland*, ed. A. Babelon (Paris, 1938), I, p. 51.

5. Carl Becker, "The Dilemma of Diderot," *Philosophical Review* XXIV, p. 58.

6. *Salon de 1767*, in Diderot's *Salons*, ed. J. Seznec and J. Adhémar (Paris, 1963), III, p. 67.

7. "Les Juifs dans l'opinion chrétienne aux XVIIe et XVIIIe siècles: Peuchet et Diderot," *Revue des Études juives*, VIII, pp. 138-44.

8. "Issues and Ideas in the Jewish World," unsigned article in *The Shofar* (May-June 1968), p. 7.

9. "Juifs, Philosophie des" ("Jews, Philosophy of"), *L'Encyclopédie, ou Dictionnaire raisonné des sciences, des arts et des métiers* (Paris, 1751–1772), IX, pp. 25b–51.

10. The reference is to the stories of the renegade of Avignon and of the Jew of Utrecht in Diderot's *Neveu de Rameau (Rameau's Nephew)*, and to his notes on a voyage to Holland (*Voyage de Hollande*, in *Oeuvres complètes*, XVII, pp. 365-425).

11. *Juden und Altes Testament bei Diderot*, diss. Bayrischen Julius-Maximilians Universität zu Wurzburg, 1932; published Wertheim am Main, 1933.

12. P. H. Meyer, "The Attitude of the Enlightenment towards the Jews," *Studies on Voltaire and the Eighteenth Century*, XXVI (1963): 1161–1205; A. Hertzberg, *The French Enlightenment and the Jews* (New York and London, 1968). "Voltaire, Diderot, and D'Holbach stand squarely arraigned, tried, and convicted of the grossest manifestations of prejudice," wrote Simon Schama, historian of the French Revolution, in his review of the Hertzberg book (*Saturday Review*, June 22, 1968, p. 33).

13. *The Jewish Element in French Literature* (Fairleigh Dickinson University Press, 1961), p. 127.

14. *The Origins of Totalitarianism*, new edition (New York, 1966), p. 23.

15. "Juifs, Hist. des" ("Jews, Hist. of"), *Encyclopédie*, IX, 24–25a.

16. (Geneva, 1973), pp. 35–54.

17. For a study of the questions of attribution and tampering in the *Encyclopédie*, see especially D. H. Gordon and N. L. Torrey, *The Censoring of Diderot's Encyclopédie and the Reestablished Text* (New York, 1947); H. Dieckmann, *Inventaire du fonds Vandeul et inédits de Diderot* (Geneva, 1951) and *"L'Encyclopédie* et le fonds Vandeul," *Revue d'histoire littéraire* (July-September 1951), pp. 318–32; J. Proust, *Diderot et l'Encyclopédie* (Paris, 1962); J. Lough, *Essays on the "Encyclopédie" of Diderot and d'Alembert* (London, 1968); and R. N. Schwab, "The Diderot Problem, the Starred Articles and the Question of Attribution in the *Encyclopédie,*" *Eighteenth-Century Studies* 2, no. 3 (Summer 1969): 370–438. Naigeon, who "rectified" the Diderot texts, was often misled by Diderot's compilational method, and Proust (p. 267, n. 70) accuses him, along with most of the critics, of having "confused Brucker's thought with Diderot's" and attributing to him many anonymous articles. "The product of these successive mix-ups is a monster that can in no wise be considered as representing Diderot's thought."

Naigeon's amendments, unidentified as such in the great Assézat-Tourneux edition of Diderot's complete works, either mitigated Diderot's praise of Jews or added derogatory language where none existed in the original Diderot manuscript (Proust, pp. 138–49 and 539–47). For a contrast of Naigeon's rigidly doctrinaire atheism with Diderot's skeptical humanism, see the "Preliminary Notice" to the *Essai sur le mérite et la vertu (Essay on Merit and Virtue)* in Assézat-Tourneux (hereafter cited as A-T), I, 7.

18. The articles "Christianisme," "Judaïsme," "Préadamites," "Prophète," "Providence," "Osée" ("Hosea"), and "Résurrection" are of unknown authorship. "Prêtres" ("Priests") and "Théocratie" are now attributed to d'Holbach (Proust, p. 538). "Asiatiques" and "Mosaïque" are believed to be by Diderot as indicated by Naigeon.

19. " . . . One must *systematically* doubt Assézat and Tourneux's choice, and *never* accept an article as Diderot's for the sole reason that it is reproduced in the *Complete Works*" (Proust, p. 119).

20. In one case, unhappy with Rousseau's article "Économie politique" after publishing it, Diderot had a second article written for a later volume under the name "Œconomie politique."

21. Jacques Basnage, *Histoire des Juifs depuis Jésus-Christ jusqu'à présent,* 15 vols. (The Hague, 1716); Jacob Brucker, *Historia critica philosophiae a mundi incunabulis ad nostram usque aetatem deducta,* 5 vols. (Leipzig, 1742–1744); Pierre Bayle, *Dictionnaire historique et critique,* 4 vols. (Rotterdam, 1697); Ephraim Chambers, *Cyclopaedia,* etc. (London, 1728–1746). On Diderot's compilational method and Brucker's influence, see R. L. Cru, *Diderot as a Disciple of English Thought* (New York, 1913), pp. 262–86.

22. "These textual borrowings are perhaps the least significant: they prove that the encyclopedist has not rethought what he transcribes, and in order for this original mind not to have given his own personal form to the ideas that he expresses, it can only be that these same ideas must have remained foreign to him" ("Sur le texte de Diderot et sur les sources de quelques passages de ses oeuvres," *Revue d'Histoire littéraire,* 22nd yr. [Paris, 1915], p. 363). Proust generally agrees with this opinion (pp. 277–78), but he modifies it by pointing to Diderot's selection and ordering of borrowed passages to serve his own fundamental criticisms of religion (p. 257).

23. "Since most of Diderot's texts supposedly demonstrating prejudice were not published in his lifetime, while those recommending universal tolerance were, Hertzberg should have placed Diderot in the line of Montesquieu's 'liberalism' rather than in the

supposedly prejudiced camp of Voltaire'' (pp. 36–37, n. 8). This formulation is not even factually correct. It will be demonstrated below that Diderot's most "prejudiced" writings were the earlier, that is, published or intended to be, and that the theme of tolerance is one of the constants of Diderot's thought.

24. Dieckmann cites testimony that Diderot did, in fact, attempt to publish in Holland some of his works that could not be printed in France. The project failed for financial reasons (*Cinq Leçons sur Diderot* [Geneva, 1959], p. 20). But the major unpublished works were circulated in his lifetime among Diderot's friends and sent in manuscript form to the courts of several German states, of Poland, of Russia, and of Sweden in the literary correspondence of his friend and collaborator Frederick Melchior Grimm (see J.R. Smiley, "The Subscribers of Grimm's *Correspondance littéraire,*" *Modern Language Notes*, LXII [1947]:44–46; and L. Schwartz, *Melchior Grimm: The "Correspondance littéraire" and the Philosophic Spirit*, [Ph.D. dissertation, University of Southern California, 1962], p. 84 and *passim*).

25. Paul Ledieu ascribes the Diderotian paradoxes to his "moral incertitude" and "intellectual anxiety," which cause him to oppose ceaselessly one view to another in order to test their validity (*Diderot et Sophie Volland*, 2nd ed., cited by O. Fellows and N. Torrey, *Age of Enlightenment* [New York, 1971], p. 211). Jacques Chouillet painstakingly demonstrates the essentially dialectical character of Diderot's thought and coins the term *dialectique d'épreuve* to describe his esthetic methodology (*La Formation des idées esthétiques de Diderot* [Paris, 1973], pp. 432–33).

26. Dieckmann avers that Diderot wrote for a small group of enlightened friends and that, "like Stendhal," his eye, ultimately, was on posterity (pp. 25, 31–33). The question of Diderot's sensitivity to his posthumous image is treated in detail by Arthur Wilson in *Diderot* (New York, 1972), pp. 508–12.

27. See especially the conclusion of Voltaire's *Treatise on Tolerance*.

28. See especially Voltaire's article on the Jews in his *Philosophical Dictionary*. Bertram Schwarzbach, in his article "The Jews and the Enlightenment," *Diderot Studies XVI*, pp. 369–70, denies that this article was intended by Voltaire for his *Philosophical Dictionary*.

29. See especially Arendt, *The Origins of Totalitarianism*, part one: "Anti-Semitism." Jean Jaurès, in his *Histoire socialiste de la Révolution française*, goes back to the time of Abbé Maury and the threat to the property of the church in the French Revolution to find "the first manifestation of [modern] anti-Semitic demagoguery" ([Paris, 1968], I, p. 685). But *political* anti-Semitism was only a sporadic phenomenon in France before the late nineteenth century.

30. The selection of the Jews as central characters in the providentially directed drama of human history was the main thesis of Bossuet, the foremost spokesman of the seventeenth-century French Catholic church, in his *Histoire Universelle*. Voltaire's historical writings were aimed in part at refuting Bossuet.

31. About the Jews in the eighteenth century, Abram Sachar has written as follows:
Jews were everywhere sunk in superstition; learning had decayed and leadership had so far degenerated that it was impossible to find a worthy champion in the libels which were concocted against Jewish literature. It was the age of Eybeschutz and his curious controversy over the miraculous powers of amulets; of Messianic imposters who, despite their incredible claims and almost patent rascality, attracted large

followings. It seemed that Judaism had become a mass of meaningless formulas, totally divorced from life, unworthy of the respect and loyalty of sincere and sensible men (*History of the Jews* [New York, 1965], p. 263).

H. Graetz wrote of the physical degradation of the Jews: "They neglected their outward appearance . . . lost all taste and sense of beauty, and to some extent became as despicable as their enemies desired them to be" (*History of the Jews* [Philadelphia, 1891–1898], III, pp. 512–13).

Gendzier (p. 37) calls the eighteenth-century French Jew "a negative phenomenon" even in the eyes of sympathetic non-Jews.

32. See especially "Hebrews and Hellenes" in Peter Gay's *The Enlightenment*, Vol. 1 (New York, 1966–69). One can only wish, wistfully, that Voltaire in particular might have lived to read Elie Wiesel's oh-so-Voltairian, twentieth-century definition of Judaism: "in spite of God to believe in God, in spite of Man to believe in Man."

33. See the dedicatory preamble to Diderot's *Essay on the Reigns of Claudius and Nero*, A-T, III, pp. 9–14.

34. Diderot used the term *la philanthropie* in the original sense of "love of humanity." See his *Correspondance inédite* (Paris, 1931), I, p. 311.

Chapter 2

1. Letter to the Abbé Diderot, May 1770, in Diderot's *Correspondance*, ed. G. Roth and J. Varloot (Paris, 1955–1970), X, p. 63. Varloot collaborated on vols. XIV–XVI.

2. His younger brother did become a churchman, rising to the rank of canon. A younger sister became a nun and died tragically in her convent.

3. *Plan of a University for the Government of Russia*, in A-T, III, p. 478. In his *Refutation of Helvétius* he tells us that he began reading Horace at fifteen (A-T, II, p. 429).

4. *Notre Jeunesse* (Paris, 1933), p. 55. Bossuet's "Sermon on the Goodness and the Severity of God" referred to the Jews as a "monstrous people" justly punished for their crimes by Divine Providence.

5. According to the *Guide Juif de France* (Paris, 1971), p. 59, there were fewer than one thousand Jews living in Paris as late as 1789. See also David Feuerwerker, *L'Émancipation des Juifs en France de l'Ancien Régime au Second Empire* (Paris, 1976), pp. 332, 349, and 351.

6. *The Story of Civilization IX*, "The Age of Voltaire" (New York, 1965), p. 623.

7. Peter Gay cites a fact that few of Diderot's freethinking contemporaries recognized, that "unlike other ancient religions, Judaism incorporated rational, rather than mythical, elements from its neighbors" (p. 93).

8. Diderot uses the expression in his two critical essays on Helvétius, dated 1758 (A-T, II, p. 270) and 1773–1774 (A-T, II, p. 285). The expression was edited into the *Encyclopédie* article on Jewish philosophy by Naigeon.

9. Franco Venturi claims that Diderot's ecclesiastical training lasted until 1740 and that he had first intended to become a Jesuit, then a Carthusian (see *La Jeunesse de Diderot*, transl. by J. Bertrand [Slatkine Reprints, 1967], p. 21). Venturi's chronology conflicts with that of Madame de Vandeul, Diderot's daughter, who has him entering a lawyer's

service around 1738 or 1739, more than two years before he met her mother in 1741 (see note 10, following).

10. "Memoirs on the Life and Works of Diderot," by Madame de Vandeul, in A-T, I, xxxii.

11. H. J. Reesink writes, "Among the subjects that the English authors treat with preference and which seem to excite great interest in the literate public on the continent . . . we note the Schism of the Anglican Church, Transubstantiation, the Trinity, the Immortality of the Soul, Witchcraft, and Ghosts. There is also the 'Rabinage,' and furthermore everything concerning the religion of the Jews, which is much discussed, and innumerable writings against Deism, Atheism, the Socinians, the Libertines, and the Freethinkers, not to forget the Mystics and Quakers" (L'Angleterre et la littérature anglaise dans les trois plus anciens périodiques français de Hollande de 1684 à 1709), in Bibliothèque de la Revue de Littérature comparée, ed. by F. Baldensperger and P. Hazard (Paris, 1931), LXVII, p. 139.

12. This 120-verse poem, Voltaire's first literary assault on the Old Testament and the Jews, was not published until the 1770s but was well known in the 1740s. In this poem, Voltaire, in the spirit of the Latin poet Lucretius, proclaims that he will tear the bands of superstition from the eyes of his readers and expose the cruel image of the biblical God. In order to accentuate the absurdity of Christian doctrine, he vilifies the Jews.

13. See Hertzberg's exposition of the anti-Jewish tenor of English deist writings (pp. 38–39).

14. By the time the translation was published in 1743 he was married.

15. This is a major theme of Toussaint's book on mores, Les Moeurs, published three years after Diderot's translation of Shaftesbury. Diderot was also closely associated at this time with Condillac, Locke's most distinguished sensationalist disciple in France. It is evident that by this time both Diderot and Condillac were prepared to spread the gospel of English philosophy in France, as Voltaire was prepared to popularize English physics.

16. A-T, I, p. 18, n. 1.

17. On the question of comparative Jewish and Christian usury, see Malcolm Hay, Europe and the Jews (Boston, 1961), p. 105.

18. "I asked him his religion. He answered me that religion had nothing to do with it, but that rectitude, which is independent of it, was all that mattered. I liked this answer. I gave him both of my hands; he took them and shook them warmly" (Correspondance, XIII, p. 13). The passage quoted here is found in a fragment, possibly of a letter from Belgium, written in June 1773.

19. A-T, I, pp. 76–77, ns. 1, 2.

20. For a more complete account of the genesis of this work, see P. Vernière's "Introduction" to the Pensées philosophiques in his edition of Diderot's Oeuvres philosophiques (Paris, 1961), pp. 3–6; and J. Chouillet, part 1, chap. II.

21. Several copies of the Testament were circulated in manuscript form. See A. Lichtenberger, Le Socialisme au XVIIIᵉ siècle (Paris, 1895), p. 76.

22. For a discussion of Diderot's revision of this negative criticism, see chapter 3 of this study.

23. "Conclusion," p. 126.

24. Diderot goes on to praise Egypt's ministers, who are as "enlightened" as their

religion is "tenebrous." In his later unpublished writings, Diderot says the same about the Christian religion. See n. 53, following, for commentary on Diderot's later references to the Egyptians.

25. It is a distinction that Diderot is not always careful to make. See p. 36.

26. *Essay on the Reigns of Claudius and Nero,* A-T, III, p. 383.

27. In his *Observations sur le Nakaz,* Diderot describes the ancient theocratic state: "At that time there was a priest-king. When these two heads were separated, the priest retained the privilege of consecrating the king. He was made to wear [the Church's] livery. What does this ceremony mean, properly interpreted? Just this: You are responsible only to God. Be a tyrant if you wish." Diderot then refers the reader to Samuel's address to the people (*Oeuvres politiques,* ed. by P. Vernière [Paris, 1963], p. 405). Vernière notes the strong influence on Diderot of Boulanger's *Recherches sur l'origine du despotisme oriental.* One may also assume the influence of Meslier's *Testament,* which extends the thesis of church-state collusion to Christian Europe.

28. "It is however not impossible to find in the *Promenade du sceptique* the indication of the great themes of reflexion that Diderot will take up again in his *History of Philosophy*" (Proust, p. 235). Proust believes that Meslier's *Testament* was the principal source of the *Promenade,* which was written in 1747 (p. 286).

29. Diderot alludes to it directly elsewhere in the *Promenade* (p. 215).

30. The word *race* was frequently use in the eighteenth century for a homogeneous group of any kind. This usage was pejorative.

31. A militant cleric in Rabelais's *Gargantua.*

32. For an analysis of Diderot's ineptness in the genre of allegorical satire, see Chouillet, p. 70.

33. The characterization of the Jews as a seditious sect was an eighteenth-century cliché. It will be shown how Diderot, in using it, reflected contemporary usage. The image of the seditious Jew came from the Roman authors, who were obviously hostile to a people that tenaciously refused to submit to Roman power. It will also be shown how Diderot later defended the Jews on this charge. On the Roman sources of the calumny on Jewish "plunder" in the Egyptian exodus, see H. Coudenhove-Kalergi, *Anti-Semitism throughout the Ages,* transl. by A. S. Rappoport (London, 1935), p. 84.

34. See Peter Gay, p. 76.

35. "Diatribe gives way to elevation," writes Jean Fabre of Diderot's writings on philosophy and religion in the post-*Promenade* period ("Diderot et les Théosophes," *Cahiers de l'Association Internationale des Études Françaises, no. 13,* [June 1961], p. 204). Diderot himself would later write, in his "Commentary on Voltaire's *Lettres d'Amabed,*" the following pertinent remarks:

> I know very well that I shall provoke screams of protest in all of Voltaire's idolators, but I shall whisper in your ear that this last work [of his] is tasteless, clumsy, unoriginal, a rehashing of all the old obscenities that the author has peddled against Moses and Jesus Christ, the prophets and the apostles, the Church, the popes, the cardinals, the priests and the monks; no interest, no fire, no semblance of truth, lots of muck, a crude frolic . . . . I don't like religion, but I do not hate it enough to consider this good (A-T, VI, 367).

Voltaire himself would regret Diderot's abandonment of the genre. See Fabre, ibid.

36. The erotic novel in an Oriental setting was enjoying a great vogue in 1747, despite strong official efforts to suppress the genre. Diderot himself would publish in Holland in the following year *Les Bijoux indiscrets (The Indiscreet Jewels)*, a work which is outside the immediate scope of this monograph, in spite of its ideological significance. On the latter point, see Michel Butor's essay, "Des *Bijoux indiscrets* à l'*Encyclopédie*." in the Club Français du Livre edition of Diderot's *Oeuvres complètes* (Paris, 1969), I, p. xxiv.

37. It is noteworthy that in spite of philosophic partiality toward the Chinese, Diderot does not hesitate to use them as an example of religious fallibility.

38. Franco Venturi doubts that *De la suffisance* dates back to this early period of Diderot's career and prefers to believe it contemporaneous with his *Additions to the Philosophical Thoughts* (1760) (p. 107). This writer has no way of dating the work with certainty and, lacking proof, prefers to adhere to the traditional date. In terms of Diderot's ideological evolution, the atheistic *Letter on the Blind* logically belongs after the deistic defense of natural religion.

39. The first seven volumes of the *Encyclopédie* appeared between 1751 and 1757 and included the letters A-G. Most of Diderot's articles on the Jews were composed *before* 1757. The principal article, on Jewish philosophy, was probably written in 1754 for the ninth volume. Because of the suspension of the publication privilege after the seventh volume, it did not appear until 1765, when the last ten volumes of text were finally authorized.

40. This is the thesis of Louis Ducros's *Les Encyclopédistes* (Paris, 1900).

41. *Les Sciences sociales dans l'Encyclopédie* (Paris, 1923).

42. " . . . a whole spectrum of successive nuances, going from the complete and sincere orthodoxy of the first *abbés* [Yvon and Mallet], from the liberal traditionalism of Boucher d'Argis, to the temerarious extremes of Diderot, d'Alembert, or Marmontel" (Hubert, p. 32).

43. Hubert, pp. 112–17.

44. Condorcet characterized the *Encyclopédie* as "a depository in which respected errors were betrayed by the weaknesses of their proofs or shaken by the mere proximity of truths which undermined their foundations" (quoted from his *Life of Voltaire*, in Hubert, p. 32).

45. "They fought against religion all the while acting as though they were defending it" (Ducros, p. 194).

46. This is the principal thesis of Voltaire's *Essai sur les Moeurs*, his answer to Bossuet's *Histoire Universelle*. The tendency to see the Jews as a unique people, selected to fulfill a mystical historical role, is clearly identified by Sartre as the psychological basis of anti-Semitism. "Let us remember that anti-Semitism is a primitive Manichean conception of the world in which the Jew's place is that of the great explanatory myth" (*Réflexions sur la question juive* [*Reflexions on the Jewish Question*] [Paris, 1954], p. 179). By demythologizing the Jews, the philosophes—whatever their prejudices regarding the character of the Jews—were asserting the essential humanity of this people.

47. The following passage in Brucker well illustrates this "standard" Philosophic view: We shall conclude our view of the state of philosophy among the Hebrews in the words of an eminent English writer: "It is well-known that the Hebrews never excelled in mathematical or philosophical learning, or liberal arts, nor were even distinguished by any ingenious discoveries . . . . Apollonius passes this severe

judgment upon them, that they were to be ranked among the most stupid barbarians, and are perhaps the only people who have never produced any single invention" (*The History of Philosophy*, transl. by W. Enfield [London, 1791], I, 23).

But there were limits to the kinds of classical clichés a philosophe like Diderot would repeat. He would never repeat the Apion-Tacitus blood-ritual calumny, which had been widely circulated in France since the twelfth century and "confirmed" by Pope Benedict XIV in 1755. See Hay pp. 131, 137.

48. "Sermon on the Goodness and Severity of God."

49. Sänger (p. 12) says that in his article on the Jews, Diderot "tended to accept" Boussuet's characterization of the Jews as "Slaves wherever they are, without honor and without liberty." This conformity of view is only apparent. The essential difference, and this is overlooked by Sänger, is that Diderot believed that the Jews had become servile because of a self-imposed sociocultural straitjacket. To Diderot this condition was curable and was not decreed by God. Diderot's views on the social problem of the Jews are examined in Chapter 4 of this work.

50. The original quotation is in the first edition of the *Encyclopédie*, VII, 904b. Proust (p. 279, n. 130) is puzzled by the laudatory wording of the original, which Diderot *added* to Brucker. He assumes that the Naigeon "rectification" is Diderot's correction of an "aberration."

51. In the article "Mosaïque et Chrétienne" Naigeon adds the word "bad" to the expression "the physics of Moses" (Proust, p. 545).

52. This may be called the "blast theory" of civilization. It will be shown in Chapter 3 of this work how this theory governs Diderot's assessment of Jewish literature.

53. Diderot's treatment of the Egyptians is full of contradictions. In his article "Bibliothèque" ("Library") he writes that "the Chaldeans and the Egyptians were probably the first whom the Jews instructed in their sciences" (XIII, p. 440). In his article "Egyptians" he says that Jewish notions were introduced into Egypt under the Ptolemys (XIV, p. 382). In the article on Jewish philosophy he denies that the Egyptians took anything from the Jews or that the latter had any science. The article "Egyptians" praises this people for their taste for useful things and calls the pyramids monuments to Egyptian science (XIV, pp. 385–86). But in his *Addition to the Philosophical Thoughts* (1770) Diderot refers to the "Égyptien imbécile" as an example of blind superstition (*Pensée* XXX).

How then should one read Diderot? Preferably outside of the *Encyclopédie*, which as has been noted and will be further demonstrated is largely mere compilation, as far as Diderot's articles are concerned.

54. This article is attributed to Diderot by Naigeon.

55. A more definitive evaluation of Maimonides is furnished in the article on Jewish philosophy. See following, pp. 63-64 of this work.

56. On the Persian Sufists: "They will pay you . . . with these kinds of comparisons which have nothing to do with God, and which are good only to mislead an ignorant people ("Asiatics," p. 375). On the Tartars: "They wallow in the grossest superstition . . . all travelers agree that the Tartars are, of all the peoples of Asia, the most uncouth, the most ignorant, and the most superstitious. Natural law is virtually unknown amongst them . . ." (pp. 376–77). On the Hindus: "If from Tartary you go on to India, you will find there scarcely less ignorance and superstition" (p. 377). On Buddhism: "We should not forget to speak here of Buddha or Xekia, so celebrated among the Indians . . . and whom these

peoples consider the greatest philosopher who ever lived. His history is so full of fables and contradictions that it would be impossible to conciliate them'' (p. 377). Diderot, translating Brucker here, then calls Buddha an imposter.

57. Sänger (p. 94) quotes d'Holbach. The opening sentence of the second paragraph of Diderot's article "Grecs" ("Greeks") clearly affirms the filiation: "The Hebrews knew what the Christians call *the true God.*" Naigeon, in his edition, adds: "as if there were false ones!''

58. This article is attributed to Diderot by Naigeon.

59. The article "Theocracy" is one of two d'Holbach articles erroneously attributed to Diderot by Sänger and used as evidence against Diderot. The other is "Prêtres" ("Priests") (Lough, p. 121). In the latter, says Sänger (p. 110), the Jewish priesthood is used as an example of the abuses of priestly power over the people. Sänger is patently mistaken. Reference is made in the article to pagan, Egyptian, druidic, and Mexican priestly abuses, to the incursions of Christian priests into the affairs of state in medieval Europe, and to the "countries where the frightful inquisition was established [which] furnishes frequent examples of human sacrifice unsurpassed in barbarism by those of the Mexican priesthood'' (XVI, pp. 406–09). There is no mention of Jewish priests anywhere in the article!

60. "Some Christians . . . seduced by the resemblance that there was between their religion and modern philosophy, fooled by the lies of the eclectics on the efficacity and wonders of their rites, but drawn especially to this kind of superstition by a *faint-hearted*, curious, restless . . . temperament . . .'' ("Eclecticism," XIV, pp. 310–11 [emphasis added]).

61. Naigeon attributes this article to Diderot. Proust and Lough accept the attribution.

62. *Émile* (Paris, 1939), p. 374.

63. Ibid., p. 380. This ungenerous appraisal of the Jews was written to appease the censor, for Rousseau, who appears really to have been sympathetic to the Jews and Judaism, also included favorable references to them in other sections of *Émile* and in the *Social Contract* (Bk. II, Ch. 7). Paradoxically, while friends of the Jews, like Mirabeau, were repeating his pro-Jewish pronouncements, the enemies of Jewish emancipation in the final days of the *ancien régime* made frequent use of his anti-Jewish "feints."

For a favorable assessment of Rousseau's views on the Jews and Judaism, see Ronald D. Margolin, *Judaism and the Old Testament in the Thought of Jean-Jacques Rousseau* (Ph. D. dissertation, University of Connecticut, 1975), and this work, p. 180, n. 7. On the quotation of Rousseau by the enemies of the Jews, see Feuerwerker, pp. 85, 94, and 114.

64. The story of Hypatia is taken directly from Brucker. The description of the Jews as "a people naturally inclined to revolt" is Brucker's (art. *"De Secta Eclectica,"* p. 353). Diderot himself did not believe that any people *as a whole* could be characterized in moral terms. Brucker's characterization of the Jews, which also appears in Basnage, was derived from Roman sources, especially Tacitus.

65. This is based on Van Helmont's linguistic theories, as may be seen in Shaftesbury's "Advice to an Author," in *Characteristics* (Gloucester, Mass., 1963), I, p. 186, n. 2. Diderot may be "simply paying lip-service to the orthodox belief," as Paul Meyer, the author of a critical edition of the *Letter* (*Diderot Studies* VII [Geneva, 1965]) has suggested in a recent letter to this writer. This does not, however, make the conscious departure from philosophic orthodoxy any the less noteworthy.

66. The term is Fabre's ("Diderot et les théosophes," p. 210).

67. Attributed to Diderot by Naigeon. Proust and Lough agree.

68. *Oeuvres philosophiques*, p. 235, n. 1.

69. The first published version of *Rameau's Nephew* was Goethe's translation in 1805. There was no authentic French edition until 1891. Whether Grimm had anything to do with Goethe's discovery of the manuscript is not known.

70. See Arthur Wilson, *Diderot* (New York, 1972), p. 443.

71. Letter to Princess Dashkoff (December 24, 1773), in *Didro v Peterburgi* (Saint Petersburg, 1884), p. 189.

72. For an account of Diderot's relations with d'Holbach, see C. Avezac-Lavigne, *Diderot et la société du baron d'Holbach* (Paris, 1875).

73. *Correspondance littéraire, philosophique et critique*, ed. M. Tourneux (Paris, 1878), III, p. 176.

74. These letters are dated February 15, 1756; May 1, 1765; and November 15, 1765.

75. D'Holbach's major work, the *Système de la nature*, published with Diderot's collaboration in 1770, methodically attacked the bases of all the world's religions without singling the Jews out for harsher treatment than the others. To the contrary, a major theme of this work is the *universality* of human behavior. "Every individual of the human species is a necessary mixture of good and bad qualities, every nation presents to us the mottled spectacle of vices and virtues" (*Système de la nature* [Hildesheim, 1966], II, p. 176). On d'Holbach's racial views, see Chapter 5, note 6.

76. Sänger dates the article on Jewish philosophy by noting Diderot's statement that 1614 years had elapsed since the supposed publication date of the Mishnah (140 A.D.). This would place the composition of the article in 1754 (A–T, XV, p. 359). It is reasonable to assume that the article "Judaism" originated at about the same time.

77. We are reminded of Montesquieu's *Persian Letters* (XXIX), where we read: "[the judges of the Inquisition] are terribly sorry to have condemned them. But, to console themselves, they confiscate all the wealth of these unfortunate people for their own profit." Interestingly, the recently published *History of the Jews in France* ("Collection Franco-Judaïca," ed. B. Blumenkranz [Paris, 1972]), calls this article "truly liberal" in its attitude toward the Jews (see following, n. 84). However Proust is not sure that Diderot is the author (p. 538).

78. The article "Jews" was divided into two parts, the first being subtitled "History of" and the second "Philosophy of." The author of the first, de Jaucourt, was a liberal Protestant and Diderot's most productive collaborator. His sensitive and sympathetic account of Jewish history in Europe is completely ignored by Hertzberg in his attack on the *Encyclopédie*. For a detailed study of this article and its influence on Diderot, see Chapter 4 of this work.

79. In *Paradoxe sur le Comédien, Oeuvres esthétiques* (Paris, 1959), p. 315.

80. The testimony of this *Salon*, which was sent to Grimm's correspondents abroad and not published in France in Diderot's lifetime, should suffice to prove the sincerity of Diderot's published praise of Moses. Even Grimm, in a private quarrel with Diderot about Numa's role in history, would attempt to win his argument by equating Numa's greatness with Moses', knowing of Diderot's admiration for the latter (*Correspondance littéraire* [December 15, 1769], VIII, p. 398). Chapters 3 and 5 will deal with the philosophical and esthetic bases for Diderot's evolving appreciation of Moses.

81. This does not exclude judging them as poets, since relevation is transmitted in Hebrew poetry.

82. The term *Juif* for Jew was standard in eighteenth-century France. Though its use

was often pejorative, it was not necessarily so. Isaac de Pinto, a Portuguese Jew and later a friend of Diderot's (see Chapter 4), would himself use the term in the title of his *Apologie pour la nation juive (Apologia for the Jewish Nation)*, published in 1762. Similarly, in 1769 there appeared a defense of the Old Testament entitled *Lettres de quelques juifs portugais et allemands à M. Voltaire (Letters of Some Portuguese and German Jews to M. Voltaire)*.

83. Diderot used Arnauld d'Andilly's translation of the *Antiquities* and *Jewish War*. It is revealing to compare Voltaire's contemptuous dismissal of Josephus (*Oeuvres complètes*, ed. L. Moland [Paris, 1877–1885], XI, p. 120) to Diderot's positive appreciation of the Jewish historian (A-T, I, 210).

84. Minor use is also made of Saint Epiphany, Eusebius, Boureau-Deslandes's *Histoire critique de la philosophie*, Calmet's *Dictionnaire de la Bible*, and Simon's *Histoire critique du Vieux Testament*. Brucker himself had used Basnage and the anti-Semitic Eisenmenger's *Entdecktes Judentum (Jewry Revealed)*, besides the Latin historians. Basnage had used, besides the Latin sources, Surenhusius, Buxtorf, and Cocceius (see Sänger, pp. 34, 119–20).

85. *Histoire des Juifs en France*, pp. 269–71 (see preceding, n. 77). None of the three articles regarded as offensive by the editors of this history of the Jews—"Messie" ("Messiah"), "Pères de l'Église" ("Church Fathers"), and "Œconomie politique" ("Political Economy")—is Diderot's.

86. Count Honoré Gabriel de Mirabeau, eminent orator of the French Revolution.

87. Paul Meyer attributes the deprecation of the Talmud by the pro-Jewish philosophe Marquis d'Argens to a need to discredit the less enlightened factions of Judaism in order to demonstrate the similarity between the ideals of *basic* Judaism and the Enlightenment (p. 1182). Diderot's praise of certain Jewish sects in this article seems to have the same objective.

88. Exceptions are John Hyrcanus, the scourge of the Samaritans (XV, p. 322); and Rabbi Akiba (erroneously written as Attibas and Atriba) and his supporter Bar-Kochba, both of whom are called imposters (pp. 358, 368). Diderot's inconsistency in the spelling of Rabbi Akiba's name betrays his hasty use of source materials and his superficial knowledge of some of the subject matter of this article.

89. This passage is from Brucker. Later, borrowing the Basnage text on the flight of the Jews into Egypt at the time of the destruction of Jerusalem, Diderot repeats Basnage's characterization of the refugees as seditious (p. 356). This is not necessarily contradictory, for the Jews, like any other people, could be loyal subjects in one set of circumstances and rebellious in another.

90. A major theme of pre-Zionist anti-Semitism was that the Jews were incorrigible Bedouins, incapable of attachment to any land.

91. "We shall be content to state here that the Egyptians, proud of their antiquity, their knowledge, and the beauty of their spirit, regarded with scorn the other nations and the Jews, as slaves who had long bent beneath their yoke before shaking it" (p. 330). Sänger merely tells us that Diderot wrote that the Egyptians scorned the Jews (p. 40).

92. Cleanliness was one of Diderot's cardinal virtues. In writing to Catherine the Great during his visit to Russia in 1774, he advised her that "I would oblige my priests to preach a great deal on the sanctity of bathing." See M. Tourneux, *Diderot et Catherine II* (Paris, 1899), p. 220.

93. This is in contrast to the cliché of the "naturally seditious Jew."

94. It was, of course, not surmised in Diderot's day that Christ may himself have been an Essene.

95. This is not the only place that Diderot defends the Jews to attack his real enemy. In the article "Jesuit" he writes, "In 1728, Berruyer [a Jesuit] parodies in the form of a romance the story of Moses, and gives the patriarchs the language of lovers and libertines" (XV, p. 280). Such irreverence!

96. For a revised view of the Pharisees, see S. Zeitlin, *Who Crucified Jesus?* (New York, 1964), pp. 86–87.

97. This image is borrowed from Diderot's *Indiscreet Jewels*, chap. XXXII, "Sultan Mangogul's Oniric Voyage." See also preceding, p. 54 and n. 79.

98. Diderot did use this literary formula several times in his two works on Helvétius, in imitation of Horace, *Satires*, i, 5. See preceding p. 27 and n. 8.

99. Sänger (p. 62) objects that Diderot has confused Haggada, or legend, with Halakah, or law, as examples of Jewish doctrine. And he protests that in giving examples of bad Talmudic precepts Diderot has mistranslated the Hebrew, that the precept that "one may push a Christian off a cliff or kill him with impunity" should read instead "push a *heretic* off a cliff or kill him with impunity." Small consolation! Sänger's objection does not answer Diderot's basic argument, that is, "that a religious book should not contain laws and precepts so obviously contrary to charity" (p. 365). Diderot acknowledges that these precepts are in the nature of "vengeance"'; he is aware of the Christian persecution of Jews. Nowhere does he imply that the Jews ever actually translated such precepts into action. Hertzberg's statement that Diderot "found *nothing* good" in the Talmud (p. 311, emphasis added), misstates the issue. One would have liked Diderot to have reported such an edifying Talmudic statement as the one holding that man is judged by God not on how or whether he has worshiped him but on how he has treated his fellow men. But the problem of the Talmud to the eighteenth-century reader was not that a religious book may contain good precepts but that it also contains bad ones.

100. This sentence has been modified by Naigeon to read: "Christ followed his ideas and spread his own *pipe dreams; there are foolish ideas, errors, and truths common to all these nations,*" etc. (see Proust, p. 542).

101. This sentence has been modified by Naigeon to read: "All that one may reasonably say in this matter is that the Talmudists made comparisons similar to Christ's but that the application that this *obscure, fanatical Jew* made of them, and the lessons that he drew from them, *generally have a graver character than those that these similarities and these parables furnished to the authors of the Talmud*" (see Proust, ibid.). Though Diderot could not have been sincere in calling Christ "the son of God," the use of the term "obscure and fanatical Jew" is out of character with Diderot's writings on Christ after 1747 and is a blatant falsification by Naigeon. The amendment of the passage on the beauties of Christ's teachings, however, does appear warranted by Diderot's expressions elsewhere.

102. Reinach (p. 141) denies that the principal pieces of the cabala text were the work of Akiba and Simeon ben Johai and blames Diderot for the perpetuation of this error as well as for two errors of fact in the life of Maimonides. Gendzier (p. 41) properly places Diderot's treatment of the cabala in the context of his time.

103. "If one wishes to make a choice among these doctors, those of the twelfth century are preferable to all the others: for not only were they bright, but they also furnished great help in understanding the Old Testament" (p. 372).

104. As usual, Naigeon makes matters worse. To the end of the account of Maimonides' "subtle" explication of a scriptural passage, he adds: "true or false, all that is of little importance" (p. 378).

105. Even Voltaire and Grimm would eventually concede this, the former in writing of the Jews of Holland (see his letter to Damilaville, August 6, 1764, quoted in *Studies on Voltaire and the Eighteenth Century*, XLVI, p. 162) and the latter in acknowledging in 1772 the great philosophical reputation of Moses Mendelssohn (X, p. 14).

106. The episode of the Jew of Utrecht in *Rameau's Nephew* (see following, pp. 132, 148-49). The subject of human diversity and its import for this study is discussed in Chapter 5.

107. An enemy of the philosophes, Élie Fréron was the publisher of the clericalist literary journal, *L'Année littéraire*.

108. *Le Drame en France au XVIIIe siècle* (Paris, 1910), pp. 78 ff.

109. Diderot, *Oeuvres esthétiques* (Paris, 1959), p. 71.

110. Chouillet calls Dorval, the hero of the play and an interlocutor of the *Conversations*, "an altogether Romantic hero" (p. 424).

111. The *Letter on the Deaf and Dumb* and the article "Beau" ("Beauty"), written in 1752 for the *Encyclopédie*, are especially worthy of note.

112. See J. Seznec, *Essais sur Diderot et l'Antiquité* (Oxford, 1957).

113. Grimm.

114. *Salons*, ed. by J. Seznec and J. Adhémar (Paris, 1957), I, p. 65.

115. Diderot comes close to reversing himself in his *Essays on Painting*, written three years later: "We shall use the expressions divine charms, divine beauty, but without some vestiges of paganism, that habit and the ancient poets sustain in our minds, they would be cold and meaningless" (*Oeuvres esthétiques*, p. 707). This quotation follows a long attack on the ugliness of Christianity. But Diderot seems to be arguing for artists with imagination, capable of investing Christian art with the kind of sensual beauty found in the pagan: "if our painters and sculptors were men to be compared with the painters and sculptors of antiquity" (p. 706). The entire passage appears paradoxical, for Diderot continued to worship Raphael and Michelangelo and to express his admiration for the Christian art of Deshays and Vien.

116. Jean Calas, a Protestant, was broken on the wheel in 1762 after having been accused of murdering his son to prevent his conversion to Catholicism. Because of the anti-Protestant hysteria surrounding the trial, it was suspected that Calas was the victim of a frame-up. Voltaire and the philosophes made a cause célèbre of the affair. Judicial error was discovered and Calas's name was cleared.

117. "Crime is a beautiful thing in history and poetry, on a canvas and in marble" (ibid.). This artistic axiom was confirmed in the *Essays on Painting*, in spite of the paradox on Christian art contained there. Diderot advises the artist or writer to "make virtue desirable, vice odious, ridicule conspicuous . . . . It is for you . . . to celebrate, to eternize great and beautiful actions, to honor unhappy, slandered virtue, to stigmatize successful, glorified vice, to frighten tyrants . . . . Lay before my eyes the bloody deeds of fanaticism.

favor, took possession of his heart, installed itself therein as a beloved despot. The evolution and achievement of Diderot's humanism are explained by the replacement of the point of view of the scientist by the point of view of the artist'' (p. 108). Chouillet modifies Thomas's formulation by contrasting Diderot's diminishing allegiance to the *mathematical* sciences (squares and circles in the sand) to his conversion to the *life sciences and the fine arts*: "In opposition to [the] 'geometrization of the universe,' the human sciences, and, in a more general way, the life sciences, blaze the trail to the future . . . . It is, significantly, with a defense of the fine arts that, in a paradoxical way, *The Interpretation of Nature* [1753] begins'' (p. 329).

15. One example should suffice. In the article "Grecs" ("Greeks") he called Orpheus's stories "a chain of puerilities," and added: "I'll say nothing about his descent into hell; I leave that fairy tale to the poets" (A-T, XV, pp. 52, 53).

16. Faiguet's Hebrew idyll is spoilt by the account of the corruption of later Hebrew society (David to Nehemiah) (p. 549).

17. Franco Venturi discerns a break with Voltaire—"typical gap between the generations" (p. 93)—as early as the *Philosophical Thoughts*. But, as has been demonstrated, the theory of passions tentatively proposed in the first *pensée* was modified in the fourth. The real break came later.

18. See *Salons*, II, pp. 184–85.

19. The words "poet" and "falsehood" (*mensonge*) require interpretation. Diderot's use of the expression "*mensonges des poètes*" is intended to mean the artist's creation of illusion, false reality. This is explained in the *Salon of 1767*: "In poetry there is always falsehood. The philosophic spirit accustoms us to discern it, and the illusion and effect are lost" (*Salons*, III, p. 157). In certain contexts Diderot's use of the term *mensonge* may be rendered in English as "fiction."

20. How closely this scene resembles that of the philosophers of the classical Academy and how different is the treatment. Diderot appears to have done a complete about-face in his appreciation of the conflicting cultures depicted in the *Promenade* of 1747.

21. "Poets, prophets, and far-sighted people are prone to see flies as elephants; near-sighted philosophers reduce elephants to the size of flies. Poetry and philosophy are the opposite ends of the telescope" (*Salons*, III, p. 232).

22. "I spent a most agitated night. How odd is the dream state. . . . Was I awake when I thought I was dreaming, dreaming when I thought I was waking? Who can say that the veil won't be torn some day, and I won't be convinced that I've dreamed all I've done and really done all I've dreamed?" (pp. 162–63).

23. "Virgil spoiled everything when he translated this part by . . . verses in which hardly a vestige of Homer's poetry and imagery is left. . . . I prefer the commonplace Latin of the Hellenized Jew, who said of the angel sent to exterminate the first-born of Egypt: *Stans replevit omnia morte et usque ad caelum attingebat, stans in terra* [*Sapientia Solomonis*, XVIII, p. 16].

Oh! My friend, what a beautiful text; if I had only happened on it sooner or had the time to go into ecstasies over it. But I'm writing hurriedly; I'm writing in the middle of a swarm of pests who are bothering me, who are keeping me from seeing and feeling . . ." (p. 305).

24. In a comment on a painting by Hubert Robert, Diderot exclaims: "I would rather see

the infernal joy of a band of Gypsies; the lair of . . . robbers; the spectacle of a peasant family's misery; . . . an adventure of Cleveland's [from the novel of Prévost] or of the Old Testament . . .'' (p. 244).

25. Diderot had himself translated parts of Ossian in 1761. For Ossian's effect on him, see *Salons*, III, p. 192.

26. The *Scattered Thoughts on Painting* (1776–1777) are the last work included in the Vernière edition of the *Oeuvres esthétiques*. The *Salon of 1781*, the only one written after this work, is relatively short and perfunctory.

27. Chouillet demonstrates the influence of the Bible in Diderot's "translation" of Shaftesbury (p. 46) and in the genesis of the title character in Diderot's second *drame* (p. 463).

28. *Correspondance*, VII, p. 87. The reference is to King David (see also IX, p. 247).

29. *Voyage à Bourbonne*, A-T, XVII, p. 342. The allusion is repeated in *Rameau's Nephew* (*Oeuvres romanesques*, p. 429).

30. On the moral utility of the arts, see also p. 260: "Images preach."

Chapter 4

1. Quoted by P. Vernière in Diderot's *Oeuvres philosophiques*, p. 600, n. 1.

2. *Diderot*, p. 236.

3. See *Réflexions sur la question juive*, p. 10.

4. Diderot's exposure to the anti-Semitic influences of his French Catholic and his classical education has been discussed in Chapter 2.

5. This was not the case in Germany, where religious prejudice was directed mainly at Jews, prompting a German liberal like Gotthold Lessing to use the issue of injustice toward the Jews as the subject of his first play, *Die Juden*, as early as 1749 (see H. I. Dunkle, "Lessing's *Die Juden*: An Original Experiment," *Monatshefte* [University of Wisconsin, November 1957], pp. 323–29. P. Meyer compares France with England and writes: "Unlike England, France as a whole had no Jewish problem to cope with until the last quarter of the eighteenth century" (p. 1166).

6. See J. Proust, p. 297.

7. Rousseau is also more unequivocally sympathetic in his later writings, as may be seen in the Altuna portrait in Book VII of the *Confessions*.

8. It is ironic that as the Protestants were forced to flee France or go underground to practise their religion, the Marranos of Bordeaux could, after 1686, drop the Christian mask and gradually return to the open practice of Judaism (*Guide Juif de France*, p. 41). Hertzberg calls the year 1686 a turning point in Jewish religious life in France (p. 25). On the issue of the relative status of Jews and Protestants in eighteenth-century France, Feuerwerker (p. 146) quotes Lamoignon de Malesherbes: "It is useful to note that in regard to [their civil status] they [the Jews] are better off in France than are the Protestants."

9. Most notably Bayle, Rousseau, and de Jaucourt.

10. See J. Proust, p. 297.

11. See the quotation from Saint Paul (A-T, XV, p. 237).

12. Diderot was not the only author of *Encyclopédie* articles dealing with religious persecution. His most faithful collaborator, Louis (*chevalier*) de Jaucourt, contributed the article "Inquisition," which contains a strong attack on the persecution of the Spanish Jews (vol. IX).

13. This is a reference to the persecution of the Huguenots after the Revocation of the Edict of Nantes.

14. Voltaire used the same reference to the persecution of the Jews in England and France in Section III of his article "Des Juifs" ("On the Jews"), but instead of deploring it he appears to justify it. There is no appeal to Christian charity in his article (*Oeuvres complètes*, XIX, pp. 523–26).

15. These are the dishonest Jew in *Zadig* ("Slavery"), the lecherous Don Issachar in *Candide*, and the Palestinian usurers in *The Princess of Babylon*.

16. See Jacob S. Wijler, *Isaac de Pinto, sa vie et ses oeuvres* (Apeldoorn, 1923 [?]), pp. 17–27, and Richard H. Popkin, "Hume and Isaac de Pinto," *Texas Studies in Literature and Language*, XII (Fall 1970): 419–20.

17. "I have rediscovered here a certain de Pinto, a Jew. He was a great libertine in Paris, and he's not too well-behaved in The Hague" (*Correspondance*, [July 22, 1773], XIII, pp. 34–35.

18. The *Système de la nature*, for which Diderot had written entire sections, appeared in 1770 and de Pinto's book was ostensibly a reply.

19. See the editor's note in Diderot's *Correspondance*, XIII, p. 35, n. 3. Reference is made to A. J. Freer's study on de Pinto in *Annale della Scuola normale superiore di Pisa*, 2nd Series (1964), XXXIII, pp. 93–117.

20. On Diderot's dislike for travel and his emotional departure from the city that he refused to leave even under threat of persecution at the height of the attack on the philosophes, see Wilson, pp. 618–19.

21. See Diderot's *Correspondance*, XIV, p. 53.

22. "One ignominious act more or less attributed to a son of Israel, what does it matter after all?" writes Reinach sarcastically. "One lends only to the rich, and the story of the Jew of Utrecht is one more proof of it to add to that of *The Merchant of Venice*" (pp. 143–44).

Reinach's "refutation" of Diderot rested on de Pinto's reputation as a philanthropist and economist and on his relations with the philosophes. Wijler (p. 17) refers to Reinach's argument as well as to a similar argument by Leon Kahn in his book on *Les Juifs de Paris au XVIIIe siècle* ([Paris, 1895], p. 3), and he seems to be persuaded that Diderot's characterization of the private de Pinto is inconsistent with his public image and therefore false. In response to Wijler, one may argue that the combination of a public image of rectitude and private immorality is not uncommon, and that writers in their private lives rarely live up to the principles espoused in their books. One may also point to evidence in Wijler's own account of de Pinto's life that he was not averse to pleasure, and that his *Essay on Luxury*, while pleading against *excessive* self-indulgence, nevertheless defended luxury as economically beneficial (see particularly the account of de Pinto's defense of the wealthy Portuguese Jews of Bordeaux, whose "luxury, prodigality, and contempt for work and business . . . whose proud gravity and noble pride . . . have nothing in common with Voltaire's criticisms of them" [p. 48]). Hertzberg also takes note of a certain ambiguity in de Pinto's character, which led him to defend the Jews of Bordeaux at the expense of the

German and Avignonnais Jews: "... unfortunately," de Pinto is quoted, "one is often reduced to empiricism in politics as in medicine" (pp. 180–81). And Hertzberg also refers to de Pinto's justification of the "womanizing" Jews of Bordeaux as one of the "vices of 'great spirits.'" Nor does Hertzberg accept the Kahnian version of de Pinto's great standing in the world of letters: "He seems to have been regarded in the literary world as a bit of a crank" (p. 143). Popkin maintains that Hume called de Pinto "a good man" (see "The Philosophical Basis of Eighteenth-Century Racism," in *Studies in Eighteenth-Century Culture* [Case Western Reserve University Press, 1973], III, p. 250), but the passage quoted by Popkin contains no such wording. Furthermore, in his article on "Hume and Isaac de Pinto" Popkin quotes Hume's joking letter to R. A. Neville, secretary of the Duke of Bedford, urging that de Pinto's claim to an English pension be honored so that the latter would stop nagging him about it (p. 418).

In all this, one finds little on which to base a charge that Diderot, who in 1773 had no reason to libel de Pinto, was portraying the private man with malicious inaccuracy. On the Diderot-de Pinto liaison, see H. L. Brugmans, "Autour de Diderot en Hollande" (preceding, Chapter 2, n. 145).

23. Reinach calls this tale "a legend, perhaps originating in Spain, and current among the Jews of Avignon [!] or of Holland, where Diderot could have gotten it" (p. 142).

24. Diderot, mistrusting Frederick the Great, avoided Berlin. "I think I would have made a pretty blunder by going looking for trouble in Berlin. That king is certainly a great man . . . [but] . . . a mean soul . . ." (letter to Madame d'Épinay, *Correspondance*, [April 9, 1774], XIII, p. 238).

25. See Wilson, p. 632.

26. *Diderot et Catherine II*, p. 534.

27. *Mémoires pour Catherine II*, ed. P. Vernière (Paris, 1966): "De l'usure," pp. 92–94; "Sur la tolérance," "Première Addition sur la tolérance," "Deuxième Addition sur la tolérance," "De l'intolérance," pp. 97–113, 185–86.

28. On April 22, 1782, Catherine issued a ukase granting Jews the right to live and trade in previously restricted cities (see Feuerwerker, p. 164).

29. Hertzberg could not be farther from the truth in stating that Diderot believed that the task of reforming the Jew "was much harder [than reforming the Christian] if not impossible because of his Oriental character and because his religion and his character were one" (p. 312).

30. (Paris, 1894), p. 115.

31. The reference is to the two Jewish episodes in *Rameau's Nephew*. Sänger's comment appears all the less justified in light of Diderot's letters from abroad. To Madame Necker he wrote of the physical strain of the voyage, the dangers of generalizing on the character of nations based on limited observations, and of his *dislike* of Russia's climate, mores, laws, customs, and usages: "I would be an ingrate if I spoke ill of them; I would be a liar if I spoke well of them" (*Correspondance*, XIV, pp. 73–75).

32. *Correspondance*, XIV, 95. See also Brugmans's article (preceding, n. 22).

33. Hertzberg is quoting de Pinto's *Apologie des Juifs*.

34. *Histoire philosophique et politique des établissements et du commerce des Européens dans les deux Indes (Philosophical and Political History of European Settlements and Trade in the Two Indies).* Raynal's book praises the economic utility of the emancipated Jews of Surinam (see Feuerwerker, p. 167).

Chapter 5

1. *Réfutation d'Helvétius*, A-T, II, p. 382.
2. W. B. Jordan, address to the American Society for Eighteenth-Century Studies Symposium on "Racism in the Eighteenth Century," University of California at Los Angeles, March 24, 1972.
3. Count Richard Coudenhove-Kalergi, "Jew-Hatred Today," in Count H. Coudenhove-Kalergi's *Anti-Semitism throughout the Ages*, p. 248.
4. Bishop Thomas Newton, *Dissertation on the Prophecies* (1765), quoted by M. Hay, p. 23. One should also take note here of Isaac de La Peyrère's pre-Adamite theory of Jewish racial differences, but this theory was not widely held and was not taught by the Church. La Peyrère's book *Preadamitae* was condemned by the Paris *Parlement* soon after its publication in 1655. For its influence on Voltaire, see following, n. 10.
5. Meyer, Hertzberg, Gay, and Schwarzbach all allude to this.
6. For an analysis of Buffon's racial views, see R. H. Popkin, "The Philosophical Basis of Eighteenth-Century Racism," pp. 250–51.
7. "And what demonstrates that they do not owe this difference to their climate is that Negroes and Negresses, transported into the coldest of countries, always produce animals of their species . . ." (*Oeuvres complètes*, XI, p. 6). Voltaire's use of the term species for race anticipates Linnaeus's human categories (see Popkin, idem, p. 248). Rousseau and d'Holbach both preferred environmental arguments to explain behavior (see Meyer, p. 1198).
8. "The more superstitious a nation is, persisting in warfare in spite of its defeats, divided into factions, shifting between royalty and priesthood, drunk with fanaticism, the more likely one is to find amongst such a people a number of citizens who unite to live in peace" (article "Esséniens," *Dictionnaire philosophique*, XIX, p. 25).
9. "One of the most honorable men in Holland" (quoted by J. Vercruysse, "Voltaire et la Hollande," in *Studies on Voltaire and the Eighteenth Century*, XLVI, p. 104).
10. Voltaire was tempted by La Peyrère's pre-Adamite theory, but unlike La Peyrère he "saw the Adamites [Jews] as a major menace to European civilization" (Popkin, in longer version of the article cited above, "The Philosophical Bases of Modern Racism," published in *Philosophy and the Civilizing Arts*, ed. C. Walton and J. P. Anton [Ohio University Press, 1974], p. 149).
11. This thesis is promulgated in two books, *De l'esprit* and *De l'homme*.
12. This preevolutionary principle was suggested to Diderot by Maupertuis's dissertation *De universali naturae systemate* (1751). See J. Proust, p. 291, n. 214; and P. Vernière in Diderot's *Oeuvres philosophiques*, p. 171.
13. The first of these arguments is illustrated below. The second, implicit in the nephew's anecdotes, is made explicit in the following exchange:

"And you stole without remorse?"

"Oh! without remorse! It is said that *if one crook steals from another, the devil couldn't care less*. The parents were loaded with a fortune acquired God only knows how. They were courtiers, financiers, bankers, business people. I helped them make restitution, I and a host of others that they employed like me. In nature all species devour each other; all classes devour each other in society. We exact justice from each other without the law's mixing in" (*Oeuvres romanesques*, pp. 426–27).

14. A character in Molière's comedy *L'Étourdi*.

15. As is clear from the context, Diderot used the French word *race* in its primary signification, that is, the family blood line. To interpret the word otherwise would be to deny the nephew's uniqueness and distort Diderot's purpose in creating this character. For an explanation of a similar use of the word *race*, see the glossary on the F. Deloffre–R. Picard edition of Prévost's *Manon Lescaut* (Paris, 1965), p. 330.

16. The famous musician Jean-Philippe Rameau.

17. *Oeuvres philosophiques*, p. 364. Diderot later modified this starkly deterministic thesis.

18. *Lettres à Sophie Volland* (November 6, 1760), I, p. 180.

19. "If I am in error," he adds, "at least I am glad to find it in the depths of my heart, and I would be very unhappy were experience or reflection ever to disabuse me" (ibid, pp. 180–81).

20. See also the *Voyage to Holland*: "One of the most common errors is to take, in any realm, particular cases for general rules, and to write . . . 'In Orleans, all innkeepers are surly and red-headed'" (XVII, p. 366).

21. The classic example of this is the story of Madame de la Pommeraye in *Jacques the Fatalist*.

Lester Crocker, in "Le Neveu de Rameau, une expérience morale" (*Cahiers de l'Association Internationale des Études Françaises*, no. 13, June 1961, p. 148), offers another interpretation by distinguishing between Diderot's "sublime" rogues, who invariably succeed (the renegade would fall into this category), and the common herd of rogues, like the nephew (and presumably also the Jew of Utrecht). But this interpretation does not adequately account for the two "sublime losers" of the novel *Jacques the Fatalist*, Madame de la Pommeraye and Father Hudson (see the *Oeuvres romanesques*, p. 684).

22. Although Diderot admired Dutch republicanism and political and intellectual freedom, it is evident in his *Voyage to Holland* that he did not admire the mercenary spirit of the Dutch: " . . . it appears that the love of gold must have singularly altered the ideas of honesty, of gratitude, of dignity, of rectitude in one and the other," writes he concerning the commercial relations between Dutch fathers and sons (XVII, p. 418). This after he has warned the reader that it is dangerous to generalize: " . . . have I taken an isolated case for the general morality? or have I judged the general morality by a few isolated cases? I don't know." Nowhere is there any suggestion that this "Dutch trait" is racial.

23. "You were born voluptuous," Diderot would later write in an imaginary conversation with Helvétius (A-T, II, p. 311).

24. A contemporary characterization of Spinoza.

25. The authorship of this article is uncertain, though it is included in the Assézat-Tourneux edition of Diderot's works.

26. See Gendzier (p. 48) for another interpretation of the Jew of Utrecht episode. Though somewhat different from this writer's interpretation, Gendzier's also relates the episode to the total novel and its purpose.

27. See the censored portion of the article "Zenda Vesta" in D. Gordon and N. Torrey, *The Censoring of Diderot's "Encyclopédie"* (New York, 1947), p. 107.

28. *Lettres à Sophie Volland* (October 6, 1765), II, p. 75. See also Diderot's characterization of the people of his native Langres: "The people of this country have a lot of wit, too much vivacity, and the fickleness of weathervanes. It comes, I believe, from the vicis-

situdes of their atmosphere, which in twenty-four hours goes from hot to cold, from calm to stormy, from balmy to rainy'' (ibid., I, p. 45).

29. *Observations sur le Nakaz*, in *Oeuvres politiques*, ed. P. Vernière (Paris, 1963), p. 349. In his *Reflections on Helvétius's Work "On the Mind"* (1758), he had expressed a similar sentiment: '' . . . in any place on earth, he who gives drink to the thirsty and food to the hungry is a good person'' (A-T, II, p. 270).

30. See also p. 296 on Locke and the moral efficacy of education.

31. Although Diderot has expressed the belief that a favorable climate can enhance the quality of the human as it does of the vegetable product, he does not say that it necessarily produces more geniuses. ''It is nature, organization, purely physical causes that prepare the genius; it is moral causes that make them bear fruit'' (p. 369). Thus he avoids the trap of absolute geographical determinism, and, in the passage quoted here, is able to attribute the apparent numerical superiority of geniuses in Athens or Rome to the superiority of their political institutions.

32. Even Voltaire is generally less harsh now in writing of the Jews. But, though he attacks the inhumanity of the Inquisition toward the Jews in his last philosophical tale, *The Story of Jenni* (Chapter II), he resurrects a story of Jewish cannibalism in the revolts against the emperors Trajan and Hadrian (Chapter VII), and contrasts this behavior with ''Greek Atticism and Roman urbanity.''

33. J. H. Meister, the continuer of Grimm's *Correspondance littéraire* with whom Diderot would continue to collaborate after 1773, would one day write: ''We shall be content to note that a large number of the arguments on which he [Cerutti] bases his enthusiasm for this people, are destroyed by the most recent accounts that we have seen of this country'' (*Correspondance littéraire* [March 1783], III, p. 284).

34. In this passage Diderot harshly berates the English for their exploitation of the Scottish and the Irish, for their war against the American colonists, and for their mistreatment of the blacks.

35. ''Damned Arab that you are who measure friendship by the importance of services rendered, go have your foreskin cut and Judaize and you can swear all you like after that'' (letter to Dr. Clerc [June 15, 1774], *Correspondance*, XIV, p. 43).

36. Most notable among these, besides the Jew of Avignon and of course Moses, are Esther (''How beautiful is Esther's grief!'' [preceding, p. 71]), Milot's ''David'' (preceding, p. 72), and Joseph, the ''worthy carpenter'' in Durameau's ''Holy Family'' (*Salon of 1767*, pp. 293–94).

37. See Grimm's *Correspondance littéraire* (July 1, 1772), X, p. 14.

38. Hertzberg sees in Spinoza, as ''the first modern adumbration of the Jew who had risen above 'the narrow prejudices of his tribe' and had therefore become 'worthy' of the world of advanced culture,'' an ''argument for the equality of all men'' (p. 38). Is there any doubt that this idea occurred to prerevolutionary France's most eloquent Spinozist?

Chapter 6

1. For an analysis of *Est-il bon? est-il méchant?* see Wilson, pp. 686–88.

2. The actual quotation is ''Judge Seneca not according to the mores of your country, but according to the mores of his country'' (*Essay on Claudius and Nero*, A-T, III, p. 75).

3. Except by Hannah Arendt (see preceding, pp. 20, 127).

4. See Alain Pons "Preface" to the *Encyclopédie*, "J'ai lu" series (Paris, 1963), p. 95. For a complete modern treatment of Diderot's materialism, see U. Winter, *Der Materialismus bei Diderot* (Geneva, Paris, 1971).

5. See R. DeHaan's review of D. D. Runes's *Karl Marx: A World without Jews*, in *Studies on the Left* I, no. 1 (Fall 1959): 77.

6. E. Silberner, *Sozialisten zur Judenfrage* (Berlin, 1962), p. 57.

7. See I. K. Luppol, *Diderot: ses idées philosophiques*, transl. from the Russian by Y. and V. Feldman (Paris, 1936), p. 25: "... he was Karl Marx's favorite author." In her introduction to M. Debré's *The Image of the Jew in French Literature from 1800 to 1908* ([New York, 1970], p. 9, n. 13), Anna Krakowski writes that Marx had drawn his anti-Jewish inspiration from Voltaire and Diderot in associating Jews with banking and commercial capitalism. This is totally at odds with Diderot's expressions of approval for the role of Jewish financiers.

8. In his article "Pour les Juifs" ("For the Jews"), *Le Figaro* (May 16, 1896), p. 1, Zola wrote as follows: "Exploiting popular revolts by making them serve religious passion, sacrificing the Jew to satisfy the claims of the oppressed in the guise of sacrificing the man of money, this is what I call a hypocritical and dishonest socialism, that should be denounced, that must be condemned." On Jaurès's denunciation of anti-Semitic demagoguery, see Chapter 1, n. 29.

Selected Bibliography

1. Editions of Diderot

Correspondance. G. Roth and J. Varloot, eds. 16 vols. Paris: Éditions de Minuit, 1955–1970.

Correspondance inédite. A. Babelon, ed. 2 vols. Paris: Nouvelle Revue Française, 1931.

Didro v Peterburgi. V. A. Bil'basov, ed. Saint Petersburg: I. N. Skorkhodov, 1884.

Encyclopédie, ou Dictionnaire raisonné des sciences, des arts et des métiers. Diderot, d'Alembert *et al.* 28 vols. Paris: F. Briasson, etc., 1751–1772.

Lettre sur les sourds et muets. Annotated ed. by Paul H. Meyer, in *Diderot Studies* VII (Geneva: E. Droz, 1965).

Lettres à Sophie Volland. A. Babelon, ed. 2 vols. Paris: Gallimard, 1938.

Mémoires pour Catherine II. Paul Vernière, ed. Paris: Garnier, 1966.

Oeuvres complètes. J. Assézat and M. Tourneux, eds. 20 vols. Paris: Garnier, 1875–1877.

Oeuvres complètes. Société Encyclopédique Française et Phil. Daudy, eds. 16 vols. Paris: Club Français du Livre, 1969–1973.

Oeuvres esthétiques. P. Vernière, ed. Paris: Garnier, 1959.

Oeuvres philosophiques. P. Vernière, ed. Paris: Garnier, 1961.

Oeuvres politiques. P. Vernière, ed. Paris: Garnier, 1963.

Oeuvres romanesques. Henri Bénac, ed. Paris: Garnier, 1962.

Salons. Jean Seznec and Jean Adhémar, eds. 3 vols. Oxford: Clarendon Press, 1957–1963.

Salons de 1759, 1761, 1763. J. Seznec, ed., "Images et Idées." Paris: Flammarion, 1967.

187

2. Other Works Consulted

Arendt, Hannah. *The Origins of Totalitarianism.* New York: Harcourt, Brace, and World, 1966.

Avezac-Lavigne, C. *Diderot et la société du baron d'Holbach.* Paris: Leroux, 1875.

Barbey d'Aurévilly, Jules-Amédée. *Goethe et Diderot.* Paris: Dentu, 1880.

Barker, Joseph E. *Diderot's Treatment of the Christian Religion.* New York: King's Crown Press, 1941.

Basnage, Jacques. *Histoire des Juifs, [etc.].* 15 vols. The Hague: H. Scheurleer, 1716.

Bayle, Pierre. *Dictionnaire historique et critique.* 4 vols. Rotterdam: R. Leers, 1697.

Becker, Carl. "The Dilemma of Diderot." *Philosophical Review* XXIV (1915): 54–71.

Belaval, Yvon. *L'Esthétique sans paradoxe de Diderot.* Paris: Gallimard, 1950.

Blumenkranz, B., ed. *Histoire des Juifs en France.* Paris: Privat, 1972.

Bossuet, Jacques-Bénigne. *Oeuvres oratoires.* Crit. ed. by Abbé Lebarq, rev. and augm. by C. Urbain and E. Levesque. 7 vols. Paris: Desclée, de Brouwer; 1922–1927.

Bougainville, Louis-Antoine de. *Voyage autour du monde.* Paris: Saillant et Nyon, 1771.

Brucker, Jacob. *Historia critica philosophiae, [etc.].* 5 vols. Leipzig: B. C. Breitkopf, 1742–1744.

———. *The History of Philosophy.* Transl. by W. Enfield. 2 vols. London: Johnson, 1791.

Brugmans, H. L. "Autour de Diderot en Hollande." *Diderot Studies* III (Geneva: E. Droz, 1951): 55–71.

Buffon, Georges-Louis Leclerc de. *Oeuvres complètes.* Ed. by M. Flourens. 12 vols. Paris: Garnier, 1853.

Butor, Michel. "Des *Bijoux indiscrets* à l'*Encyclopédie*" in Diderot's *Oeuvres complètes.* Ed. by the Société Encyclopédique Française et Ph. Daudy (see preceding editions of Diderot), I, xv–xxxiii.

Chambers, Ephraim. *Cyclopedia, [etc.]* 2 vols. London: J. and J. Knapton, etc. 1728–1746.

Chouillet, Jacques. *La Formation des idées esthétiques de Diderot*. Paris: Colin, 1973.

Coudenhove-Kalergi, H. *Anti-Semitism throughout the Ages*. Trans. by A. S. Rappoport. London: Hutchinson and Co., 1935.

Crocker, Lester. *"Le Neveu de Rameau*, une expérience morale." *Cahiers de l'Association Internationale des Études Françaises* (Paris, 1961): 133–55.

―――. *Two Diderot Studies: Ethics and Esthetics*. Baltimore: Johns Hopkins Press, 1952.

Cru, R. L. *Diderot as a Disciple of English Thought*. New York: Columbia University Press, 1913.

De Haan, R., review of D. D. Runes. *Karl Marx: A World without Jews* in *Studies on the Left*, I, no. 1 (Fall, 1959): 75–79.

Dieckmann, Herbert. *Cinq Leçons sur Diderot*. Pref. by J. Pommier. Geneva: E. Droz, 1959.

―――. "Diderot's Conception of Genius." *Journal of the History of Ideas* II (1941): 152–82.

―――. *Inventaire du fonds Vandeul et inédits de Diderot*. Geneva: E. Droz, 1951.

―――. "L'*Encyclopédie* et le fonds Vandeul." *Revue d'Histoire littéraire* (July–September 1951): 318–32.

Ducros, Louis. *Les Encyclopédistes*. Paris: Champion, 1900.

Dunkle, H. I. "Lessing's *Die Juden*: An Original Experiment." *Monatshefte* (University of Wisconsin, November 1957): 323–29.

Durant, Will and Ariel. *The Story of Civilization*. Vols. 9, 10. New York: Simon and Schuster, 1965, 1967.

Fabre, Jean. "Diderot et les Théosophes." *Cahiers de l'AIEF* (Paris, 1961): 203–222.

Fellows, Otis, and Torrey, Norman. *Age of Enlightenment*, 2nd ed. New York: Appleton-Century-Crofts, 1971.

Feuerwerker, David. *L'Émancipation des Juifs en France, [etc.]*. Paris: Albin Michel, 1976.

Gaiffe, Felix. *Le Drame en France au XVIIIᵉ siècle*. Paris: Colin, 1910.

Gay, Peter. *The Enlightenment*. 2 vols. New York: Knopf, 1960–1969.

Gendzier, Stephen J. "Diderot and the Jews." *Diderot Studies* XVI (Geneva: E. Droz, 1973): 35–54.

Gordon, Douglas H. and Torrey, Norman. *The Censoring of Diderot's Encyclopédie and the Re-established Text.* New York: Columbia University Press, 1947.

Graetz, Heinrich. *History of the Jews.* 6 vols. Philadelphia: The Jewish Publication Society of America, 1891–1898.

Grimm, Frederick Melchior. *Correspondance littéraire, philosophique et critique.* Ed. by M. Tourneux. 16 vols. Paris: Garnier, 1877–1878.

Guide Juif de France. Ed. by R. Berg, C. Chemouny, and F. Didi. Paris: Éditions Migdal, 1971.

Hay, Malcolm. *Europe and the Jews.* Boston: Beacon Hill Press, 1961.

Hermand, Pierre. "Sur le texte de Diderot et sur les sources de quelques passages de ses ouvrages." *Revue d'Histoire littéraire* (1915): 361–70.

Hertzberg, Arthur. *The French Enlightenment and the Jews.* New York: Columbia University Press, 1968.

Hill, Emita. "The Moral *Monstre.*" *Diderot Studies* XVI (Geneva: Droz, 1973): 91–117.

Holbach, Paul-Henri T. d'. *Système de la nature.* 2 vols. Hildesheim: Georg Olms, 1966.

Hubert, Réné. *Les Sciences sociales dans l'Encyclopédie.* Paris: F. Alcan, 1923.

Jaurès, Jean. *Histoire socialiste de la Révolution française.* 7 vols. Paris: Éditions Sociales, 1968–1973.

Krakowski, Anna. Introduction to *The Image of the Jew in French Literature from 1800 to 1908,* by M. Debré. New York: Ktav, 1970.

Legras, Joseph. *Diderot et l'Encyclopédie.* Amiens: Société Française d'Éditions Littéraires et Techniques, 1928.

Lehrmann, C. C. *The Jewish Element in French Literature.* Rutherford, Madison, Teaneck: Fairleigh Dickinson University Press, 1971.

Lichtenberger, A. *Le Socialisme au XVIIIe siècle.* Paris: Alcan, 1895.

Lough, John. *Essays on the "Encyclopédie" of Diderot and d'Alembert.* London: Oxford University Press, 1968.

Luppol, I. K. *Diderot: ses idées philosophiques.* Transl. from Russian by Y. and V. Feldman. Paris: Éditions Sociales Internationales, 1936.

Margolin, Ronald D. *Judaism and the Old Testament in the Thought of Jean-Jacques Rousseau.* Ph.D. dissertation, University of Connecticut, 1975.

Maritain, Jacques. *Anti-Semitism.* London: G. Bles (The Centenary Press), 1939.

May, Georges. "Diderot, artiste et philosophe du décousu." *Europäische Aufklärung: H. Dieckmann, zum 60. Geburtstag* (Munich: W. Fink, 1967): 165–88.

————. *Le Dilemme du roman au 18e siècle.* New Haven: Yale University Press, 1963.

Mayer, Jean. *Diderot, homme de science.* Rennes: Imprimerie Bretonne, 1959.

Meyer, Paul H. "The Attitude of the Enlightenment Towards the Jews." *Studies on Voltaire and the Eighteenth Century* XXVI (Geneva: l'Institut et Musée Voltaire, 1963): 1161–1205.

Montesquieu, Charles de Secondat de. *Lettres persanes.* Paris: Garnier-Flammarion, 1964.

Mornet, Daniel. *Diderot, l'homme et l'oeuvre.* Paris: Boivin, 1941.

Naville, Pierre. *Paul Thiry d'Holbach et la philosophie scientifique au XVIIIe siècle.* Paris: Gallimard, 1943.

Péguy, Charles. *Notre Jeunesse.* Paris: Gallimard, 1933.

Pons, Alain. Preface to *Encyclopédie.* Paris: ("J'ai lu") L'Essentiel, 1963.

Popkin, Richard H. "Hume and Isaac de Pinto." *Texas Studies in Literature and Language* XII (Fall 1970): 417–30.

————. "The Philosophical Basis of Eighteenth-Century Racism." *Studies in Eighteenth-Century Culture* III (1973): 245–62; and expanded version, "The Philosophical Bases of Modern Racism," in *Philosophy and the Civilizing Arts.* Ed. by C. Walton and J. P. Anton. Athens, Ohio: Ohio University Press, 1974.

Proust, Jacques. *Diderot et l'Encyclopédie.* Paris: A. Colin, 1962.

Reesinck, H. J. "L'Angleterre et la littérature anglaise dans les trois plus anciens périodiques français de Hollande de 1684 à 1709" in *Bibliothèque de la Revue de Littérature comparée.* Ed. by F. Baldensperger and P. Hazard. Paris: E. Champion, 1931. LXVII: 167–96.

Reinach, Theodore. "Les Juifs dans l'opinion chrétienne aux XVIIᵉ et XVIIIᵉ siècles: Peuchet et Diderot." *Revue des Études juives* VIII: 138–44.

Renan, Ernest. *Histoire du peuple d'Israël.* 5 vols. Paris: Calmann Lévy, 1887–1893.

Rousseau, Jean-Jacques. *Émile.* Paris: Garnier, 1939.

———. *Les Confessions.* Ed. by L. Martin-Chauffier. Paris: Pléiade, 1951.

Sachar, Abram. *History of the Jews.* New York: Knopf, 1965.

Salesses, Raymond, "Mystères de la jeunesse de Diderot." *Mercure de France* (December 15, 1937).

Sänger, Hermann. *Juden und Altes Testament bei Diderot.* Wertheim am Main: Hinckel, 1933.

Sartre, Jean-Paul. *Réflexions sur la question juive.* Paris: Gallimard, 1954.

Schwab, Richard N. "The Diderot Problem, the Starred Articles and the Question of Attribution in the *Encyclopédie.*" *Eighteenth-Century Studies* II (Spring, 1969): 240–85; (Summer, 1969): 370–438.

Schwartz, Leon. *Melchior Grimm: The "Correspondance littéraire" and the Philosophic Spirit.* Ph.D. dissertation, University of Southern California, 1962.

Schwarzbach, Bertram. "The Jews and the Enlightenment." *Diderot Studies* XVI (Geneva: Droz, 1973): 361–74.

Seznec, Jean. *Essais sur Diderot et l'Antiquité.* Oxford: Clarendon Press, 1957.

Shaftesbury, Anthony Ashley Cooper, Earl of. *Characteristics, [etc.].* 2 vols. Gloucester, Mass.: P. Smith, 1963.

Silberner, E. *Sozialisten zur Judenfrage.* Berlin: Colloquium Verlag, 1962.

Silberschlag, Boris. *Hebrew Literature: An Evaluation.* New York: Herzl Institute Pamphlet no. 12, 1959.

Smiley, Joseph R. "The Subscribers of Grimm's *Correspondance littéraire.*" *Modern Language Notes* LXII (1947): 44–46.

Thomas, Jean. *L'Humanisme de Diderot.* Paris: Société d'Édition Les Belles Lettres, 1938.

Tourneux, Maurice. *Diderot et Catherine II.* Paris: Calmann Lévy, 1899.

Venturi, Franco. *La Jeunesse de Diderot.* Transl. by J. Bertrand. Paris: Skira, 1939.

Vercruysse, J. "Voltaire et la Hollande." *Studies on Voltaire and the Eighteenth Century* XLVI (Geneva: l'Institut et Musée Voltaire, 1966): 9–212.

Voltaire. *Oeuvres complètes.* Ed. by L. Moland. 52 vols. Paris: Garnier, 1877–1885.

Wade, Ira O. *The Clandestine Organization and Diffusion of Ideas in France from 1700–1750.* Princeton: Princeton University Press, 1938.

Wijler, Jacob S. *Isaac de Pinto, sa vie et ses oeuvres.* Apeldoorn: C. M. B. Dixon, [1923?].

Willard, N. "La Folie et le génie vus par Diderot à travers ses oeuvres" in *Le Génie et la folie au 18e siècle.* Paris: Presses Universitaires, 1963.

Wilson, Arthur. *Diderot.* New York: Oxford University Press, 1972.

Winter, Ursula. Der Materialismus bei Diderot. Geneva: Droz; Paris: Minard, 1972.

Zeitlin, S. *Who Crucified Jesus?* New York: Bloch, 1964.

Zola, Émile. "Pour les Juifs." *Le Figaro* (May 16, 1896), p. 1.

Index

Abraham, 44, 54, 71, 80, 131, 154, 175
Acosta, Uriel, 126
Aeneid, 119
Aeschylus, 51, 95, 109
African (black, Negro), 135, 151, 183, 185
Aine, Suzanne d', 97
Akiba (Akiva), rabbi, 62, 172, 173
Alembert, Jean Le Rond d', 32, 39, 67, 168, 177
Alexander III, pope, 126
Al-Manzor, prince, 74
Alsace, pogroms in, 125
Altuna, Ignatio Emanuel de, 180
Americans, 96, 185
Amyot, Jacques, 178
Anabaptist, 82, 85, 138
Anacreon, 26, 119
Anaximander, 127
Andilly, Arnauld d', 172
Antigonus Sochaeus, 57
Anti-Semitism: and attacks on Talmud, 56, 60; Christian, 36, 41, 128, 141, 165, 169; English, 28, 116; essence of, 125, 168; French, 26, 36, 125, 164, 180; German, 172, 180; Greco-Roman, 27, 41, 94, 128, 167, 168–69, 170, 180; modern, 17, 24, 164; other, 92, 172; socialist, 160, 186. *See also* Enlightenment; Grimm, Frederick Melchior; Holbach, Paul H. T., baron d'; *Moïsade, La;* La Peyrère, Isaac de; Naigeon, Jacques A.; Newton, bishop Thomas; Race; Voltaire
Apion, 169
Apollonius, 168

Apologie de l'abbé Galiani (Diderot), 129
Arabs, 30, 44, 105, 185
Arendt, Hannah, 20, 127, 164, 186
Argens, Jean Baptiste, marquis d', 172
Aristotle, 108, 177
Asia (Asiatic, Oriental), 30, 43–44, 83, 92, 98, 100, 105, 135, 151, 169, 177, 178, 182
Assézat, Jules, 21, 43, 54, 78–79, 136, 163, 176, 184
Athalie (Racine), 98
Atticus, 33
Augustus, emperor, 94
Averroës, 74

Babylonia, 55, 60
Bacon, Francis, 50
Bacon, Roger, 51, 109, 127
Balzac, Honoré de, 150
Banians, 77
Barbey d'Aurévilly, Jules, 176
Bar-Kochba, 62, 172
Basnage, Jacques, 22, 54, 55, 56, 60, 61, 64, 122, 163, 170, 172
Bayle, Pierre, 22, 27, 29, 30, 32, 33, 41, 47, 57, 149, 163
Beaumont, Christophe de, 82
Becker, Carl, 16, 22, 23, 162
Benedict XIV, pope, 169
Ben Johai, 62, 173
Bergson, Henri, 161
Bernhardt, Sarah, 161
Berruyer, abbé, 101, 173
Bible (Old Testament): and art, 72, 97–98; Buffon and, 39, and celibacy, 45; "chosen people,"

41, 49, 76–77, 158, 159, 168; in Diderot's education, 26–27, 101; in Diderot's daughter's education, 97, 177; and Diderot's humor, 97; and Diderot's literary style, 98, 121–22, 180; divinity of, 27, 31,101; in England and Holland, 27–28, 100; God's cruelty, 31, 75, 166; holy books, 89; and Ibn Ezra, 63; inconsistency of, 24, 31, 46, 47; intolerance in, 84; irrationality, 27, 101; and Jewish culture, 25, 100, 118–19; as literature, 25, 31, 35–36, 97, 101, 116, 119, 122, 177, 180; and monarchy, 87; and Philosophes, 24, 48, 79, 89, 159; prophecy and revelation, 31; and Rousseau, 48, mentioned, 172, 174. *See also* Bayle, Pierre: *Encyclopédie*; Poetry; Prophets; Voltaire

Bijoux indiscrets, Les (Diderot), 80, 168, 173

Bizet, Georges, 161

Blount, Charles, 27

Bohemia, 137

Bolingbroke, Henry St. John, viscount, 28

Bossuet, Jacques Bénigne: exaltation of Moses, 35; *Histoire Universelle*, 32, 164; "mystery" of Jews, 77, 168; sermons relative to Jews, 26, 41, 165, 169

Boucher d'Argis, Antoine G., 40, 168

Bougainville, Louis A. de, 81, 176

Boulanger, Nicolas A., 40, 103, 114, 167, 197

Boureau-Deslandes, André F., 172

Brahman, 45

Briard, Gabriel, 71

Brucker, Jacob, 22, 42, 54, 55, 60, 64, 106, 122, 163, 168, 169, 170, 172, 178

Buddha (Buddhism), 43, 168

Buffon, Georges Louis L., count de, 39, 50, 142, 152, 177, 183

Buxtorf, Johannes, 172

Cabala, 43, 56, 62–63, 64, 173, 178

Caesar, Julius, 101, 115, 151

Calas, Jean, 69, 174

Calmet, Dom Augustin, 172

Calvinist, 85, 138

Canada, 152

Carib, 30

Caroline Henrietta Christina, landgravine, 132

Catherine II (the Great), empress: Diderot's visit to, 82, 132, 133–36; and Diderot's writings, 52, 87–89, 99, 123, 136, 150, 182; and the *Encyclopédie*, 52; and Falconet, 78; and Grimm, 52; and Jews, 134–35, 176, 182; mentioned, 151, 154, 176

Catholic(ism): biblical canon, 46; collaborators on the *Encyclopédie*, 40; Diderot most opposed to, 96; intolerance, 125, 126; mentioned, 83, 85, 116, 138. *See also* Christian; Church

Cato, Marcus Porcius, 115

Cerutti, Giuseppe A., 185

Chaldeans, 48, 169

Chambers, Ephraim, 22, 46, 53, 163

Chateaubriand, François R. de, 112

Chinese: antiquity of, 34–35, 40, 48; character, 113, 150, 185; enlightenment of, 92–93; government, 155; religion, 38, 168

Chouillet, Jacques, 51, 84, 164, 166, 167, 174, 178, 179, 180

Christ. *See* Jesus

Christian(s): Alexandrian, 49; caricatured, 158; common humanity with Jews, 85; convent system, 73, 144–45, 165; cosmogony, 45; credulity, 27, 75; crimes and cruelty, 30, 69, 71, 127, 128; Diderot's aversion to, 96; divination, 45; "false image of

Christians(s) (*continued*)
man," 81; fantasies, 101; hell, 92;
"heretical naturalism," 38;
ignorance, 43; impermanence, 37;
insincerely praised, 31, 47;
Messianism, 87; and Mohammed,
74; mistreatment of Jews, 53,
125–26, 128, 173; morality
compared to Jewish, 29–30, 59,
75, 111, 182; morality compared
to Tahitian, 81; and Petrobrusians,
126; political meddling, 45,
87–88, 93, 167, 170; religion
attacked, 30, 34–35, 41, 59, 75,
76, 87, 96, 100, 158–59, 166,
167, 175–76; religion as art theme,
68–71, 174, 175; resurrection
doctrine, 45; revelation, 27, 77;
sentimental appeal of, 90, 116;
theology and Jews, 41, 43, 48,
101, 141, 158, 164, 165; and
Therapeuts, 59; usury, 29; versus
Enlightenment, 32. *See also*
Catholic; Church;
Convulsionaries; Diderot, Denis;
Inquisition; Jansenist; Jesuit
Church: Diderot persecuted by, 96;
Encyclopédie threatened, 41, 48,
52, 74; establishment of, 87, 158;
opposed to progress, 39; and
Prades affair, 46–47; not racist,
183; Voltaire attacks, 167. *See
also* Enlightenment
Cibber, Colley, 148
Cicero, Marcus Tullius, 27, 33, 118,
151, 152
Classical. *See* Greek; Roman
Claudius I, emperor. *See Essai sur les
règnes de Claude et de Néron*
Clement XIII, pope, 67
Cocceius, Johannes, 172
Condillac, Étienne B. de, 32, 39, 166
Condorcet, Antoine C., marquis de,
168
Convulsionaries, 31
Corneille, Pierre, 69

Correspondance littéraire (Grimm),
52, 139, 164, 171, 178, 185
Crébillon, Claude, 37, 38
Crocker, Lester, 184
Cynics, 45

Damiens, Robert F., 66
Daniel, 54
Dashkoff, Princess Catherine, 95, 171
David, king, 54, 72, 122, 175, 179,
180, 185
Deffand, Marie, marquise du, 32
Deicide, 31, 175–76
Deist (deism, theism, natural
religion), 28, 30, 31, 32, 33, 34,
36, 37–38, 40, 46, 59, 96, 166
*De la suffisance de la religion
naturelle* (Diderot), 37–38, 49,
168
De l'Esprit (Helvétius), 67. *See also
Réflexions sur l'ouvrage
d'Helvétius*
De l'Homme (Helvétius), 19, 90, 151.
*See also Réfutation . . . de
l'ouvrage d'Helvétius*
Democracy, threat of religion to, 88
Demosthenes, 152, 153
Descartes, René, 126, 178
Deshays, Jean B., 69, 174
Dickens, Charles, 150
Diderot, abbé Didier P., 98, 99, 165
Diderot, Antoinette, madame, 177
Diderot, Denis: as art critic, 68–73,
76, 84, 108, 114–15, 174, 175;
canon, 20–23, 40, 42, 54, 163,
169; Catholic childhood, 17, 26,
165, 180; correspondence, 23,
96–99, 131; deist period, 17, 30,
34, 37–38, 168; dualism, 83–84,
101, 112–19, 178–79;
Encyclopedist period, 38, 39–66,
73–74, 131; equalitarianism, 58,
111, 151–52, 153, 156–57, 185;
esthetic sensitivity, 30, 68,
101–23, 175, 178–79, 179–80;
and experimental science, 30, 48,

50–51, 65; and genius, 19, 51, 55, 83, 91–92, 105–10, 115–16, 118–21, 151–52, 153–54, 160, 177, 178, 185; Hellenism of, 36, 101–19, 179; Helvétius answered, 90–93; and human diversity, 20, 65–66, 73, 74, 142–46, 149–56; and human perfectibility, 34, 40, 91–92, 116, 135–36; imprisoned, 39, 66; and "inspirationism," 50–51, 65; materialism (atheism) of, 17, 29, 30, 34, 39, 40, 51, 57, 65, 76, 83, 85, 90–92, 98, 115–16, 131, 141, 144–47, 148–49, 152–53, 160, 168, 185; on national character, 150–55, 184, 185; and Péreire, 177; as Philosophe leader, 32, 67; and Prades affair, 46–47; preromanticism, 51, 68, 102–23, 174, 175, 178; on religious tolerance, 29, 31, 36, 78, 82, 84, 85, 88, 99, 126–27, 136, 138, 155, 163, 166; sensationalist psychology, 39, 46, 49, 51, 102–3, 166; voyage to Holland and Russia, 82–89, 132–39, 181–82. *See also titles of Diderot's works*

Diderot, Denis, and Jews: early attitude, 26–27, 28–30, 33–37, 158; on de Pinto, 130–31, 132–33, 136, 139, 181–82; in his *Encyclopédie* articles, 42–65, 105, 110–11, 125, 127–29, 159, 168–69, 172, 173; evolving attitude, 68, 75, 78, 84–87, 108, 123, 124–25, 129, 131, 154, 155–56, 184; Jews as art theme, 71–73, 111–60; on the Jewish question, 124–40; on Jewish sects, 57–60, 172; visit to Jews of Holland, 85–87, 137–39

Diderot, Denis, literary career: early period, 28–39; maturity, 66–82, 111–12, 129, 131; as novelist, 73, 76, 90, 95, 114–46, 147–50; as playwright, 67–68, 158, 175; last works, 93–99

Diderot, Denis, religion attacked by: Bible, 34–35, 46, 84; Christian Church, 32, 34–36, 37–38, 39, 46, 59, 75, 96, 167; final causes, 51; general, 28, 30–31, 46, 65, 74, 75, 76, 82–83, 87–90, 93, 96, 97, 98, 145, 150, 155, 159, 160, 167, 173; Judaism, 29, 33, 34, 36, 38, 49, 56–63, 64–65; paganism, 42; sectarianism, 38. *See also* Egyptians; Mohammedan; *etc*.

Diderot, Denise, 98, 177

Diderot, Marie-Angélique. *See* Vandeul, Marie-Angélique de (née Diderot)

Dieckmann, Herbert, 79, 163, 164

Diodorus, 63

Discours sur la poésie dramatique (Diderot), 68, 112, 143, 144

Dreyfus Affair, 24

Druid, 170

Duclos, Charles, 67

Ducros, Louis, 136, 168

Dumarsais, César C., 30

Durameau, Louis, 185

Durant, Will and Ariel, 26, 177

Dutch. *See* Holland

Eclectic, 49, 105–6, 170

Egyptian(s): antiquity of, 48; celibacy, 45; civilization source, 43, 75; contradictory treatment of, 169; divination, 45; "Égyptien imbécile," 75, 169; irrationality or superstition of, 105, 150; and Jews, 43, 55, 56–57, 61, 63, 169, 172, 178; Joseph among, 54; and Mark, 59; practicality of, 178; religion, 29, 31, 166–67; and Romans, 94; science or wisdom of, 44, 166, 169; and theocracy, 98, 170

Eidous, Marc A., 28

Eisenmenger, Johannes A., 172

Elijah, 62
Elizabeth, empress of Russia, 134
Elizabeth I, queen, 141, 151, 153
Éloge de Richardson (Diderot). *See*
Richardson, Samuel
Émile. See Rousseau, Jean Jacques
Encyclopédie: Bayle's influence,
32–33, 41; Biblical criticism, 33,
46–48; and Catherine II, 52; and
Church, 39, 41, 48, 52, 53, 67,
76, 108, 127, 168; collaborators,
40, 168; completion of, 74;
Diderot's contributions, 20–22,
32, 74, 163, 169, 172, 181;
empirical-rationalist, 48; and
Grimm, 52; and d'Holbach, 52;
Jews and Judaism in, 41–46,
47–49, 53–65, 105, 127–29, 171;
and Marxists, 160; "Preliminary
Discourse," 40; mentioned, 38,
102, 186
Encyclopédie articles:
"Androgynes," 42;
"Antediluvian," 42; "Arabs,"
44; "Asiatics," 43, 163, 169–70;
"Beauty," 102–3, 106, 174, 178;
"Bible," 46; "Canon," 46;
"Celibacy," 45; "Chaldeans,"
48; "Chaos," 42, 47;
"Children," 45; "Chinese," 93;
"Christianism," 165; "Church
Fathers," 172; "Costerels"
("Cotereaux"), 126; "Cowl," 41;
"Crusades," 124–26;
"Divinations," 45;
"Eclecticism," 49, 105–6, 127,
170; "Egyptians," 43, 169, 178;
"Geneva," 67; "Genius," 106–8;
"God," 40; "Greeks," 42–43,
170, 179; "Hosea," 163;
"Inquisition," 181;
"Intolerance," 127; "Ionic,"
127; "Jesuit," 173; "Jews,
History of," 53, 127–29, 159,
171; "Jews, Philosophy of," 17,
49, 53, 54–65, 105, 158–59, 160,
168, 169, 171, 172; "Judaism,"
49, 53, 163, 171; "Library," 169;
"Messiah," 172; "Mosaic," 163;
Mosaic and Christian," 42, 45,
169; "Nobility," 40; "Political
Economy" ("Économie
Politique," "Œconomie
Politique"), 40, 163, 172;
"Preadamite," 42, 163;
"Priests," 163, 170; "Prophet,"
163; "Providence," 163;
"Representatives," 40;
"Resurrection," 45, 163; "Sacred
Chronology," 46, 47;
"Saracens," 74, 108;
"Scholastics," 127;
"Theocracy," 45–46, 163, 170;
"Theosophists," 51, 55, 73–74,
95, 109–10, 154, 178; "Usury,"
110–11, 118, 129; "Wood of
Life," 49, 178; "Zenda Vesta,"
184
English: and Jews, 53, 128, 137, 139,
176, 180, 181, 182; language, 27,
28, 105, 139; mentioned, 30, 51,
80, 117, 141, 150, 151, 153, 154,
155, 166, 185. *See also* Deist;
Enlightenment
Enlightenment: Catherine II and, 135;
Church and, 11, 24, 32, 95,
158–59; Diderot and, 16;
Encyclopédie and, 39–40; free
expression, 32, 93; importance of,
34; Jews and, 17, 24–25, 64, 87,
129, 155, 158, 162, 171, 172. *See
also* Philosophes
"Enquiry Concerning Virtue or Merit,
An" (Shaftesbury), 28
Entretiens sur le Fils naturel
(Diderot), 67–68, 147, 175
Epicurean, 34
Épinay, Louise de la Live d', 130,
132, 139, 176, 182
Epiphany, Saint, 172
Essai sur le mérite et la vertu
(Diderot), 28–30

Essais sur la peinture (Diderot), 76, 174

Essai sur les règnes de Claude et de Néron (Diderot), 93–94, 95, 123, 140, 155, 156, 162, 185

Essenes, 45, 55, 58–59, 142, 173, 183

Esther (Racine), 98

Esther, queen, 71, 175, 185

Euripides, 26, 73, 110, 119

Europe: Jews in, 76, 100, 128, 141, 155; mentioned, 135, 151

Eusebius, 172

Eybeschutz, Jonathan, 164

Fabre, Jean, 51, 65, 167, 170

Faiguet (de Villeneuve), Joachim, 110–11, 118, 129, 179

Falconet, Étienne M., 23, 78, 97, 98, 122, 131, 175, 176

Fénelon, François de Salignac de la Mothe-, 111

Feuerwerker, David, 165, 170, 180, 182

Fez, massacre of Jews in, 74

Fielding, Henry, 148

Fils naturel, Le (Diderot), 68

Fleury, Claude, 125

Fo, 97

Formey, Jean Henri S., 40

France: intolerance in, 88–89; Jews in, 26, 53, 87, 128, 139, 157, 160, 165, 180, 181; monarchy troubled, 95; Protestants persecuted in, 126, 128–29, 180; mentioned, 135. *See also* French

Frederick II (the Great), 52, 84, 176, 182

French: Academy, 67; language, 103–4, 105; people, compared to Jews, 111; and Romans, 151; poetry, 117. *See also* France

Fréret, Nicolas, 79, 80, 176

Fréron, Élie, 67, 174

Freud, Sigmund, 161

Galiani, abbé Ferdinando, 71, 72, 129

Galitzin, Prince Alexander, 132

Gallion (proconsul), 94

Garand, Jean B., 16, 17

Gassendi, Pierre, 30

Gay, Peter, 141, 165, 167, 183

Gendzier, Stephen, 20, 23, 165, 173, 176, 184

Geoffrin, Marie Thérèse, 32

German(y), 51, 52, 53, 78, 80, 84, 89, 131, 132, 138, 164, 180, 182

Ghebers, 77

God (Almighty, Divinity, gods, Lord, Providence, Supreme Being), 19, 25, 31, 32, 36, 37, 38, 40, 41, 43, 46, 55, 57, 58, 61, 62, 63, 64, 75, 76, 78, 81, 83, 85, 87, 88, 89, 90, 93, 98, 109, 110, 122, 156, 165, 166, 167, 169, 170, 173

Goens, R. M. Van, 136

Goethe, Johann W. von, 106, 112, 116, 171, 176

Goudar, Ange, 127

Graetz, Heinrich, 165

Greek(s): atomism, 30; anti-Semitism, 94; celibacy, 45; culture, compared to Jewish, 25, 33, 36, 43, 65, 71–72, 101–23, 155, 177, 185; Diodorus among, 63; divination, 45; genius, 19, 73, 108, 118, 151, 153, 154, 156, 185; language, 27, 98, 103, 105, 108; mores, 59, 92, 135, 151; mythology or religion, 42, 58, 93, 105, 175, 179; philosophy, 19, 156; poetry, 73, 117; priests, 93, 127, 155; state, 135; themes in art, 68, 72, 175; tragedy, 175

Grégoire, abbé Baptiste H., 160

Greuze, Jean B., 17, 175

Grimm, Frederick Melchior, 51–53, 64, 67–68, 69, 78, 79–80, 92, 107, 131, 132, 134, 136, 159, 171, 174, 175, 176, 177, 185. *See also Correspondance littéraire*

Gymnosophists, 45

Hadrian, emperor, 185
Hallé, Noël, 71
Hasidim, 56
Hegel, Friedrich, 119
Hebrew language, 75, 98, 103, 108, 177
Helmont, Franciscus M. Van, 103, 104, 170, 178
Helvétius, Claude A., 19, 90–93, 140, 142, 147, 151–55, 165, 173, 184, 185. *See also Réfutation . . . d'Helvétius*
Herbert of Cherbury, 27
Hermand, Pierre, 22
Hertzberg, Rabbi Arthur, 19, 21, 54, 56, 60, 79, 124, 125, 127, 138–39, 148, 162, 163, 166, 171, 173, 176, 177, 180, 181, 182, 183, 185
Hierophant, 45
Histoire Naturelle (Buffon), 142
Hitler, Adolf, 24
Hogarth, William, 148
Holbach, Paul H. T., baron d', 40, 52–53, 60, 64, 76, 80, 104, 159, 162, 163, 170, 171, 176, 183. *See also Système de la nature*
Holland: Diderot in, 65, 82, 84–87, 122, 130, 132, 133, 136–39, 162, 184; Jews of, 19, 81–82, 85–87, 126, 128, 130, 132–33, 137–39, 148–49, 155, 174, 176, 232; publishers in, 80, 164; religions in, 27–28, 85; "Utrecht, Jew of," 81, 132–33, 148–49, 162, 174, 181, 184
Homer, 26, 73, 108, 110, 118, 119, 121, 152, 179
Horace, 26, 27, 119, 165, 173
Hubert, René, 39, 41, 43, 168
Hume, David, 131, 181, 182
Hutcheson, Francis, 102, 178
Huysmans, G. C. (Joris Karl), 114
Hypatia, 49, 127, 170
Hyrcanus, John, 57, 172

Ibn Ezra, Abraham, 63, 64
India, 169
Inquisition, 61, 67, 124, 125, 127, 133, 170, 171, 181, 185
Introduction aux Grands Principes (Diderot), 76–78
Irish, 185
Isaac, 54
Isaiah, 175
Italy (Italian): intolerance, 89; language, 27, 105; mores, 151; poetry, 17; states, 151; usury, 110. *See also* Rome; Tuscany

Jacob, 54, 71, 110
Jacques le Fataliste (Diderot), 23, 52, 90, 95, 140, 150, 184
Janin, Jules, 160
Jansenists, 26, 82, 176
Japanese, 46
Jaucourt, Louis, *chevalier* de, 20, 53, 128, 129, 130, 135, 138, 159, 171, 181
Jaurès, Jean, 160, 164, 186
Jerusalem: academies, 61; destruction of, 55, 60, 82, 172; temple of, 85
Jesuits, 26, 95, 173
Jesus (Christ), 35, 48, 51, 60, 62, 69, 71, 75, 78, 80, 83, 95, 97, 109, 141, 154, 167, 173, 175–76, 178
Jews (Hebrews, Israel, Jewish): academies, 61; Alexandrian, 49; antiquity of, 35, 40, 48, 50, 54; Babylonian captivity, 55; biblical chronology, 46–47; caricatured, 34–35; celibacy, 45; civil rights of, 87, 128–29, 134, 137–38, 180; compared to pagans, 42, 43; compared to Jansenists, 82; in Christian theology, 35, 41, 43, 48, 101, 141, 158, 164, 165; credulity, 27, 35, 61, 78; and Crusades, 124–26; culture in eighteenth century, 25, 100, 164–65; deicide charge, 31, 175–76; Diderot's ignorance of, 65, 122, 129; Diderot's new

sensibility toward, 68, 84, 101–23, 129, 131; in Diderot's novels, 76, 81, 126, 130, 132–33, 139, 145–49, 156; Diderot's visit to Dutch Jews, 85–87, 122, 137, 154, 155; diversity of, 66, 137, 138–39, 181; divination, 45; economic utility, 127, 128, 130, 135, 137–38, 154, 160, 182, 186; in Egypt, 35, 43, 56–57, 172; emancipation of, 157, 160, 170; in *Encyclopédie*, 22, 41, 42–65, 105, 100–11, 124, 127–29, 159, 172, 173; and English deists, 27–28, 166; in eighteenth-century Europe, 24–25, 141, 164–65, 180; fantasies or mythopoeia, 25, 36, 65, 101, 105, 108, 117; Fez massacre, 74; in France, 26, 53, 87, 124–28, 157, 160, 162, 171–72, 176, 180, 181; inventions, 100, 177; "Jewish Enlightenment," 156; Jewish *pathétique* as art theme, 69–73, 111, 160, 175; "lustful Jew" stereotype, 148–49; materialism, 29, 57; Messianism, 85–87; Moses as representative of, 118–21; negative appraisals of, 19, 24–25, 27–28, 31, 33, 36, 41, 43, 45, 47–49, 56, 64, 65, 78, 100–101, 111, 159, 167, 170, 172, 173; and Philosophes, 17–20, 24–25, 29, 41, 45, 48, 64, 78–80, 100, 125, 141–42, 154, 168; philosophy, 43–44, 53–65, 100, 169; poetry, 19, 35–36, 73, 84, 101, 108, 110, 117, 123, 160, 169, 171; religion and state (theocracy), 45–46, 98, 167, 170; revelation, 27, 48, 64, 76; Romans, war with, 58, 185; Samaritans, persecution of, 56; science, 19, 45, 60, 63–64, 65, 169; sects, 57–60; and socialists, 160–61, 186; Spanish Jews, expulsion of, 89; Spanish Jews, sages of, 55, 63–64, 100, 174; state's obligation to protect, 94; survival as nation, 77, 128; the "unreconstructibility" canard, 92, 138, 156, 177, 182; usury, 28–29, 35, 110, 118, 166. *See also* Bossuet, Jacques Bénigne; Diderot, Denis; *Encyclopédie*; Jaucourt, Louis, *chevalier* de; Judaism; Moses; Prophets; Rousseau, Jean Jacques; Voltaire; *geographical names*

Joinville, Jean de, 83

Joseph, 54, 97, 184

Joseph II, emperor, 52

Josephus (Flavius), 55, 57, 58, 59, 100, 101, 172, 178

Judah the Holy (the Prince), 61

Judaism: in Augustan Rome, 94; compared to Christian and other religions, 29–31, 33, 44–45; dangerous to praise, 48; degeneration in eighteenth century, 164–65; in the *Encyclopédie*, 53–65; factions of, 172; and fanaticism, 56, 59–60, 64; as "heretical naturalism," 38; in Holland, 85–87; humanism of, 165; impermanence of, 37; importance to Jewish survival, 77, 128; and intolerance, 61; "Judaize," 185; "mother" of Christianity and Mohammedanism, 128; moral superiority claim, 49; rarely mentioned in Diderot's correspondence, 96, 98; rationalism of, 165; revived interested in, 28, 166; satirized, 36–37; and superstition, 60, 64; and women, 49; mentioned, 51, 149, 170, 180. *See also* Jews; Moses

Julian, emperor, 31, 82

Kahn, Leon, 181

Karaites, 55, 56, 57–58

Koran, 44

Krakowski, Anna, 186

La Mettrie, Julien O. de, 30
La Peyrère, Isaac de, 183
La Rochefoucauld, François de, 15
Lazarus, Emma, 96
LeBreton, André F., 21
LeDieu, Paul, 164
Lehrmann, Charles C., 19, 79
Leibnitz, Gottfried W., 106, 143, 156
Le Monnier, abbé, 97
Lessing, Gotthold E., 156, 180
Lettre sur les aveugles (Diderot), 38–39, 49–50, 168
Lettre sur les sourds et muets (Diderot), 50, 105, 108, 170, 174, 178
Lettre à Mlle *** (Diderot), 178
Lettres à Sophie Volland (Diderot). *See* Volland, Sophie (Louise Henriette)
Levant, Jewish trading posts, 138
Linnaeus, Carl von, 183
Livy (Titus Livius, historian), 101
Locke, John, 27, 32, 40, 46, 102, 166, 185
Louis IX, king (saint), 83
Louis XV, king, 52, 66
Lucretius, 166
Lutheran(s), 82, 85, 96, 138

Maimonides, Moses, 44, 63–64, 74, 169, 173, 174
Malesherbes, Chrétien G. Lamoignon de, 180
Mallet, abbé Edme, 168
Marcus Aurelius, emperor, 115
Marmontel, Jean F., 67, 168
Marx, Karl (Marxists), 160, 186
Maupertuis, Pierre L. M. de, 183
Maury, abbé Jean S., 164
Maux, Jeanne Catherine de, 89
May, Georges, 95
Meister, Jacques H., 139, 185
Mémoires pour Catherine II (Diderot), 182
Mendelssohn, Moses, 156, 174

Meslier, Jean, 30, 167
Messiah, 85–87, 172
Meyer, Paul H., 11, 19, 139, 148, 162, 170, 172, 176, 180, 183
Mexican, 170
Michelangelo, 71, 72, 111, 121, 174
Milot (artist), 72, 185
Mingrelian, 30
Mirabeau, Honoré G., count de, 56, 160, 170, 172
Mirabeau, Victor R., marquis de, 131
Mishnah, 55, 61, 171
Mohammed(an) (Moslem), 29, 38, 47, 51, 74, 76, 80, 83, 95, 109, 128
Monarchy, 88, 167, 177
Montaigne, Michel E. de, 15, 64, 156, 176, 178
Montesquieu, Charles de Secondat, baron de, 15, 16, 31, 32, 33, 93, 125, 126, 128, 136, 139, 141–42, 152, 171
Moïsade, La, 21, 55, 78–80, 176
Moses (Mosaic): in art, 71, 121, 175; Berruyer's "parody," 95; celibacy, 45; in Christian thought, 48; chronologies, 47; cosmogony, 46; Diderot's ambivalence toward, 83–84, 95, 110; Diderot "suckled on," 26, 101; and Egyptians, 43; genius of, 51, 54–55, 73, 95, 105, 108, 109, 110, 118–21, 171; Jewish culture incarnate, 25, 118, 119, 121; laws, 37, 44, 59; miracles, 78; "a Moses among the carp," 97; Naigeon's
• "rectifications" on, 169; and revelation, 76–77; satirized, 34–35, 78–80; the sword-bearer, 83; and the Talmud, 61; and theocracy, 45–46; and Voltaire's "obscenities," 80, 167; mentioned, 185

Naigeon, Jacques A., 21, 42, 43, 55, 61, 80, 107, 163, 165, 169, 170, 173, 174, 177

National character, 150–55
Necker, Suzanne, 82, 182
Nehemiah, 179
Nero, emperor, 17. *See also Essai sur les règnes de Claude et de Néron*
Neveu de Rameau, Le (Diderot), 23, 66, 76, 81, 84, 92, 95, 111, 112, 126, 132–33, 139, 114–46, 147–49, 162, 171, 174, 180, 182, 183–84
Newton, Bishop Thomas, 183
Noah, 44, 76
Numa, 171
Nun, The. See Religieuse, La

"Observations sur l'église Saint-Roch" (Diderot), 68
Observations sur le Nakaz (Diderot), 87, 167, 185
Orpheus, 42, 69, 113, 179
Ossian, 180

Pagan(s), 29, 33, 38, 42, 43, 54, 59, 68, 72, 93, 98, 170, 174, 177
Palissot, Charles, 74, 76
Paracelsus, 51, 95, 109
Paradoxe sur le comédien (Diderot), 23, 171
Paris, Jews of, 26, 131, 165
Parsees, 150
Pascal, Blaise, 30
Pathos (passion): and humanism, 116, 175; as inspiration for art, poetry, *grandeur*, 68, 71, 102–23, 178, 179; Jewish *pathétique*, 69–71; "pathetic realism," 73; primacy of feeling, 91, 121
Paul, saint, 94, 180
Péguy, Charles, 26, 125
Pensées détachées sur la peinture (Diderot), 121, 180
Pensées philosophiques (Diderot), 30–32, 68, 74, 102, 107, 179
Pensées sur l'interprétation de la nature (Diderot), 50–51, 65–66, 67, 95, 105, 142–43, 179
Père de famille, Le (Diderot), 68, 98

Péreire, Jacob R., 131, 177
Peripatetics, 55, 65
Persian(s), 98, 105, 169
Peruvian, 30
Peter I, czar, 78, 135, 151, 154
Peuchet, Jacques, 17, 162
Phädon (Mendelssohn), 156
Pharisees, 55, 57, 59–60, 173
Philadelphus, 56
Philo, 59
Philosophes: attitudes toward Jews, 17–20, 24–25, 41, 45, 87, 100, 121, 129, 141–42, 154, 159, 168. *See also Encyclopédie*; Enlightenment; *names of individuals*
Pindar, 51, 109, 118, 154
Pinto, Isaac de, 130–31, 132–33, 136, 138–39, 148–49, 154, 172, 181–82
Pissarro, Camille, 161
Plan d'une université (Diderot), 23, 88
Plato, 26, 33, 116, 117, 119
Pliny (the Elder), 27
Plutarch, 27
Poetry: "antique heads," 118; and madness, 114; as opposed to science, philosophy, reason, 101, 104–5, 108, 116–17, 119, 123, 179; primitive, 112–13, 117; and religion, 68
Poland, 137, 164. *See also* Stanislas II
Popkin, Richard, 181, 182, 183
Portugal, 89
Poussin, Nicolas, 71, 72, 175
Prades, abbé Jean M. de, 46–47
Prévost d'Exiles, abbé, 180, 184
Promenade du sceptique (Diderot), 33–37, 54, 73, 84, 101, 102, 105, 106, 158, 167, 179
Prophets, 26, 71, 99, 101, 119, 122
Protestant (Huguenot), 40, 46, 83, 96, 126, 129, 171, 174, 181
Proudhon, Pierre J., 160

Proust, Jacques, 21, 42, 163, 167,
    169, 170, 171, 173, 180, 183
Ptolemy(s), 169, 178
Ptolemy Lagus, prince, 56
Pythagorean, 45, 59

Quaker ("Quakeress"), 58, 142, 157,
    166

Race (racism), 17, 19, 60, 64, 66,
    136, 141–42, 147–51, 156, 183.
    See also Anti-Semitism
Racine, Jean, 15, 69, 98, 108
Rameau's Nephew. See Neveu de
    Rameau, Le
Raphael (painter), 71, 72, 111, 174
Raynal, abbé Guillaume, 139, 156,
    158, 177, 182
Réflexions sur l'ode (Diderot), 116
Réfutation suivie de l'ouvrage
    d'Helvétius intitulé l'Homme
    (Diderot), 19, 23, 91, 93, 140,
    147, 151–55, 183
Reinach, Theodore, 17–19, 20, 22,
    54, 66, 133, 148, 173, 181, 182
Religieuse, La (Diderot), 23, 73, 95,
    144–45
Rembrandt H. van Rijn, 69, 97
Renou, Antoine, 71
Réve de d'Alembert, Le (Diderot), 23,
    52, 76, 81, 95, 115, 131, 146–47
Richardson, Samuel, 55, 73, 108,
    110, 131, 175
Rome (Roman): anti-Semitic writers,
    27, 169, 170; art, 68; divination,
    45; genius, 151, 153, 185; morals,
    92, 94, 153, 155, 185; mythology
    or religion, 58, 93; philosophy, 33;
    poetry, 117; war with Jews, 58,
    185; mentioned, 147
Romanticism, 68, 160
Rousseau, Jean Jacques: and the
    Bible, 121–22; compared to
    Diderot, 15, 16; his Confessions
    and the Jews, 180; in Diderot's
    circle, 32, 51; his Émile and the

Jews, 48, 170; and the
    Encyclopédie, 40, 67; and the
    enemies of Jewish emancipation,
    170; on environment and human
    character, 183; and Péreire, 177;
    on the social utility of religion, 93;
    mentioned, 139
Russia: Diderot's voyage to, 52,
    82–84, 132, 133–36, 172, 182;
    and Grimm's Correspondance
    littéraire, 80, 164; ignorance in,
    154; Jews in, 134–35, 176, 182;
    mentioned, 131. See also
    Catherine II; Peter I

Saadi, 152
Sachar, Abram, 164
Sadducees, 55, 57
Sainte-Beuve, Charles A., 160
Saint-Lambert, Jean F. de, 107
Saint-Mard, Rémond de, 178
Salesses, Raymond, 177
Sallust, 101
Salons (Diderot), 19, 23, 52, 55,
    68–73, 76, 80–81, 97, 108,
    111–12, 115, 117–21, 131, 156,
    171, 174, 175, 179, 180
Samaritans, 55, 56, 71, 172
Samson, 72
Samuel, 45, 87, 98, 167
Sänger, Hermann, 19, 21, 22, 31, 36,
    42, 53, 55, 60, 63, 97, 122,
    124–25, 136, 139, 169, 170, 171,
    172, 173, 182
Sartre, Jean-Paul, 91, 125, 127, 168
Scaliger, Joseph J., 63
Schama, Simon, 162
Schwarzbach, Bertram, 164, 183
Scottish, 185
Seneca, 17, 25, 94, 123, 159, 177
Shaftesbury, Anthony A. Cooper, earl
    of: his "Enquiry Concerning
    Virtue or Merit," 28–30, 166,
    180; and the Pensées
    philosophiques, 30, 100; and the
    "stupid Jew," stereotype, 75; and

the theory of passions, 102; and
    Van Helmont, 170, 178
Shakespeare, William, 51, 95, 108,
    109, 154
Simon, Richard, 172
Slavery, 78, 94, 151, 156
Socinian, 67, 96, 166
Socrates, 33, 50, 105, 156
Solomon, king, 54, 122
Sophocles, 73, 110
Spain, 54, 61, 89, 100, 122, 128, 181
Spencer, John, 44
Spinoza, Baruch (Benedictus), 25,
    27, 30, 32, 33, 51, 56, 100, 126,
    142, 149, 156, 178, 184, 185
Spirit of the Laws (Montesquieu), 126
Stanislas II Augustus, king, 52, 131
Stendhal (Henri Beyle), 112, 164
Sufists, 169
*Supplément au Voyage de
    Bougainville* (Diderot), 23, 81,
    176
Surenhusius, Guilielmus, 172
Surinam, Jews of, 182
"Sur la tolérance," (Diderot), 82–83
Sweden, 52, 164
"Synagogue, the," 52
Système de la nature (d'Holbach),
    131, 171, 181

Tacitus, 27, 94, 169, 170
Tahiti, 16, 81–82
Talmud, 55, 56, 60, 61–62, 100, 172,
    173
Tartars, 169
Terence, 26, 119
Theosophists, 51, 55, 74, 95, 109,
    178
Therapeuts (Healers), 55, 59
Thomas, Jean, 15, 23, 81, 84, 108,
    116, 176, 177, 179
Thucydides, 35
Tindal, Matthew, 28
Tolerance. *See* Diderot, Denis;
    Encyclopédie article

"Intolerance"; Inquisition;
    Montesquieu; "Sur la tolérance";
    Voltaire
Tourneux, Maurice, 21, 43, 54, 78,
    79, 134, 136, 171, 172, 176, 184
Toussaint, François V., 28, 166
Trajan, emperor, 185
Turgot, Anne Robert J., 160
Tuscany, 128

Usury, 28–29, 35, 110–11, 118, 129,
    166
"Utrecht, Jew of." *See* Holland

Valabrègue, Israel B. de, 160
Vandeul, Marie-Angélique de (née
    Diderot), 79, 97, 165, 177
Van Loo, Michel, 16, 17, 36
Venturi, Franco, 74, 165, 168, 176
Vernière, Paul, 51, 67, 84, 106, 166,
    167, 176, 178, 180, 182, 183, 185
Vien, Joseph M., 174
Virgil, 26, 108, 119, 152, 179
Volland, Sophie (Louise Henriette),
    15, 23, 74, 80, 81, 97, 98, 147,
    164, 175, 184
Voltaire (François Marie Arouet):
    anti-"Mosaism," 80, 167; article
    "Jews," 24, 164, 181; Calas
    affair, 69, 174; on Christianity,
    76, 167; compared to Diderot, 15,
    16, 125, 139; criticized by
    Diderot, 80, 167; and the
    Encyclopédie, 67; "Epistle to
    Urania," 28, 34, 36, 166; *Essay
    on Mores*, 142; Hellenism of, 108;
    on the Inquisition, 185; on
    "Jewish cannibalism," 185; and
    Jewish suffering, 124, 181; his
    Jewish villains, 129, 148, 150,
    181; Jews, his dislike of, 24, 64,
    100, 119, 121, 125, 131, 139,
    154, 162, 164, 172, 174, 181;
    Philosophical Letters, 37, 58, 142;
    and Marx, 186; on the Pharisees,
    60; racial theory, 136, 142, 143,

Voltaire (*continued*)
164, 168, 183; rationalism, 112,
176, 179; on religious art, 68;
satirical manner, 33; on the social
utility of religion, 93; his *Treatise
on Tolerance*, 24, 164; mentioned,
26, 32, 38, 69, 98, 116, 165
Voyage en Hollande (Diderot). *See*
Holland, Diderot in

Walckenaer, baron Charles A., 79,
176
Webb, Daniel, 72
Wiesel, Elie, 165
Wijler, Jacob S., 181

William III, king of England, 137,
138
William IV, stathouder of Holland,
130
Wilson, Arthur, 11, 124, 134, 164,
171, 181, 182
Wolf(f), baron Christian von, 156

Xekia. *See* Buddha

Yvon, abbé Claude, 168

Zabians, 44
Zohar, 62–63
Zola, Émile, 160, 186
Zoroaster, 76